Overseas Students in Higher Education

During the past decade there has been a substantial expansion in the provision of both undergraduate and postgraduate programmes for overseas students in British universities and colleges. Over the same period, higher education institutions have become increasingly concerned with the quality of their teaching and the learning experiences they provide for students, as they have had to face public audit and assessment.

The focus for this text is the provision of quality teaching and learning for overseas students. It brings together, for the first time, contributions from major authorities in the field. Offering sound practical advice, successive chapters discuss key findings from current research and explore a range of ways in which the teaching of overseas students might be improved.

The book will be of particular interest to all staff in higher education institutions who have a measure of responsibility for teaching overseas students. It refers to a wide range of students' overseas backgrounds, including the Pacific Rim, China and the European Community.

Both editors are based at the University of Hull. **David McNamara** is a member of the Department of Educational Studies and Professor of Education. **Robert Harris** is Pro-Vice-Chancellor and Professor of Social Work.

Overseas Students in Higher Education

Issues in teaching and learning

Edited by David McNamara and Robert Harris

London and New York

First published 1997
by Routledge
11 New Fetter Lane, London EC4P 4EE

Transferred to Digital Printing 2003

Simultaneously published in the USA and Canada
by Routledge
29 West 35th Street, New York, NY 10001

Typeset in Palatino by Routledge

British Library Cataloguing in Publication Data
A catalogue record for this book is available from the British Library

Library of Congress Cataloguing in Publication Data

A catalogue record for this book has been requested

ISBN 0–415–13199–5 (hbk)
ISBN 0–415–13200–2 (pbk)

Contents

Illustrations

Contributors

Jim Ackers is Course Director for Teaching English to Speakers of Other Languages at the University of Newcastle Centre for International Studies in Education. Previously he worked for the Overseas Development Agency and British Council in Senegal as an adviser and teacher trainer at the British–Senegalese Institute. He has also worked overseas as a teacher of English as a Foreign Language in Saudi Arabia and Morocco. He has conducted overseas consultancy work for the ODA and is currently developing an overseas taught programme. He is interested in the developmental impact of modes of education and training.

John Barker is a Lecturer at the Centre for Hazard and Risk Management in Loughborough University's Business School. He has substantial experience teaching and tutoring overseas students, particularly at postgraduate and post-experience levels. He is a regular contributor to the Loughborough University International Students' pre-sessional programme. He was a member of the research team that investigated the experiences of overseas students at Loughborough and Nottingham Universities from 1986 to 1988 and he contributed to the resulting book, *The Learning Experiences of Overseas Students*, published by The Society for Research into Higher Education and the Open University in 1990.

John Brennan is Head of the Quality Support Centre, The Open University. He held academic posts at Lancaster University and Teesside Polytechnic before becoming Director of the Quality Support Group at the Council for National Academic Awards. He is currently developing a higher education management course with the Dutch University of Twente that will be delivered internationally by the Open University. He has written extensively on higher education policy and practice, and recent publications include (with others) *Changing Conceptions of Academic Standards*, The Open University, and 'The rise of quality assessment in higher education', in *Higher Education Management*.

Nadine K. Cammish is Tutor in Modern Languages at the School of Education, University of Hull, where she is engaged in initial and in-service teacher training programmes for language teachers from both home and abroad and in comparative education courses. Her overseas experience includes serving as French adviser in the Seychelles and teaching in the British Virgin Islands and Hong Kong. Her research in gender issues in education in developing countries has taken her to Sierra Leone, Cameroon, Jamaica, India, Bangladesh, Pakistan and Vanuatu; her most recent publications are in this field.

David Chan is an Associate Professor at the Department of Applied Social Studies at the City University of Hong Kong. He is currently finishing his PhD at the University of Nottingham. He received his masters' degree from Stanford University in the United States. Hence, he has first-hand experience as an overseas student in two different countries. The focus of David's research is the sociology of education and he has published on the educational developments of Hong Kong.

Martin Cortazzi is Senior Lecturer in Linguistics and Education at the University of Leicester, where he has been training teachers and supervising international research students since 1979. He has taught in Iran, China, Turkey and the Lebanon. He is visiting professor at the Universities of Nankai (Tianjin), Renmin (Beijing) and Hubei (Wuhan). His research interests and publications are in narrative analysis, discourse, teaching methodology and cross-cultural communication.

Glenn Drover is Professor of Applied Social Studies at the City University of Hong Kong. Previously he was Director of the School of Social Work, University of British Columbia for eleven years. Prior to that, he taught at Carleton University and McGill University in Canada. He has published widely in the fields of social work and social welfare. He has been an active volunteer for many years in multi-cultural and international development agencies. He is currently doing research on social security in Asia and the welfare implications of free trade.

Adrian Furnham is Professor of Psychology at the University of London. He grew up in South Africa but was educated at the London School of Economics and the University of Oxford. He is the author of twenty books and 350 scientific publications, a number of which are concerned with culture. Having once been an overseas student he is particularly interested in the process of adaptation to new countries and cultures. Currently all of his doctoral students are from overseas. He travels widely and lectures annually at the University of Hong Kong. He is currently working on a second edition of *Culture Shock* (Methuen, 1986).

Robert Harris is Pro-Vice-Chancellor and Professor of Social Work at the University of Hull. He has long experience of teaching overseas students (particularly from Hong Kong); he has worked on postgraduate educational development in Malaysia on British Council funding, taught in Hong Kong and Japan, and researched aspects of professional accreditation and freedom of movement within the European Community on EU funding. He has published widely in the field of quality and accreditation in higher education as well as in international and comparative aspects of social welfare and criminal justice.

Lixian Jin is Lecturer in Linguistics at De Montfort University where she teaches general linguistics, sociolinguistics, syntax and clinical linguistics. She has taught TESOL and linguistics courses and trained teachers for over ten years at universities in China, Turkey and Britain. She is visiting professor at Renmin (Beijing) and Hubei (Wuhan) universities. She has published in the areas of her research interests, namely cross-cultural communication, academic cultures, cultures of learning, second language acquisition and narrative analysis.

Murray Macrae was Senior Lecturer in Educational Management Policy and Planning to international students at the University of Newcastle for thirteen years and also became Director of the Centre for International Studies in Education. He is currently an international development consultant in human resource development with Macrae Mason Development in Newcastle. He has professionally visited and conducted consultancies in some sixteen countries and has authored over fifty publications, including thirty-eight textbooks, with worldwide sales, especially in Africa and the Caribbean.

David McNamara has been Deputy Director of the School of Education at the University of Lancaster and Professor of Education at the University of Durham. Currently he is Professor of Education at the University of Hull, where he helps coordinate the Educational Development Team responsible for providing advice and training in teaching methods for academic staff. He also directs the EduLib project, which has a national remit for developing higher education librarians' teaching expertise. He has directed a number of educational research projects and written extensively on the relevance of the social sciences to educational practice and on teacher education policy. His latest book is *Classroom Pedagogy and Primary Practice* (Routledge, 1994).

Othman Mohamed is Associate Professor and Deputy Dean in the Faculty of Educational Studies in the Universiti Pertanian Malaysia. He is a counselling psychologist and counsellor educator with twenty years experience as a counselling practitioner. He has wide experience with overseas students, particularly with South-East Asian students studying in the USA and with foreign graduate students in Malaysia. He has published research works on career development and counselling, learning styles and adolescent development.

Elizabeth S. Todd is Lecturer in Psychology in the Department of Education at the University of Newcastle upon Tyne. She worked as an educational psychologist before lecturing in educational psychology and mathematical education at the University of the South Pacific in Fiji. This involved teaching undergraduates and postgraduates and developing consultancies in several Pacific island countries. She has also lectured at Newcastle's Centre for International Studies in Education, teaching international MEd students. Her current research interests include postgraduate supervision, social constructivist learning and aspects of special educational needs.

Caroline Wright is Lecturer in the Centre for the Study of Women and Gender at the University of Warwick. She has considerable experience of teaching overseas students both at Warwick (where more than half the students in her Centre are from overseas) and at the universities of Manchester and Hull. Her research concentrates on gender and development and she has recently authored 'Gender research and development: looking forward to Beijing', *Journal of Gender Studies*, 1995, and 'Gender awareness in migration theory: synthesising actor and structure in Southern Africa', *Development and Change*, 1995.

Acknowledgements

Chapter 2 is an amended and updated version of "Overseas students in the United Kingdom university system," a paper first published in *Higher Education*, vol. 29, 1995, pp.77-29. The Editors are grateful to the journal for granting permission.

Introduction

David McNamara and Robert Harris

The United Kingdom's higher education system has changed dramatically during the past decade. Government has decreed that the life and work of universities and colleges should become increasingly accountable to public scrutiny. The system must demonstrate that public funds are used responsibly and effectively to promote high quality teaching and research. Increasingly funding for both research and teaching is being linked to the quality of provision. Institutions are being encouraged to rely less exclusively upon funding sourced from taxation and to seek other means of raising their income by becoming more entrepreneurial within the wider educational marketplace.

It is the pressures upon higher education which, in part, provide the impetus for this book. One of the distinctive ways in which institutions are aiming to expand their activities and increase their income is by developing significantly the courses that they offer for overseas students. There have been dramatic increases in the numbers of undergraduate and postgraduate overseas students within the system. As this aspect of university and college activity has burgeoned it has become apparent that the quality of the teaching and learning offered to overseas students must be maintained and enhanced and also become subject to audit. The central aim of this book is to draw upon the developing literature, expertise and experience which focus upon the delivery of courses for overseas students and to offer a useful resource for those academic staff who have a measure of responsibility for teaching and sustaining the quality of overseas students' learning experiences. In addition, it is hoped that the book will be of interest to overseas students who are contemplating or embarking upon programmes of study in the United Kingdom.

The expansion in overseas students numbers has been noteworthy during the past decade. In 1973 there were 35,000 international students in HEs in the UK. This was followed by a decline in the early 1980s, and by dramatic growth in the early 1990s so that by 1992 numbers had risen to 95,000 (CVCP 1995a: 2.2). This increase can be accounted for by a decline in the real cost of courses for overseas students, steady per capita growth in the principal consuming countries, and the expansion of the student base in UK institutions (ibid.). Currently one third of overseas students are postgraduates, and international students are concentrated in three main academic areas: Engineering, Technology, Social Science, and Business and Finance (ibid.: 2.3).

Within the global context (setting aside the USA's dominant 70 per cent share) the UK is a major player in the provision of courses for overseas students and has 17 per cent of the total overseas student population, with one third from the European Union (CVCP 1995a: 5.3). It should be noted that it is predicted that the global supply of overseas student places will increase, and expected that the UK will endeavour to expand its volume in response to constraints in home student numbers, the higher fees international students command and the move to increase postgraduate numbers (ibid.: 5.5).

Overseas students are having a significant impact upon the economies of UK higher education institutions. In broad terms their economic impact arises from the export of educational services from the UK so that student fees and expenditure represent an injection into the circular flow of income (CVCP 1995a: 3.2–3.3); even discounting EU students, funded at undergraduate level and paid for by the UK Treasury, the value of fees of fully funded overseas students was £310 million in 1992–3 (ibid.: 3.31). In addition, their expenditure on UK-produced goods and services is estimated to be at least £405 million in 1992–3 (ibid.: 3.32). In total this sums to twice the value of UK exports of coal, gas and electricity in the same year (ibid.: 3.33). In terms of the benefit to institutions themselves, on average 5.1 per cent of 'old' university income depends on international students and 2.2 per cent in 'new' universities. There are also, of course, non-economic benefits arising from overseas student provision such as the promotion of the English language and culture and fostering understanding between races. In such circumstances it is hardly surprising that the government is keen to promote the export of educational services as a means of promoting economic growth (see for example DTI 1995).

According to a wide ranging recent survey, the main reasons why overseas students decide to study in the UK rather than anywhere else are: that the English Language is spoken; UK qualifications are recognised by the home government and companies; the standard and quality of education in the UK; the international reputation of UK education; the presence of well known universities; and that students are already used to the English system of education (Allen and Higgins 1994: 22, table 20). The two main reasons they decided to go to their current institution rather than elsewhere in the UK were the academic reputation of the institution (for 27.8 per cent) and the content of the course (for 20.8 per cent) (ibid.: 39, table 27).

Given the importance that overseas students attach to the quality of UK institutions and the courses they offer, it is essential that quality is maintained. There have, however, in recent years been concerns that the rapid expansion in overseas courses could have an effect upon quality. For instance an editorial in the *Times Higher Education Supplement* (1994) opined that there was a danger that the recruitment of overseas students was being driven too much by the pursuit of money to support an under-funded system and too little by genuine educational considerations. The need to maintain quality has been recognised within the system and the Committee of Vice-Chancellors and Principals (CVCP) has recently issued a relevant Code of Practice (CVCP 1995b). The introduction by the Chairman of the CVCP demonstrates higher education's determination to maintain high standards and quality control. As he says: 'The Committee of Vice-Chancellors and Principals seeks to encourage the commitment of institutions to providing value for the investment made by and on behalf of their international students by developing and applying consistent procedures in the recruitment and support of such students.'

It is evident that higher education institutions must pay particular attention to the quality of the teaching and learning which they offer for overseas students. With the establishment of a quality assurance system which ensures that higher education teaching is scrutinised on a regular basis and that external assessors' ratings are published (see for example HEFCE 1996; HEQC 1995), institutions have become very much more aware of the importance of teaching and concerned to enhance academic staff expertise in this crucial aspect of their roles. Many institutions now provide formal training in teaching methods and linked higher education teaching qualifications for their staff (SEDA 1996), and have established staff and educational development units to offer appropriate advice and support. There is an ever growing body of literature which brings together the pertinent research and expertise on teaching and learning in higher education and offers academic staff a valuable resource (see for example Brown and Atkins 1988; CVCP 1992a; Ramsden 1992; Wilkin 1995). There is, however, within the available corpus very little mention of overseas students and the special problems they present when studying in the UK environment (but see Makepeace 1989; and Ballard and Clancy 1991 for an Australian example). It is an apposite time, therefore, to make available for the wider academic community the burgeoning body of information on teaching and learning which has a direct bearing upon overseas students studying in the UK higher education system. This book comprises invited chapters from colleagues who have experience and a particular interest in working with overseas students. The aim is not to supply 'tips for teachers' but rather to bring to tutors' attention theoretical perspectives, empirical studies, informing principles and experience which have a bearing upon overseas students' learning in the UK as the host country. It is hoped that the information will help sensitise academic staff to the problems encountered by both students and tutors and also offer interpretive frameworks which will aid reflection upon practice and develop proposals for improving practice.

In education there is no easy distinction between an entity known as 'theory' and another referred to as 'practice'. Theory should have some bearing upon the 'real world' of practice and our actual practices are always informed by either covert or overt theoretical assumptions. As we all know, there is nothing so practical as a good theory. The contributors to the book have, depending upon their substantive subject matter and the manner in which they treat their topics, given different emphases to theoretical and practical matters. We have used this consideration as the principle for arranging the sequence of chapters. We begin with those that place a greater stress upon policy issues which may inform and guide educational practices and we move on to those which give a greater emphasis to practical considerations. We divide the chapters up into two sections, Part I, 'Principles: perspectives and orientation' and Part II, 'Practice: supporting learning', but we are well aware that the division between them is somewhat arbitrary.

PART ONE

An essential starting point for the overseas student's tutor is to try to understand the learner's perspective and to appreciate study in the host country from his or her point of view. We begin, therefore, with **Adrian Furnham's** chapter in which he raises some salient issues. He draws upon the academic research which has investigated foreign and exchange students' experience of sojourn in the host country. He focuses upon important processes associated with being an overseas student. These include culture shock, homesickness, social support and friendship networks, and poor adaptation. He then moves on to review the training programmes which provide forms of orientation to the host country. He offers a hard-headed and critical review and exposes terms which we may be disposed to deploy too readily, such as 'culture shock' to critical scrutiny. He argues that, overall, the evidence indicates that despite the best efforts of host institutions, overseas students may remain vulnerable to culture shock. People working in culturally different environments require some sort of orientation programme. There are a variety of alternative forms available and he suggests that simple skills training is the most cost-effective.

Robert Harris contextualises and addresses the learning needs of overseas students in UK universities and locates the provision of courses for international students within historical and policy contexts. At the outset, among other things, he identifies the 'unfortunate contradiction' that the factors which have pressured institutions to take more overseas students (which are essentially economic) have also led to a decline in the resources available to support them. He identifies an historical shift from a position in which students were the recipients of post-colonial *noblesse oblige* to one where they become potential customers for institutions keen to offer their educational services. He then reviews the evidence which has investigated studying abroad from students' perspectives. He pursues the economic motif which informs his analysis by suggesting that overseas students are becoming increasingly assertive and regarding overseas study as a means of securing an economic advantage. He then goes on to illuminate the overseas student experience by locating it within a life-cycle model which begins with the period prior to arrival in the host country, moves on to the moment of arrival and the stay abroad, and concludes with the return home. This perspective should help tutors to appreciate that their impact upon students is not confined to the time that they are in their charge. For instance, students will have developed expectations prior to arrival and may return home disillusioned or invigorated. Finally, Harris considers the learning needs of overseas students and demonstrates how important it is for tutors to attend to their concerns. An interesting aspect of his discussion is the suggestion that the adoption of innovatory teaching practices which tutors may think will foster learning may actually cause problems for some overseas students.

David Chan and **Glenn Drover**, writing from Hong Kong whence, for the time being at least, so many overseas students come to the United Kingdom, locate student mobility at the macro level in terms of the globalisation of trade and communications; at the mezzo level in the post-colonial policies and experiences of Hong Kong itself; and at the micro level in the educational behaviour of Chinese students. Chan and Drover offer an invigorating defence of the learning styles and strategies of Confucian-heritage cultures which are so misunderstood by westerners, who confuse repetitive learning (which facilitates accurate recall) with rote learning (which entails learning mechanically and unthinkingly). Repetitive learning, for all its unpopularity in the West, works rather well as a deep learning strategy and might just be worth revisiting by those whose eschewal of it stems less from philosophical or empirical refutation than from an overarching hedonistic approach to learning. Perhaps Confucian-heritage students have remembered what too many educators in the West have forgotten: that learning cannot always be fun, nor teaching always a five-star spectacular. Sometimes learning is a hard slog, painful and dull at the time but, one hopes, worthwhile in the end. It need hardly be added that, particularly when set alongside the critical studies of standards in the UK higher education system reported by Brennan, a gloss can be put on these observations which makes them by no means complimentary to some central aspects of the United Kingdom's contemporary educational philosophy and practice.

John Brennan sets the themes of this book within a European context in a chapter which both considers the ERASMUS scheme from a political as well as educational perspective, and which raises some issues to be considered if quality is to be conceived of and addressed transnationally. While there is about Brennan's chapter a comforting sense that the United Kingdom is not alone in grappling with the problems associated with creating a mass higher education system which retains much of the character and quality of the former élite one, his review of the experiences of users of the ERASMUS scheme will bring little comfort to domestic readers. This review does, however, demonstrate just how crucial is the debate about standards initiated by the Major administration but likely to continue into the next century. While some comfort can be taken from the fact that on the whole EU students studying in the UK enjoyed themselves and appreciated some of the character of our universities, the fact that they also claimed that the academic level of a degree was lower in the UK than elsewhere in Europe is profoundly disturbing, professionally, politically and commercially – the more so since this critical student comment is supported by peer evaluation at discipline level.

Martin Cortazzi and Lixian Jin begin with the premise that learning to communicate is important in higher education, for both students and staff. Both parties, therefore, need to develop inter-cultural skills, entailing *learning to communicate across cultures* and *communicating for learning across cultures*. Their chapter surveys ways in which hidden assumptions about culture infuse communication and learning. They develop their theme with reference to academic cultures (norms and expectations involved in academic study), cultures of communication (expected ways of communicating and interpreting others' communication in a cultural group), and cultures of learning (cultural beliefs and values about teaching and learning). They argue persuasively that learning across cultures means considering overseas students as bearers of culture. These are deep rooted and change may be a threat to identity. Hence there are problems associated with expecting overseas students to assimilate British ways. They propose that there is a basic need for participants in higher education to be aware of the variations in communication and learning which can lead to different understandings. They commend a process of cultural synergy, through which both teachers and students make mutual efforts to understand each other's cultures.

Caroline Wright draws on over two decades of research in general education in order to demonstrate that gender is an important axis around which educational experiences may be structured and one which is pivotal to initiatives promoting equal opportunities in education. An initial difficulty which she has, as she eloquently demonstrates, is that essentially the literature on overseas students is 'gender blind'. She is thus presented with the formidable task of recasting the available literature as the basis for initiating discussion of gender issues within the context of overseas students. She first explores the emergence of gender as an important issue in education generally, before examining the neglect of gender in the higher education literature and its scant consideration in the literature on overseas students. She then turns to three major issues concerning overseas students, namely access, welfare, and teaching and learning. Where possible she draws on the wider discipline of gender studies and also makes suggestions for a more gender-sensitive approach to the education of overseas students. Wright explores why there has been a neglect of gender in the research on teaching and learning in higher education and makes suggestions for a research agenda. Throughout she stresses that we must reject accounts of women's disadvantage which are premised upon their inherent qualities *qua* women. Instead, we must be aware of structural factors within the university system and the wider society which may constrain the capacity of overseas women as a group and enhance those of overseas student men as a group.

John Barker draws upon empirical evidence in order to review three issues which are central to the learning experiences of overseas students. He first asks what may seem a simple question, namely, why are they studying? He goes on to consider whether their responses have implications for the courses and subjects offered to them. He then asks whether there are any significant features of the attitudes, values and motivations which overseas students bring to the classroom, an awareness of which might cause academic staff to modify their approach. Finally, he explores both student and staff expectations and reviews how we may be able to take these into account. A central theme which informs Barker's commentary is that we should avoid generalisations when considering overseas students. They come from many different cultural backgrounds and even from a particular mix of circumstances in their home countries. They may have nothing more in common than the fact that they are 'overseas students'. As an example, consider students' motivation for study; the theories of motivation we draw upon for explanatory purposes are largely western Anglo-Saxon and motivation itself encompasses a complex set of individual human behaviours even within a single culture. It is therefore difficult to arrive at a secure understanding of what staff should do in order to motivate their overseas students. In his chapter he also discusses the awkward problem of 'cheating' and considers how tutors should approach dealing with a form of behaviour which may be acceptable in one culture but not approved of in the UK.

PART TWO

When embarking upon any new experience first impressions and being made welcome are all important, and as far as overseas students are concerned, their systematic introduction into their new academic environment is a process which is likely to colour their subsequent sojourn. **Murray Macrae** discusses the induction of overseas students and how higher education institutions may most effectively prepare them for academic life. He provides much advice which will prove useful for tutors responsible for establishing students in their departments. He begins with the issue of identifying language needs and emphasises the all-important point that it is much preferable to identify competence in English before students embark upon their course of study. He then addresses the induction of students to study facilities, including laboratory, library and computing provision. He finally offers sound advice on how to help overseas students adjust to the academic modes that they are likely to encounter in the UK, with suggestions for resolving particular problems such as being unable to participate fully in seminars; developing academic self discipline; acquiring adequate feedback on performance; coping with the variety of assignments; and understanding examination methods and developing appropriate techniques.

Tutors need to be especially aware of the daunting challenge presented to students who are learning at an advanced level through the medium of a second language. **Nadine Cammish** begins her exploration of the issues by pointing out that the type of experiences encountered by students when they were learning English in their home countries will affect their linguistic competence. Some students will have learned English in school as a foreign language subject. The way they are taught, the methods used and the educational assumptions informing English language methodology will all influence linguistic capability. Some will have learned the language in contexts where it is culturally decontextualised (she gives the pointed example of the boy on a Caribbean island reading a story called 'How we nearly froze to death'), while others will have used teaching materials which reflect the traditions and values of the learners' country (and who may therefore have difficulty relating their learning to the UK context). She then proposes that successful study at advanced level requires developing communicative competence in English in four language skills, namely listening, speaking, reading and writing. She elaborates on each one and identifies key issues which tutors need to be aware of, and her insights have a direct bearing upon practical teaching.

Othman Mohamed offers a thought-provoking discussion of aspects of cross-cultural counselling designed to be of value to a wide range of supervisors of South-East Asian students. He stresses the inter-relatedness of the emotional and intellectual aspects of a student's life, the heterogeneity of the South-East Asian student population in particular, and the fact that not only do such students have to adapt to cultural differences overseas which may pose fundamental questions about their own values and way of life, but, such is the rate of social and economic development in much of the Western Pacific Rim, while they are abroad their own countries may be undergoing such transformation as to deny them any fixed point in their own lives. In such a situation not only can the immediate need for support be incontrovertible but the prospect of returning home can provoke a form of reverse culture shock with which they have also to deal. Drawing on Malaysian research Othman addresses the familiar experience of academics dealing with South-East Asian students (and by implication, East Asian students) whose academic single-mindedness borders on obsession but for whom success proves elusive. He shows that a planned and structured training approach based on achievement motivation training can improve academic performance. So central is academic success to the self-perception of such students (and the perceptions others will have of them on their return home) that, almost literally, if this goes wrong nothing else can go right.

Elizabeth Todd considers the learning support needs of students from overseas, particularly but not exclusively postgraduates, challenging the view that the core difficulty is language. While language is (virtually by definition) important, Todd argues that to see it as the root problem rather than as part of a configuration of issues to be addressed is a mistake: crack one language problem, she says, and, *ceteris paribus*, another will pop up to take its place. Language cannot be severed from meaning, culture and context, and Todd affirms the necessity of locating language support in this broader framework. After all, she implies, the rules of discipline discourse are, to an outsider, arcane if not arbitrary. While part of the process of 'joining' a discipline in an overseas setting entails learning the rules, helping overseas students understand what the rules are and how to play effectively by them is a big step towards helping them close the gap between what they know and what they write. Only by such means are examiners able with confidence to distinguish between overseas students' discipline ability and their adjustment to cultural and geographical 'difference'. Though both are important parts of the overseas student experience, they are still different, and to assess the latter when one thinks one is assessing the former is both incompetent and unfair.

It is salutary to remember the key role which overseas students themselves may play in providing feedback on the courses provided for them. **Jim Ackers**, drawing on long experience at home and overseas, asks how best to evaluate courses from the point of view of overseas students and their sponsors. Skilfully maintaining a balance between the demands of the commercial world and the traditions of the academy, he reminds us of the importance of a 'cradle to grave' approach to student support. Keep in touch with prospective students when they are still applicants, he implies, and you will be off to a good start – and even if they never arrive you will have done your bit to enhance the reputation of UK higher education as a whole. And at the other end of the higher educational process, when reintegration is being negotiated, your graduates may need help too. He notes wryly that in many African countries people have turned from the time-honoured Landrover to Japanese four-wheel-drives because the Landrover has no support systems in terms of garages and spare parts. How many of our institutions provide effective after-sales care to their students?

Finally, as will be evident, there is a considerable literature on overseas students being established and which has been drawn upon by our contributors. We hope that the composite bibliography will provide a valuable resource for staff in colleges and universities who wish to pursue further study and research in the field of teaching and learning for overseas students.

Part I

Principles: perspectives and orientation

Chapter 1

The experience of being an overseas student

Adrian Furnham

INTRODUCTION

What is it like being a foreign student? Do they do as well as natives? How well do they cope with the culture of the country in which they are studying? Is there much evidence of psychological distress among foreign students the world over? Foreign and exchange students have been the topic of academic research for a long time (Bock 1970; Brislin 1979; Byrnes 1966; Tornbiorn 1982; Zwingmann and Gunn 1963). Over thirty years ago in a book delightfully entitled *Colonial Students*, Carey (1956) looked at how different groups of students adapted to life in Britain. Consistent themes running through this book were the excessively optimistic, followed by the chronically disillusioned expectations of the students. Another theme was the importance of the British beliefs about and attitudes to the students. Carey wrote:

> Both favourable and unfavourable stereotypes exist in relation to Asians and Africans: thus Asians are 'highly civilised', 'very brainy', philosophers who often perform truly astounding feats of memory; but they are also 'treacherous', cunning and cruel; 'you can't trust any of them'. Africans, on the other hand, are either 'savage' and 'primitive', with enormous sexual powers, or alternatively kind, loyal darkies, childlike and grateful for any kindness bestowed on them. But it is significant that of the stereotypes about Asians, some at least are unqualifiedly favourable; while those about Africans are favourable only in a highly patronising way, and hence unacceptable to African students.
>
> (Carey 1956: 145)

In the mid 1960s, two psychologists arranged an essay competition for foreign students concerning their reactions to Britain (Tajfel and Dawson 1965). The best were published in a book entitled *Disappointed Guests* and they found, in a content analysis of these essays, six times as many negative and unfavourable comments as favourable ones. Overseas students found the British profoundly ignorant of their native country, reserved, patronising, superior, conservative, critical and unfriendly!

The experience of studying in a foreign country leaves a powerful impression on young people that may last all their lives. For a few the experience is negative and they recall the loneliness and rejection of the foreign country, but for most the experience is very enriching so much so that some people prefer never to return home and to continue living in their new country. As a result of the increase in student movement much has been written on this topic (Jenkins 1983; Kagan and Cohen 1990; Searle and Ward 1990). The diversity, quality and increase in the number of studies on 'foreign' or international students is probably a function of a number of issues (Crano and Crano 1993; Furukawa and Shibayama 1993, 1994; Kagan and Cohen 1990; Harris 1995; Sandhu 1994). These include the large increase in their numbers; the fact that a significant number fail, drop out or have serious psychological and medical problems whilst abroad and problems of adapting once they return; developing theoretical work on the experience of sojourners and the existence of specialist academic journals that focus on the issues associated with foreign student exchange.

Furnham and Tresize (1983) have suggested that problems facing the foreign student are threefold: problems of living in a foreign culture (racial discrimination, language problems, accommodation difficulties, separation reactions, dietary restrictions, financial stress, loneliness, etc.); problems of late-adolescents/young adults asserting their emotional and intellectual independence; and the academic problems associated with higher educational study. It is no wonder then that some experience problems. For some young people it is the most important experience of their lives and one that turns them into loyal advocates of the country they study in. But even the most successful adaptation has its problems. This chapter will focus some of the more important processes associated with the experience of being a foreign or overseas student.

CULTURE SHOCK: THE SHOCK OF THE NEW

The culture shock 'hypothesis' or 'concept' implies that the experience of visiting or living in a new culture is an unpleasant surprise or shock, partly because it is unexpected, and partly because it may lead to a negative evaluation of one's own and/or the other culture.

The anthropologist Oberg (1960) was the first to have used the term. In a brief and largely anecdotal article he mentions at least six aspects of culture shock. These include:

- *Strain* due to the effort required to make necessary psychological adaptions.

- A *sense of loss and feelings of deprivation* in regard to friends, status, profession, and possessions.
- Being *rejected* by and/or rejecting members of a new culture.
- *Confusion* in role, role expectations, values, feeling and self-identity.
- *Surprise, anxiety*, even *disgust* and *indignation* after becoming aware of cultural differences.
- *Feelings of impotence* due to not being able to cope with the new environment.

The flavour of Oberg's observations may be gathered from this quotation:

> Culture shock is precipitated by the anxiety that results from losing all our familiar signs and symbols of social intercourse. These signs or cues include the thousand and one ways in which we orient ourselves to the situations of daily life.... All of us depend for our peace of mind and our efficacy on hundreds of these cures, most of which we are not consciously aware. Some of the symptoms of culture shock are: excessive washing of the hands; concern over drinking water, food, dishes, and bedding; fear of physical contact with attendants or servants; the absent-minded, far-away stare (sometimes called 'the tropical stare'); a feeling of helplessness and a desire for dependence of long-term residents of one's own nationality; fits of anger over delays and other minor frustrations; delay and outright refusal to learn the language of the host country; excessive fear of being cheated, robbed or injured; great concern over minor pains and eruptions of the skin and finally, the terrible longing to be back home.
>
> (Oberg 1960: 176)

Research since Oberg has identified culture shock as a frequently occurring process of adaption to cultural differences. Others have attempted to improve and extend Oberg's definition and concept of culture shock. Guthrie (1975) has used the term *culture fatigue*, Smalley (1963) *language shock*, Byrnes (1966) *role shock* and Ball-Rokeach (1973) *pervasive ambiguity*. In doing so different researchers have simply placed the emphasis on different problems – such as language, physical irritability and role ambiguity. Bock (1970) has described culture shock as primarily an emotional reaction that follows from not being able to understand, control and predict another's behaviour. When customary experiences no longer seem relevant or applicable, people's usual behaviour changes to becoming 'unusual'. Lack of familiarity with environment (etiquette, ritual) has this effect, as do the experiences of use of time (Hall 1959). This theme is reiterated by all writers in the field (Lundsteldt 1963; Hays 1972).

Culture shock is seen as a temporary stress reaction where salient psychological and physical rewards are generally uncertain, and hence difficult to control or predict. Thus a person is anxious, confused and apparently apathetic until he or she has had time to develop a new set of cognitive constructs to understand and enact the appropriate behaviour. Writers about culture shock have often referred to individuals lacking points of reference, social norms and rules to guide their actions and understand others' behaviour. This is very similar to the attributes studied under the heading of *alienation* and *anomie*, which include powerlessness, meaninglessness, normlessness, self and social estrangement, and social isolation. In addition, ideas associated with *anxiety* pervade the culture shock literature. Observers have pointed to a continuous general 'free-floating' anxiety which affects people's normal behaviour. Lack of self-confidence, distrust of others and psychosomatic complaints are also common (May 1970). Furthermore, people appear to lose their inventiveness and spontaneity, and become obsessively concerned with orderliness (Nash 1967).

Most of the culture shock investigations have been descriptive, in that they have attempted to list the various difficulties that sojourners experience, and their typical reactions. Less attention has been paid to explain for whom the shock will be more or less intense (for example the old or the less educated); what determines which reaction a person is likely to experience; how long they remain in a period of shock, and so forth. The literature seems to suggest that all people will suffer culture shock to some extent, which is always thought of as being unpleasant and stressful. This assumption needs to be empirically tested. In theory some people need not experience any negative aspects of shock: instead they may seek out these experiences for their enjoyment. Sensation-seekers, for instance, might be expected not to suffer any adverse effects but to enjoy the highly arousing stimuli of the unfamiliar. People with multi-cultural backgrounds or experiences may also adapt more successfully. For instance, Adler (1975) and David (1971) have stated that although culture shock is more often associated with negative consequences, it may, in mild doses, be important for self-development and personal growth. Culture shock is seen as a transitional experience which can result in the adoption of new values, attitudes and behaviour patterns. As Adler remarks:

> In the encounter with another culture the individual gains new experiential knowledge by coming to understand the roots of his or her own ethnocentrism and by gaining new perspectives and outlooks on the nature of culture.... Paradoxically, the more one is capable of experiencing new and different dimensions of human diversity, the more one learns of oneself.
>
> (Adler 1975: 22)

Thus, although different writers have put emphases on different aspects of culture shock, there is by-and-large agreement that exposure to new culture is stressful. Fewer researchers have seen the positive side of culture shock, whether for those individuals who revel in exciting and different environments, or for those whose initial discomfort leads to personal growth. The quality and quantity of culture shock has been shown to be related to the amount of difference between the visitors' (sojourners', managers') culture and the culture of the country they are visiting or working in. These differences refer to the numerous differences in social beliefs and behaviours.

HOMESICKNESS AND THE FOREIGN STUDENT

References to homesickness occur in all languages over many centuries. In the eighteenth century, medical texts occasionally explained pathology in terms of homesickness. It is, of course, experienced by people who move *within* rather than *between* countries as they too have left their home. The key psychological features of homesickness appear to be a strong preoccupation with thoughts of home, a perceived need to go home, a sense of grief for the home (people, place and things) and a concurrent feeling of unhappiness, dis–ease and disorientation in the new place which is conspicuously not home.

In a number of studies, Fisher investigated the causes and correlates of homesickness (Fisher et al. 1985; Fisher and Hood 1987). While she was unable to identify factors which were good predictors of homesickness, she did find a number of factors that clearly discriminated between students who did not report homesickness and those who did. They included:

- they lived further from home;
- the university they were attending was not their first choice;
- they were less satisfied with their current residence;
- they were less satisfied with present, relative to past, friendships;
- they expected their friendships to be better in the future than at present.

Fisher's studies also identified an association between homesickness reporting and a greater number of cognitive failures, poor concentration, handing in work late and decrements in work quality. These data suggest that homesickness is a potentially important phenomenon that may exercise a considerable influence on academic performance, at least over the short term. More recently, Brewin et al. (1989) investigated some of the determinants of homesickness and reactions to homesickness in two samples of first-year English psychology students who had left home for the first time. Homesickness was found to be a reasonably common but short-lived phenomenon, and was predicted longitudinally by greater self-reported dependency on other people and by higher estimates of the frequency of homesickness among students in general. Although homesickness was equally common in men and women, women were much more likely to discuss their feelings with others and to respond by being more affiliative. Greater anxiety and depression about home-sickness were also associated with more confiding behaviour. There was a suggestion that homesick male students were more likely to seek out others, the more common they perceived homesickness to be. They note:

> Like examination failure, homesickness appears to be a consistent source of stress to a considerable number of students, and lends itself to the testing of hypotheses about aetiology and coping behaviours. The present study has identified attitudinal precursors of home-sickness that implicate attachment style and expectations about the transition to university.... Further research is necessary to confirm these findings and to clarify the meaning of homesickness. For example, although it is often assumed to be a wholly negative experience, for some individuals homesickness may represent a positive affirmation of the importance of their personal relationships rather than an unwanted interference in the transition to a new environment.
>
> (Brewin et al. 1989: 476)

SOCIAL SUPPORT AND FRIENDSHIP NETWORKS

To what extent do foreign students' friendship networks buffer them against culture shock? Does the presence of a reasonably large number of students from the same area (country, region, linguistic area) inoculate against culture shock? Despite current interest in the social support hypothesis, little work has been done on the social support and social networks of foreign students (for a review see Church 1982). The voluminous literature on social networks and social support suggests that these factors reduce stress by providing the individual with information, emotional, monetary and moral support. According to Cobb (1976) social support provides a person with three sorts of information: namely that they are cared for and loved; esteemed and valued; and that they belong to a network of communication and mutual obligation. Hence it may be predicted that foreign students with a strong and supportive friendship network may be happier and better adjusted than those without such a network.

Although a great deal of work has been done on the friendship networks of students, very little has been done on the friendship networks and preferences of foreign students, despite its obvious and important application. The work of Bochner is, however, an important exception. Recently, Bochner and his co-workers (Bochner et al. 1976, 1977; Bochner and Orr 1979; Furnham and Bochner 1986) have shown some interesting results concerning the friendship networks of foreign students. In a study of foreign students in Hawaii, Bochner et al. (1977) provided a functional model for the development of overseas students' friendship patterns stating that sojourners belong to three distinct social networks. They are:

- A *primary, monocultural network*, consisting of close friendships with other sojourning compatriots. The main function of the co-national networks is to provide a setting in which ethnic and cultural values can be rehearsed and expressed.
- A *secondary, bi-cultural network* consisting of bonds between sojourners and significant host nationals such as academics, students, advisors and government officials. The main function of this network is to facilitate instrumentally the academic and professional aspirations of the sojourners.
- A *third multi-cultural network* of friends and acquaintances. The main function of this network is to provide companionship for recreational, 'non-cultural' and non-task oriented activities.

As Bochner et al. (1977) have noted:

> Thus monocultural (co-national) bonds are of vital importance to foreign students, and should therefore not be administratively interfered with, regulated against, obstructed, or sneered at. On the contrary, such bonds should be encouraged and, if possible, shaped to become more open to bi- or multi-cultural influences. In particular, mediating individuals who function as links between different cultural networks, should be identified and supported. Bi-cultural (foreign student–host national) bonds should be expanded to reach beyond their initial task-orientated and instrumental function. This often happens spontaneously, and ways and means should be found to capitalize on this tendency. Multi-cultural associations (bonds between non-compatriot foreign students) could likewise be expanded beyond their recreation-oriented function toward the non-superficial learning of each other's cultures.
>
> (Bochner et al. 1977: 292)

Although Bochner did not interpret his findings within a social network framework, others have found that the degree of social interaction between the host national and the sojourner is related to the latter's adjustment. For example, Sewell and Davidson (1961) reported a significant relationship between the social interaction of Scandinavian students with Americans and their satisfaction with their sojourn. Richardson (1974) noted a difference in the friendship patterns of satisfied as opposed to dissatisfied British migrants to Australia having more compatriot and fewer host national friends. Sellitz and Cook (1962) found that sojourners who had at least one close host national friend experienced fewer problems than sojourners with no close host national friends. Based on the findings of a study in Australia, Au (1969) reported that the degree of personal contact between Chinese-Malaysian students and host nationals positively related to the student's attitude towards Australia.

The social support hypothesis places more importance on the *quality* and *quantity* of support compared to the nature (i.e. the nationality) or source of that support, and would thus expect the degree of adjustment to be related simply to these quantity and quality aspects of one's social networks. Others, however, such as Bochner (1982) place more emphasis on the *source* of support and would suggest that the social support and help from a host national network is of far greater importance for adjustment compared to that from a co-national network. It is, of course, possible that these two approaches are confounded; that is, the fact that the support complex from a co-national (who possibly shares the same language, values, religion, etc.) is qualitatively different from one that comes from a host national. Furnham and Alibhai (1985) replicated and extended Bochner's work and found that foreign students showed a stronger preference for co-nationals than host nationals and other nationals.

WHAT CAUSES CULTURE SHOCK AND POOR ADAPTATION?

The extensive but different educational psychological, psychiatric and sociological literature on sojourners' adjustment has been heavy on data but light on theory. Various commonsensical hypotheses have been found wanting, while most research tends to be more exploratory than specifically theory-testing. The explanation of why foreign students experience difficulty, however, is far from trivial. Most importantly, the explanations have implications for how they can be helped. Furnham and Bochner (1986) have outlined and discussed at least eight possible explanations for the exact empirical data. These are outlined below.

Loss, grief and mourning

The concept of loss, and more particularly the work on grief, mourning and bereavement, has been applied to many areas of human experience. Furnham and Bochner (1986) have pointed out that the loss, or bereavement, literature has been used to describe the experience of such diverse phenomena as divorce, and more recently, unemployment. Grief is a ubiquitous, extremely stressful reaction to the real or imagined loss of a significant object or role, which may be resolved when a new object or personal relationship is established. It has been suggested that concepts from this research area may also be used to shed light on the reactions of migrants. Migration (but to some extent all forms of geographic movement) involves being deprived of specific relationships or significant objects. These include family, friends and occupational status as well as a host of important physical factors ranging from food to weather patterns. The loss may be followed by grief (a stereotyped set of psychological and physiology reactions, biological in origin) and mourning (conventional bereavement behaviour determined by the mores and customs of society). Indeed, it is the similarity between various documented symptoms of grief and the stages or phases of grief which have most interested researchers on migration and mental health. And because bereavement behaviour is to some extent culturally determined, this may account for various differences in the reaction pattern of migrants and sojourners from different cultures.

However, there are a number of problems with the analogy between grief and migration. First, it is presumed that all migrants, sojourners and travellers experience negative, grief-like reactions, which is clearly not the case. For some people migration is a blessed escape. Second, although the grief literature does take into account individual and cultural differences, it makes no specific predictions as to what type of people suffer more or less grief, over what period or what form the grief will take. Third, counselling for the grieving would seem highly inappropriate for migrants, who need information and support as much as therapy.

Fatalism (locus of control)

There is a considerable literature in personality and social psychology on a person's perceived locus of control. *Fatalism* is the generalised expectation that outcomes are determined by forces such as powerful others, luck or fate and is the opposite of *instrumentalism*, which is the generalised expectation that outcomes are contingent on one's own behaviour. The dimension has also been described as a perception of *general self-efficacy and control* over events in one's own life. The fatalism or locus-of-control explanation for the relationship between migration and mental health is potentially interesting but does have problems. It suggests that those who come from cultures or societies where instrumentalism (as opposed to fatalism) is encouraged, tend to adapt faster and more successfully. The explanations should be able to account for the different distress rates of different immigrant groups. For instance, immigrants from a country whose religion is fatalistic should have more difficulty in adjusting than migrants from a country where personal responsibility is valued. However, there is ample evidence to suggest that this is not the case. For instance, Cochrane (1983) has shown that Indians adjust particularly well when migrating to Britain yet supposedly come from a fatalistic culture. Another problem lies in self-selection. In order to voluntarily migrate (as opposed to being a refugee) one has to assume considerable personal responsibility and control over one's own affairs, such as financial, social and familial aspects. It may be argued, therefore, that most people who migrate have by definition an internal locus of control and are therefore relatively homogeneous irrespective of their culture or origin. There must therefore be other factors which account for the relationship between geographic movement and psychological well-being.

Selective migration

One of the oldest and most popular explanations for the different patterns of reaction to new environments by migrants is the neo-Darwinian idea of selective migration. It is an extension of the principle of natural selection, which states that all living organisms that cope best with the exigencies of the environment become the prevailing type. When people are selected for a new environment to which they are particularly suited, they will cope better than others who are not so well matched.

There are a number of appealing features to this approach. First, it describes why different migrant groups to the same country at the same time may adapt differently because of different selective processes. Second, it tends to highlight which combination of general coping strategies are most appropriate to the particular requirements of a certain country. Hence it can explain why people who were 'selected' by similar processes from the same country may adjust well in a particular 'new' country but not in others. The explanation therefore pays special attention to the types of selection processes and the coping strategies of various groups. One should, however, be aware of the fact that, being nearly always retrospective, the selective migration thesis is tautological rather than explanatory. There are many other references in the literature on mental health and migration which explicitly or implicitly refer to a selective-migration hypothesis. However, this hypothesis has a number of limitations. First, considering the selective processes of the migrants themselves, it is not clear which barrier or obstacles select for adaptation and which do not. The sheer number of obstacles alone may predict a certain type of fitness or motivation but does not imply that those people necessarily adapt well. For instance, education, physical fitness, language ability and financial security may be important positive factors with regard to selection, while others such as religion may not. Rarely, if ever, do the optimally adaptive selectors exist in isolation from those factors that do not discriminate. Furthermore, the positive selector obstacles may differ from country to country.

Expectations

The idea of this theory is straightforward. The more accurate, objective and comprehensive a sojourner or migrant's expectations of the visited country, culture, university, the more successful that adaptatation. Most of the research has suggested that high expectations that cannot and are not fulfilled are related to poor adjustment and increased mental illness.

Although he does not refer directly to the expectancy-value hypothesis, Cochrane (1983) clearly believes that positive expectations are inversely related to adjustment. As regards British immigrants he notes:

> West Indians typically come to this country with high expectations of achievement in terms of material well-being and also probably in terms of achieving integration within the wider community. Alienation results from a failure both to meet these expectations and to reach the assimilation that the immigrant has set for him or herself.
>
> (Cochrane 1983: 97)

Expectancy-value theories have proved useful in predicting people's reactions to various types of adversity. Yet this theoretical approach is not without its problems. First, it should be pointed out that the migrants have a wealth of expectations, some relating to social, economic, geographic and political aspects of life in their new country. They are bound to be wrong about some, expecting too much or too little. What is unclear is which expectations about what aspects of life in the new country are more important to adjustment than others. Second, the way in which unfulfilled expectations lead to poor adjustment is far from clear. For instance, do disappointed or unfulfilled expectations lead to anxiety, depression or anger? Third, from the above literature it would seem that having low expectations may be better for adjustment but worse for overall social mobility. Further, apart from refugees, few people would voluntarily migrate if their expectations were too low.

However, research on applying expectancy-value theory to the area of migration and mental health is comparatively new, and many of the above problems have simply not been addressed.

Negative life-events

For nearly twenty years psychologists, psychiatrists and sociologists have been collecting evidence on the relationships between recent stressful life-events and psychological and physical illness. The basic idea is that negative life-events, such as the death of a spouse, divorce or losing one's job, make people ill; the more negative in terms of intensity of the duration and consequences of the events, the more severe the illness. Some research has also shown that any change in one's daily routine, not necessarily a negative one, has similar deleterious effects, although these findings have been questioned (see later in this chapter). Negative life-events have been associated with responses as varied as depression, neurosis, tuberculosis, coronary heart disease, skin diseases, hernias and cancer.

Although the mechanism by which negative life-events influence health and illness is by no means clear, most studies have demonstrated a significant relationship between the two. Monroe (1982) has listed three reasons for the growth in this research area: first, it allows one to examine the attractive but elusive link between psycho-social processes and physical/psychological functioning; second, its conceptual basis is congruent with other areas of research; and third, the clinical implications seem clear and straightforward.

What is perhaps most surprising is how little the life-event literature appears to have filtered into the migration and the mental health literature. Though it may not serve to account for a great deal of variance, the range, intensity and perceived threat of migrants' life-changes may go some way towards explaining the nature of the link between mental health and migration.

Social support networks: reduction in social support

There is a rapidly growing and already considerable body of literature in clinical, community, medical and applied psychology regarding the supportive functions of interpersonal relationships. In the main the available evidence suggests that social support is directly related to increased speed and quality of adaptation as well as breaking the clear links between stress and illness.

As is probably true with all areas of research, the social support literature is somewhat equivocal, and fundamental processes have yet to be fully described. Differences in populations, measures, as well as social support definitions and stresses may account for the contradictory findings in this area. Nevertheless, there is enough consistent literature to indicate that a relationship does exist between social support and psychological disorder; suggesting that the various types of support provided by interpersonal relationships play a crucial role in determining a person's general adaptive functioning and sense of well-being. This literature draws on various traditions, including attachment theory, social network theory and various ideas in psychotherapy. Of relevance in the present context are the findings that the social networks of neurotics differ significantly from those of normal people and that people with a well developed primary group are substantially protected against neurotic symptoms. Because migration often involves the leaving behind of family, friends and acquaintances, such as work colleagues and neighbours, sources of social support are reduced and there is, according to the theory, a consequent increase in physical and mental illness. Supportive relationships with family and friends are no longer available to the same extent to sustain migrants and sojourners.

Value differences

The differences in values that exist between many cultures have also been used to try to account for the misunderstandings, distress and difficulties experienced by cross-cultural travellers. Ever since the work of Merton (1938) on the relationship between social structure and anomie, sociologists and psychologists have seen a link between deviance, delinquency and mental disorder, and a conflict in cultural values. There is a rich, interdisciplinary literature on the definition of and consequences of values.

To understand the consequences of value differences for migrants it is important to take three variables into consideration: the quality and quantity of differences in salient values between the hosts' and migrants' societies; the tolerance for varying cultural value systems within the same society; and individuals' cognitive complexity, ability and motivation to change their cultural value system. Certain values – like stoicism and self-help – are perhaps more adaptive than others (Hofstede 1984). It may, however, be that the values relate more to the reporting or non-reporting of illness and unhappiness than to how people cope with stress. Value systems, then, may be useful predictors of both how much strain travellers feel and how they cope with the strain.

Again, it is not being argued that values are the only important variable in determining culture shock but rather that they account for a significant proportion of the variance.

TRAINING FOR INTER-CULTURAL SKILLS

Few people would disagree with the proposition that men or women working in culturally different environments require some sort of orientation programme. Many techniques are available which differ according to theoretical orientation, length of training, type of training, etc. For instance, Brislin (1979) has listed five such sorts of programmes: self-awareness training (in which people learn about the cultural bases of their own behaviour); cognitive training (where people are presented with various facts about other cultures); attribution training (where people learn about the explanation of behaviour from the point of view of people in other cultures); behaviour modification (where people are asked to analyse the aspects of their culture that they find rewarding or punishing); and experiential learning (where people actively participate in realistic simulations). These techniques do overlap and are not mutually exclusive. Furnham and Bocher (1986) (see below) have examined some of these in grater detail.

Information giving

The most common type of cross-cultural orientation usually involves providing prospective sojourners with specific information about their new culture. Students are presented with all sorts of facts and figures, either in written form or in lectures or films, about topics such as the climate, food, sexual relations, religious customs and anything else the trainers may consider important. However, the effectiveness of such illustrative programmes is limited, because, first, the facts are often too general to have any clear specific application in particular, notably business circumstances; second, the facts emphasise the exotic yet tend to ignore the mundane but more commonly occurring happenings, such as how to hail or pay a taxi; third, such programmes give the false impression that a culture can be learned in a few easy lessons, whereas all that they convey is a superficial, incoherent and often misleading picture which glosses over the culture's hidden agendas; and finally, even if the facts are recommended they do not necessarily lead to action, or the correct action. It would be absurd to teach people how to operate a machine by only giving them information about how to do it. If the cognitive information training is to be of any practical use it must be combined with some form of practical experiential learning in the appropriate setting.

Cultural sensitisation

Programmes based on this approach set out to provide trainees with information about other cultures, as well as to heighten their awareness about the cultural basis of their own behaviour, and how the practices of their society differ from those of the host country. The aim is, therefore, to compare and contrast the two or more cultures, look at various behaviours from the perspective of each society, and thus develop a sensitivity to, and awareness of, cultural relativity. This view holds that many human values, beliefs and behaviours are absolute and universal, and that what a particular individual believes to be true and good will depend on the norms prevailing in that person's society; these may be norms that other societies may reject. Such programmes often operate at two levels: they aim to achieve self-awareness about the modal values and attitudes that are typically held by members of one's society; and also to gain insight into one's personal traits, attitudes and prejudices. Culture sensitisation and self-awareness programmes, being essentially cognitive techniques, suffer from many of the same limitations as information giving.

Isomorphic attributions

Many researchers have pointed out that a potential obstacle to effective cross-cultural communication is the inability of the participants to understand the causes of each other's behaviour, that is, to make correct attributions about the other's actions. Effective intercultural relations require isomorphic attributions, which means observers offer the same cause or reason for actors' (others') behaviours as they would for themselves. The likelihood of making isomorphic attributions decreases as the divergence between the subjective cultures of the participants increases, and explains why intercultural relations are often characterised by mutual hostility, misunderstanding and poor effect.

One solution is to train the individuals to understand the subjective culture of the other group, which in practice means teaching them how to make 'correct' behavioural attributions. This is done through the cultural assimilator, which in effect is a programmed learning manual. The booklet contains descriptions of episodes in which two culturally disparate individuals meet. The interactions are unsuccessful, in that each incident terminates in embarrassment, misunderstanding, or interpersonal hostility. The trainee is then presented with four or five alternate explanations of where they went wrong, corresponding to different attributions of the observed behaviour. Only one of these attributions is 'correct' from the perspective of the culture being learned. The trainees select the answer they regard as correct, and are then instructed to turn to a subsequent page, where they are either praised if they selected the 'right' answer, or told why they were wrong if they selected an 'incorrect' answer. A great deal also depends on which particular critical incidents are selected to form the basic curriculum. Inevitably, exotic, strange and hence less common events tend to be given greater prominence than the less interesting but more frequently encountered day-to-day problems that make up the bread-and-butter content of inter-cultural contacts.

Learning by doing

The limitations of information-based orientation programmes led to various attempts to expose trainees to supervised real or simulated second culture experience. Most organisations do not have or are unwilling to commit the substantial resources required for experiential culture training. More typically, behaviourally based culture training programmes rely on role-playing encounters between trainees and persons pretending to come from some other cultures, or other-culture professional personnel if they are available. In this respect these techniques are similar to those employed by social skills trainers. Some programmes also contain a behavioural evaluation component, which may take the form of a team of psychologists evaluating and training the performance of the candidates in the field.

It should be emphasised that the vast majority of sojourners, or those who come into contact with members of other cultures in their own societies, receive no systematic culture training whosoever. The little 'training' that does occur is done informally by experienced migrants who pass on useful information to the new visitors. This in itself may not be such a bad thing. One of the requirements of a successful culture trainer is to be a mediating person, i.e. one who is intimately familiar with both cultures and can act as a link between them representing each to the other. In theory experienced sojourners should have this special capacity, but in practice some may have highly specialised, distorted, or even prejudiced views of one or both of their cultures, and perpetuate these distortions in the informal training they impart to highly impressionable newcomers.

Intercultural (social) skills training

Although there are a number of different approaches to social skills training they share various elements in common. The first is an assessment or 'diagnosis' of a particular problem (e.g. assertiveness) or type of situation (e.g. chairing meetings) that the person has or is likely to encounter. The second is an analysis or discussion of the elements in the problem areas, possibly followed by a modelling exercise where a trainer enacts the role. This in turn is followed by role-play by the trainee with critical feedback in length following each practice. The number, range and variety of contexts in which the role-plays are enacted add to the generalisability of the training. Trainees are also encouraged to do homework exercises between role-play and feedback sessions.

CONCLUSION

The worldwide growth in overseas students in the late twentieth century has been remarkable. In Europe alone the rise has been exponential. In 1987 there were about 3,000 ERASMUS students, by 1995 over 100,000. Despite being bright and adaptable many of these sojourning students suffer homesickness and culture shock. Various causes of culture shock have been considered, each of which implied a form of cure. Of all the ways of helping overseas students simple skills training was considered the most cost effective. Studying overseas changes young people and marks them for life. In an increasingly international world they can be fine ambassadors of good international relations. Yet they remain vulnerable to the debilitating effects of culture shock which educational authorities would do well to be sensitive to, and be ready to treat accordingly.

Chapter 2

Overseas students in the United Kingdom university system
A perspective from social work

Robert Harris

This chapter contextualises and then addresses the learning needs and practical experiences of overseas students in the UK university system, straddling the literature on educational policy and process. It begins by identifying some historical milestones in policy development, showing that from the time when overseas students arrived in UK universities privately funded, with no policies either to promote or restrict their doing so and no structured concern for their welfare, we have moved to a situation where their presence reflects the economic pressures experienced by individual universities and the system as a whole.

The first main section traces how this has come about, concluding that the environment in which overseas students are admitted cannot be divorced from their learning needs once here or from the manner in which universities respond to them. The equation is a difficult one:

- In a context in which a declining unit of resource means that almost all universities need to generate revenue independent of the funding councils, many have sought to do so by expanding overseas student intakes;
- the full-cost fee environment makes this strategy both attractive and competitive. The system has in consequence become increasingly price-sensitive, placing the traditional fee cartel of the older universities under intolerable strain. It is often the universities with the weakest student support structures which charge bargain basement fees, attracting academically vulnerable students unable to meet the admissions requirements of more prestigious institutions. The students themselves, however, are unlikely to grasp the complex politics of the expanded university system or the nature of the trade-off they are making between the level of course fee and the extent of support available to them;
- hence, in an unfortunate contradiction, the very factors which make the pressure to take more overseas students, including some academically modest ones, irresistible have led to a decline in the resources available to support them.

The problem is further complicated by the fact that the supposed market in which this inter-institutional competition occurs is in fact increasingly tightly controlled. Part of this control is expressed through an emphasis on 'quality' and its expression not only as an intrinsic good but comparatively, through rankings and league tables. While in England and Wales teaching rankings do not carry direct resource implications their indirect implications are potentially considerable; nowhere is this likely to be more so than in relation to a course's attractiveness to overseas students. Yet since it is not centrally imposed criteria but an institution's own aims and objectives which teaching assessment examines, the process may not address quality issues raised by overseas students. Such students are not, therefore, even justified in making the seemingly reasonable assumption that a unit graded 'excellent' in teaching quality is at all excellent in relation to their particular needs.

It is in turn hard for universities to address these needs given the limited research which exists on what they are, how they are experienced by different categories of overseas students (who are, of course, by no means an homogeneous grouping) and to what extent they are distinct from those of home students, some of whom also experience loneliness, confusion, poverty and culture shock. There are, however, some incontrovertible differences, of degree if not kind. It is striking, for example, that while the cultural problems presented and faced by overseas students are generally recognised, less attention has been given to how culture itself shapes cognition and learning. For example one consequence of full-cost fees is that many overseas students now originate in Pacific Rim countries whose educational cultures characteristically value a highly deferential approach to teachers, and who are widely believed to place considerable emphasis on rote learning, an approach normally associated with surface or reproductive learning (though for a critique of this belief, see Chan and Drover, this volume). Such an approach would be at variance not only with the more intellectually robust and egalitarian ambience of many arts and social science faculties in UK universities, but with officially encouraged teaching innovations which utilise participative methods and problem-solving strategies to ensure deep transformational learning (Denicolo et al. 1992; Committee of Scottish University Principals 1992).

These considerations lead into the second main part of the chapter, which addresses what we know of the student experience by reviewing the literature and illustrating it by reference to a small cohort of Hong Kong students on a postgraduate course in an older English university. In that it derives from a literature review supported by illustrations from practice not empirical research the review is exploratory not definitive, part of what has been termed the logic of discovery – the reasons for entertaining a hypothesis – not of proof – the reasons for accepting one (Kaplan 1964). This may be no bad thing if it encourages productive discussion which in turn prepares the ground for future detailed empirical study of a topic likely to be no less important over the next decade than it has been over the last.

HISTORICAL BACKGROUND AND POLICY DEVELOPMENT

There is nothing new about the participation of overseas students in the universities or the problems associated with them. Whether or not the account of King Henry III chastising the citizens of Cambridge for their lack of 'restraint and moderation' towards such students (Kinnell 1990: 1) is accurate, the tradition of the wandering scholar travelling Europe and studying in different universities antedates by many centuries contemporary preoccupations with credit transfer and mutual recognition procedures within European higher education (Harris and Lavan 1992):

> Ever since the first universities were founded in Italy and France the free interchange of ideas has been jealously guarded and, in their early days, the freedom of movement of students from university to university meant that one might start studying in Padua and later move on to Paris or Cordoba. Universities were used to having students from all over Europe in their midst.
>
> (Dunlop 1966: 11)

This is not to say, however, that overseas governments were oblivious to the potential usefulness of western university education. As early as the eighteenth century, as part of an attempt to improve the intellectual standing of the Russian clergy and create a theological faculty at Moscow University, Tsarina Catherine II sent theology students to study at Oxford, Leyden and Göttingen (Cross 1985) and early this century, as part of his modernisation policy in Siam, King Chulalongkorn sent students to Britain on Government Scholarships, creating in 1904 the post of Superintendent to Siamese students at his Embassy in London. Notwithstanding such examples, the entry into British higher education of significant numbers of non-European students is largely a product of Empire (Dunlop 1966: Part II). There the intervention of Government stemmed initially from political embarrassment at the difficulties experienced by the sons of affluent Indian families sent to England ill-informed about their courses and ill-prepared for living there. Worries about these students had already led to the institution of several welfare associations, notably the National Indian Association (1875), the Northbrook Society (1879) and the Victoria League (1901), but concerns continued and in 1907 the Secretary of State for India appointed a Committee of British and Indian membership to enquire into the

conditions of the 700 Indian students then in Britain. An Advisory
Committee was set up in 1909 and an Educational Adviser to Indian
Students appointed, and in 1912 the Indian Students Department was
established at the India Office, albeit that it was widely perceived by the
students as a surveillance device (Dunlop 1966: 13).

A few students were also sent to study in Britain under scholarships
provided by the Colonial Territories, and in 1902 the Colonial Office
appointed a Director of Colonial Students. Nevertheless, in spite of the
support and scholarships offered by the British Council and the Overseas
Development Administration, the development of an overseas students
'policy' was for many years hindered both by governmental reservations
about constructing a policy on the basis of 'propaganda in peacetime'
(Wallace 1981) and by the prestige and autonomy of the universities
which, unconstrained by financial considerations, maintained virtually
complete control over admissions.

It was not until the Robbins Report in 1963 that any attempt was made
to provide a realistic estimate of the costs involved. Robbins calculated
that overseas students received an effective annual subsidy of £9,000,000
and, though not unsympathetic to the subsidy, argued that it should be
regarded as part of overseas aid policy, its merits being weighed against
competing policy options (*Report of the Committee on Higher Education
1963*: para 175). Clearly such an approach clashed with the liberal
bilateralism of the universities which presupposed that overseas
students gave as much to the system culturally and intellectually as
they took out financially. With hindsight it is clear that this was the
moment at which overseas students began to be conceived politically
and economically as a dimension of UK commercial interests and
cultural and foreign policy (Williams 1981):

> the issue is essentially how to assess student interchange among the
> various instruments available for the pursuit of cultural relations.
> Bringing foreigners to Britain for periods of study...is an activity
> comparable to, and complementary to, other forms of sponsored visits
> to Britain: to the dispatch of British lecturers and teachers to
> institutions overseas; to the provision of British books, equipment,
> and films to schools and universities in other countries, and to the
> support of links between them and equivalent institutions in Britain.
>
> (Wallace 1981: 115)

In 1967 fee differentials for overseas students were introduced in the
face of university and student opposition, but at a time when system
expansion and student unrest were contributing to a diminution of the
universities' traditional prestige and influence. For over a decade the
practical effects of the differential fee policy were mitigated by the
cheapness of the pound, the influence of pre-existing historical links, the

lingua franca status of English and the continuing international prestige of the British universities. Accordingly overseas student numbers rose to an all-time high in 1979, albeit that the distribution of countries of origin was shifting markedly to then newly developed countries such as Hong Kong and some Middle Eastern nations.

The introduction of full-cost fees in 1980, however, led to reduced numbers and further changes in the nature of cohorts. In addition to the preponderance of Middle- and Far Eastern students an increasing emphasis on postgraduate training, particularly the MBA, developed. This trend was facilitated not only by economic and cultural changes within the system which paved the way for franchising and validation arrangements but by the transformation of global communications technology. This in turn made possible the institution of distance-taught contract courses, directed at specific nationality groups, taught in the students' own country and tailored in structure and content to the demands of the students' workplace. It is no longer unusual for students to graduate from a university they have never visited.

Full-cost fees must, however, be comprehended politically as well as economically, and their introduction presaged other more radical shifts in university politics in the 1980s. Full-cost fees gave overseas students the economic role of supporting the university infrastructure and the ideological role of providing a focus for inter-institutional competition. Accordingly, in the (admittedly *ersatz*) internal market of the 1980s and 1990s the vigorous and competitive pursuit of overseas students became inevitable. Equally inevitably the ending of the binary divide in 1992 ensured that the system became increasingly quality- and price-sensitive, putting irresistible pressure on the fee cartel and leading to the practical abandonment of the tradition that a UK university degree was of equal standing irrespective of origin.

These trends have been addressed by government and the funding councils by imposing unprecedented levels of centralised monitoring and control on the supposed market (for examples of monitoring as a broader aspect of public policy see Henkel 1991a; 1991b). In the universities this has been expressed in part by the production of quality not only as an intrinsic good but as a comparative phenomenon to be measured competitively in league tables.

While the teaching quality exercise may, in spite of widespread concern at the methodology applied, have served to sharpen aspects of teaching as well as its public representation it has paid little attention to pedagogy as it relates to overseas students in particular. In an environment in which such students have long ceased to be recipients of post-colonial *noblesse oblige*, becoming instead fair game for increasingly desperate universities, it is helpful to review our knowledge of their experiences, attitudes and learning styles, how these relate to the expectations of the universities, and how the universities might best address their needs.

STUDYING ABROAD: THE STUDENT PERSPECTIVE

Given the policy developments outlined in the last section and the increasingly crucial economic role played by overseas students in the university system, there is a surprising dearth of recent research or writing in relation either to their experiences and attitudes or to their learning needs and how these may best be met. Nevertheless such literature as does exist spans some thirty years, offering a generally plausible if superficial portrayal of the experiences and attitudes of overseas students (see for example Political and Economic Planning 1955, 1965; Livingstone 1960; Burns 1965; Tajfel and Dawson 1965; Morris 1967; Kendall 1968; Sen 1970; Reed et al. 1978; Williams 1982, 1985; Kinnell 1990).

In spite of its limitations this is all we have to go on and it is possible, with proper caution, for universities desirous of enhancing the education of overseas students to derive from it a preliminary agenda for the purposes of internal discussion and staff development. Though differences must clearly exist in the experiences of student categories (not only from different nations or cultures but, for example, native English speakers and others, those from western industrialised societies and others, those financially self-sufficient and others, visible minorities and others, familied and single people, and men and women), such specifics have not been researched, and the existing literature, being inadequate to address them, is itself accordingly in urgent need of augmentation.

In the absence of such data some key points are illustrated from experience at the author's own university. Though as a method of research this approach would clearly be worthless, because the illustrations resonate with and enrich the findings of existing research they can legitimately be 'read' as having heuristic purpose but not as reliable in themselves. It is hoped, however, that their presentation will provoke discussion among readers and encourage further study of this neglected but topical area of study. With this significant caveat we draw intermittently on the experiences of a cohort of eleven former students on the University of Hull's social work MA, as reported to the author through both formal and informal channels.

The student experiences are presented under two subheads. The first, reflecting what appears a potentially fruitful approach to future research, is termed a 'life cycle', offering a natural history of the student experience in its broadest sense from the point of selection to the point of reintegration to the home country. The second draws together what we know of their more specific educational experiences.

The subtext of the section as a whole is that responsible universities, defined in this context as those which seek the reality as well as the appearance of quality, should develop an holistic approach to identifying and addressing the particular needs of their overseas students. Almost by definition these needs will vary on the basis of the kinds of variables already identified, but in the absence of an empirically verified approach a quality loop comprising effective dialogue and follow-up action is necessary if 'goodness of fit' is to be secured between the needs of the students and the resources of the universities.

The ecological concept 'goodness of fit' is of much importance. The belief that problems seemingly presented by overseas students have their cause in the personality, experience or behaviour of the students themselves has increasingly given way to a perspective in which they are seen as arising from a mismatch between the needs of the students and the responses of the universities. The basis of this shift is partly intellectual (Kinnell 1990), partly economic (the combination of the full-cost fee system and the changing patterns of university funding making such students the objects of inter-university competition) and partly political, reflecting the contemporary ideology of consumer choice and quality assurance. Similarly, in a relatively recent shift from the idea that the student must assimilate into a pre-existing structure to the idea that the institution must accommodate to the needs of more diverse student cohorts (Ecclesfield 1985; see also Kinnell 1990) it has been claimed that there is no coherent overseas students policy in much UK higher education:

> An example of this is the employment of overseas student advisers. In institutions which have such a post, how many have developed a policy in relation to the post? Further, how many of these advisers contribute to curriculum development, staff training or policy making? How many even have access to senior management outside their own department?
>
> (Ecclesfield 1985: 619)

Not surprisingly, given that the full-cost fee environment has raised the stakes for students and sponsors alike, an increasingly assertive attitude is visible among many overseas students. In many cases studying abroad is less an end in its own right than a vehicle for securing economic advantage, and full-cost fees have fed what has been memorably termed the 'Diploma Disease' (Dore 1976). Certainly in Hull the presence of the overseas social work students is predominantly an economic response to occupational rationing in a competitive, individualistic and post-colonial society: in Hong Kong social work salary levels are heavily weighted in favour of senior posts; such posts are available only to graduates; and there remain, in spite of considerable expansion, insufficient higher education places in Hong Kong to meet demand.

THE LIFE-CYCLE APPROACH TO THE OVERSEAS STUDENT

Prior to arrival

There is widespread agreement in the literature that the experiences of overseas students must be catalogued from the point of selection (normally in the home country) through the point of arrival and stay in the host country to the return home (Dunlop 1966: 16), where it is normally hoped that as loyal and appreciative alumni they will serve subsequently as volunteer recruiting sergeants.

Where students are personally selected by a member of faculty the interview has declaratory as well as substantive purpose, and it is clear that advice given at this time may be remembered in detail well after the event (Leung et al., 1995). Though we know of no evidence as to the respective take-up rates of offers made by personal interview and paper selection, a well-publicised visit generates interest among those who would not themselves initiate a written enquiry; it is also our experience that making the selector the personal supervisor provides a thread of continuity between past and present worlds which is much valued by students.

Though it is widely considered good practice to prepare students in advance for the course, the university and living in the UK (Kinnell 1990), there is no evidence either on whether/how this is done or on the relative effectiveness of different methods of doing it. As there is, however, evidence that student satisfaction with their quality of life in Britain correlates positively with their evaluation of course quality (Williams 1985), it is reasonable to assume that to the extent that advance preparation improves students' adaptation to the life and culture of the host country it may also increase academic satisfaction. Advice about accommodation, climate, clothing (and whether to buy it in the home country or the UK), the cost of living, scholarships and methods of staggered fee payment are obvious examples of practical information which can help promote the university as a concerned and well-organised institution.

There is evidence that students' expectations of the care which 'their' university will provide are often unrealistic irrespective of information to the contrary (Reed et al. 1978), though it is not clear whether these expectations result from fantasy or prior experience of more caring universities overseas. There is also anecdotal evidence that some universities, in the grip of the economic pressure already described, experience tensions between promoting themselves attractively and giving honest information to prospective students. Though when the sun always shines in the brochures it may be hard to tell students to equip themselves with thick coats and umbrellas, not to do so means that students' first sight of campus is liable to be accompanied by feelings of disappointment or resentment which may take some time to dissipate.

The literature indicates, unsurprisingly, that costs are a major worry. There may be anxieties about 'hidden costs' (for example for language tuition, vacation accommodation or college fees), fee hikes during the course and the respective costs of different forms of residence (including distance from campus and the cost of public transport). Such individual concerns are most obviously dealt with by the designation of individuals at both institutional and departmental levels as responsible for pre-arrival support. Experience suggests that periodic and friendly letters to prospective students can lead to a decline in withdrawal and no-show rates, but again this appears not to have been systematically researched.

The moment of arrival and the stay abroad

The moment of arrival is of much significance, and there is evidence that experiences there may colour subsequent attitudes (Lewins 1990). Meeting arrangements coordinated by the British Council and the National Union of Students seem to be valued, but there is no known study of their effectiveness or consistency, and experience exists of system breakdown when promised accommodation is not ready, or is inaccessible as a result of out-of-hours arrival. To students from the Far East in particular this is incomprehensible, offering as it does evidence not only of organisational inefficiency but of inhospitality and discourtesy to a guest. Where twenty-four hour cover is not provided, clear instructions on how to proceed are important: at Hull advice is sent on a step-by-step basis from the moment of landing at Heathrow or Gatwick Airport, and includes such mundane but not obvious information such as the fact that there are no washrooms on London Underground stations and that if the last train to Hull has gone it is unwise to think of spending the night on King's Cross Station.

On the experiences of students in the United Kingdom the evidence is less clear. Many students claim to prefer reciprocal friendship to 'set piece' hospitality (Morris 1967) – though experience suggests that set-piece hospitality, particularly when it includes senior university staff, is highly valued, and indeed commented on in letters home. Though examples exist of cross-cultural embarrassment and misunderstanding, for instance as a result of students accepting invitations which they have no intention of honouring for fear of causing offence by refusal (Political and Economic Planning 1955), socially most students seem to manage well (Burns 1965), especially those in communal accommodation such as halls of residence (Sen 1970). Though a significant minority experiences loneliness and isolation this is doubtless true of home students too, and we know of no comparative work on this subject.

There are, however, obvious differences. For example, while Hull as a city has many advantages for overseas students, it is not without its challenges: it is a predominantly white city with a minority population of a little over 1 per cent and a known Chinese population of only 537, most of them spread thinly over the city and working long hours in the restaurant and take-away trades. Though there is a Chinese Cultural Centre only a minority of the Chinese population attend it, not least because it only comes to life after the take-aways have closed. In addition to this unsatisfactory piece of timetabling there is evidence that many Chinese people in the catering trade are poorly educated rural dwellers from the New Territories region of Hong Kong (Chiu 1993), few of them therefore constituting 'natural' supports for the upwardly mobile young professionals or intellectuals attending university courses. Accordingly, though normally the Hong Kong students are a mutually supportive group it is on the resources of the University that they of necessity fall back, and it is for the University to ensure that the resources are sufficient to meet the need.

Some visible minority students have reported racism, or at least racially related awkwardness (Political and Economic Planning 1955), though no recent study on this is known to us. This is sometimes poignant (Tajfel and Dawson 1965), may be underreported (Morris 1967), may be directly related to course experience, whether inside or outside the university (Leung et al. 1995) and has historically focused on specific tension points such as seeking private accommodation and opposite-sex relationships. Here the difficulties are of several distinct kinds, though the literature almost certainly simplifies a complex set of issues in this hard-to-research area. For example, male students have reported hesitancy in seeking relationships with British female students (Morris 1967: 34) and female students from Muslim countries have found themselves in confusion and distress as a result of the relative sexual liberation of western youth:

> I have had to accept many things I do not approve of and it is such a shock to me because of my own customs. It is as though everything I have been taught at home and all my values do not count for anything here and I must become a different person to cope with it all. I think if my family could see me now they would think I had changed very much, to accept such things that are completely against my upbringing.
>
> (Anonymous 1985: 642)

For many students costs remain a constant source of anxiety; and while this clearly is true for home as well as overseas students we have found at Hull that in the phenomenology of the Hong Kong students, economic anxieties have a strong psychological dimension. Not only does the character of Hong Kong society make it especially shameful to return home a failure, but the modes of financial support secured by the students raise the stakes further. Most students are supported by their families by payment or loan, and on graduation are expected to provide similar help for younger brothers and sisters. This sense of obligation is fundamental in Chinese culture, where the western individualised 'ego' is culturally alien and, in more traditional families, the notion of 'I' and 'family' as distinct entities without meaning.

It would be easy to simplify or idealise this perception. The collectivity can fragment at times of difficulty, and examples exist of the withdrawal of family support to compel students to return home prior to the completion of study – either at a time of family crisis or simply because the student was 'missed'. This withdrawal may either be a continuing threat or imposed suddenly, without warning, when the necessary maintenance cheque fails to arrive. In one case the death of the father and his replacement as head of the family by a married elder brother shifted the micro-politics as well as economic priorities of the family – a phenomenon not unknown to readers of Hong Kong fiction (Mo 1978). Visa restrictions on paid employment mean that there is no legal means for students so placed to gain financial independence from their families and continue their studies.

Such factors help explain the nature of students' anxiety and vulnerability, feelings which reflect those of many respondents to the studies reviewed in this section. Characteristically these anxieties and vulnerabilities, though they may have their roots in Hong Kong itself, are expressed as concerns about academic attainment, social isolation, language and money – more immediate and tangible difficulties which can be pursued with less personal disclosure or betrayal of family confidence.

The return home

Relatively little is known of the capacity of former students to reintegrate into their own societies or their career advancement (though see Ackers in this volume for a helpful discussion). Such evidence as previously existed was somewhat out of date, for as several authors in this book point out, with improved travel and telecommunications, market shifts and an emphasis on postgraduate professional or business qualifications, the face of the overseas student population has been transformed. Equally the cost of visits home has reduced markedly since these studies were undertaken and it is not unusual for Hull's Hong Kong students to return home several times in the course of their two year stay.

It remains relevant, however, that many who are marginal or vulnerable in their own countries are even more so abroad (Sen 1970) and more likely to have problems reintegrating on their return (Political and Economic Planning 1955). This is of particular interest given a hint in the literature that it is sometimes socially detached people who are most willing to uproot themselves to study abroad – though again we know of no evidence to support this view.

One study noted that disillusionment on returning home was typical (Political and Economic Planning 1955: 162). Not only were facilities in the home country compared unfavourably with those of the United Kingdom, but the value of the degree was not invariably acknowledged. This study, however, concentrated largely on African students and is unlikely to be applicable in the Western Pacific Rim, where any disillusionment with facilities is more likely to be experienced on arrival in Britain. In Hull the main adjustment problem for returning Hong Kong students has been the need to adjust to a faster pace of life and more sultry weather conditions – passing matters only – and in meeting alumni in Hong Kong we have seen no evidence of prolonged difficulty even among those whose career aspirations have not been fully met. The general view, in fact, is that for most alumni the increased salary they command can make the 'payback period' for the degree as short as two years.

TEACHING AND LEARNING

In a political context in which, as we have seen, overseas students have come to constitute a major focus of inter-institutional competition it is surprising that greater attention has not been paid to the promotion of individual universities as receptive to and skilled in teaching them. The fact that the choices of many such students are influenced by recommendations from alumni or teachers means that an oral tradition already exists in the main provider countries about the respective merits of universities X and Y; but few universities have gone beyond the sometimes patronising platitudes of the glossy brochure in their attempts to woo overseas students in particular. It seems inevitable, however, that just as the best informed overseas students ask now about the research rankings of different departments, so will they come to consider teaching quality and support structures, as quality assessments and student charters ensure that these activities become more and more transparent.

While clearly to refer to 'overseas students' as though they were homogeneous is a misleading piece of shorthand, the evidence adduced in the first section that one of the consequences of full-cost fees was that a greater proportion of overseas students came from the Western Pacific Rim and the Middle East allows slightly greater scope for generalisation than hitherto. So far as Far Eastern students are concerned it is a truism that, raised in a conformist educational system, they are happier with memorising and reproducing information than with problem-oriented and more active teaching strategies; it is also reasonable to assume that the financial investment which their stay in the United Kingdom represents will not increase the likelihood of risky educational behaviour on their part.

In fact such evidence as there is on overseas students' preferred modes of academic study is contradictory, but this reflects precisely the different educational and cultural traditions of respondents to which we have referred, as well as the varied nature of their experiences in Britain. So Burns's study of trainee teachers found:

> the educational value of discussion groups had come as a revelation to a great many students, and indeed many said that they were determined to introduce these into their own teaching on their return home.... Some students, it seems, experienced a feeling of shock when they were first asked to share in the informal student-teacher relationship which obtains in a British university. It seems difficult not to jump to one's feet whenever a lecturer comes into the room and quite intolerable to discuss serious matters with him on a basis of equality.
>
> (Burns 1965: 15–16)

On the other hand, educational innovations such as problem-focused strategies were not invariably perceived as progressive by those students whose main concern was to obtain surface knowledge and pass examinations. Genuine differences in study styles exist (British Council 1980) and though the 'human contact' elements of education are perceived as important by home as well as overseas students (Elsey 1990), well-presented lectures supported by clear handouts and structured guidance are more compatible with the traditional pedagogic educational modes favoured in the countries whence many overseas students come.

Though there has been an attempt recently to remove the anecdotal stereotype of the South-East Asian student in particular (Kember and Gow 1991), such modes are more consistent with the instrumentalist perspective fostered by contemporary educational politics in general and the full-cost fee system in particular – aspects of the 'Diploma Disease' (Dore 1976). Where problem-focused and interactive teaching modes are used extensively, particular consideration needs to be given to the means of training overseas (in particular non-western) students to make best use of them and to ensuring they are aware of the learning strategies involved.

The quest for the security of 'the facts' is as widespread as it is understandable among full-fee students from many non-western cultures.

There is however a point which, like much else in this chapter, requires testing. Though studies of adult learning acknowledge the existence of a range of different learning styles and strategies, the majority of these are individually rather than culturally based (see for example Marton and Saljo 1976a; Marton and Saljo 1976b; Marton and Saljo 1984; and in social work in particular Gardiner 1989). It is to be expected therefore – an expectation which experience has done nothing to disturb – that differences in learning style and strategy encountered among western subjects would appertain too in the case of Chinese students, many of whom must be serialist learners by acculturation not personal inclination. If this is correct it follows that it is feasible to bring such students to a point of greater learning versatility by the use of educational techniques designed to do just this (see for example Entwistle and Hounsell 1975; Pask 1976).

It is also probable that the experience of being an overseas student itself encourages a cautious serialist approach to learning. This tendency is most likely to be manifested in liberal arts and social science subjects where to embrace a holist learning style necessitates a broad grasp of the empirical realities of the social world. While the 'language' of mathematics or computer science, for example, stands largely independent of external phenomena that of social scientists self-evidently does not. This is particularly relevant to postgraduate professional students, whose discourse necessitates constant movement, physical as well as intellectual, between theoretical abstraction and empirical reality; for them new learning must build especially directly on the foundations of prior learning (Ausubel et al. 1978).

For social work students these difficulties are especially manifest in the practicum, when to uncertainties about how 'the system' works are added major uncertainties about social behaviour and conventions. In professions such as teaching, general medical practice, nursing and social work where a substantial part of background knowledge is what one has experienced oneself – how schools operate, what a council house is, how the unemployment benefit system works – to practise where not only does one not know this but where one lacks a sufficiently consonant cultural background to be able to make an informed guess is inevitably challenging and stressful.

Certainly it is not conducive to making informed generalisations or engaging in conceptual analysis. To be sufficiently confident to do that foundation knowledge is necessary, and to identify and implement the most effective means of information supplementation is an important task for universities. It is important to stress that to provide such information in conventional format is not to develop an educational strategy contrary to the principles of active and depth learning but precisely to offer overseas students an opportunity to engage in those more innovative aspects of learning which lead to understanding as well as knowledge (see for example Harris 1983, 1985, 1987; Blumenfeld et al. 1987; Entwistle and Entwistle 1991; Smith 1992).

It is scarcely surprising that in the arts and social sciences factors such as these impact on performance, rendering the production of a fair assessment of achievement and ability difficult to attain. Universities need to provide not only linguistic support for overseas students but a subject-sensitive marking frame which acknowledges cultural as well as linguistic differences and does not make the error of assuming that concept and grammar can be simply unyoked. Merely refraining from deducting marks for poor grammar or spelling, for example, does not address the problem of the intellectual self-censorship of second language students: if one cannot express a complex idea the idea will not appear. To address this reality – for example by triangulating assessment methods – without lowering standards is a challenge for universities which wish to take both overseas students and academic rigour seriously; but to create within a competitive educational culture the acknowledgement that there is more than a single, traditional pathway to success may necessitate an institution-wide cultural shift.

CONCLUSION

This chapter has offered a brief historical account of the involvement of overseas students in the UK university system and a review of the literature on student attitudes to their stay, relating this to the contemporary experiences of a small cohort of students on a post-graduate professional training course. This second field of enquiry has, in a context of deficient empirical knowledge, suggested that pre-course preparation is valued; that the first days of arrival are crucial; that universities must address themselves to the overall living experience of overseas students – for some students the experience of living in Britain and of the course are analytically indivisible; and that students value personal contact based on reciprocity of interest.

A number of 'visible minority' students have experienced racism, but while overt racism does not emerge as a major concern in the research cited there were indications from some of the literature that active and possibly avoidable discomfort was experienced by many students at specific points in their stay. Further, since public sensitivity to this issue has increased since the studies we have cited were published, and rather broader definitions of racism are now in common usage, it is possible that within the terms of this wider definition there is a problem waiting to be uncovered and addressed.

We have also considered briefly the importance of universities paying serious attention to the particular learning needs of overseas students. Though these will clearly vary depending on variables which include the cultural origins of the students and the academic demands of the course, for overseas students from many non-western countries the teaching innovations encouraged in UK universities may cause surprise and unease.

This is not to say, however, that they should be jettisoned for overseas students, for this would serve only to diminish those students' educational experience. They may, however, require an explanation of the nature and purpose of the methods and sufficient background information about relevant aspects of their host country for them to be able to make good use of educational innovation. For many overseas students the economic context of full-cost fees is likely to inhibit risk-taking; but our experience at Hull is that where students steeped in traditional pedagogy can be encouraged to participate in more diverse educational experiences their learning curve is steep and the benefits accrued are considerable, both directly in relation to course performance and indirectly through the increased social interactions with home students which active learning strategies seem to facilitate.

Chapter 3

Teaching and learning for overseas students
The Hong Kong connection

David Chan and Glenn Drover

INTRODUCTION

Studying overseas has a long history in Hong Kong. Driven by limited academic spaces at home and attracted by opportunities in foreign universities, the territory's students, initially as undergraduates and increasingly as graduates, have gone abroad in search of academic excellence. Like students elsewhere, they have found their search shaped by the globalisation of the labour market and by cultural identity. While globalisation has influenced the choice of courses and universities, cultural identity has influenced individual perceptions and behaviour. While globalisation has transformed the national boundaries of educational institutions, cultural identity has challenged the mode of teaching and learning.

To understand Hong Kong, one has to look at it in the context of the global economy. To understand Hong Kong students, one has to understand their occupational expectations and social values. Our analysis, therefore, is guided by the twin processes of globalisation and cultural identity. First, we discuss the significance of globalisation and cultural identity in shaping the role and function of educational institutions in general. Second, we consider how these two factors have shaped the aspirations of Hong Kong students in the past and how they are likely to influence them in the future. Third, we describe Hong Kong student migration and experiences overseas. Fourth, we consider teaching and learning the Hong Kong way. Fifth, we examine the emergence of overseas institutions in Hong Kong. Finally, we make some recommendations.

GLOBALISATION AND CULTURAL IDENTITY

In many respects Hong Kong represents the essence of contemporary global interaction – a tension between the homogenisation of production and the heterogenisation of culture (Appadurai 1990). While Hong

Kong's relationship to the global economy and to China has changed over the years, there is little doubt that its economic and cultural impact has increased significantly (Johnson 1994). Situated on the southern tip of East Asia, Hong Kong is in many ways the economic engine of southern China and a dynamic financial market in all of Asia (Li and Lo 1993; Jao 1993). Its per capita income is among the highest of developed economies; its economic growth rate over the past forty years has been among the highest in the world; its stock market is among the busiest and most sophisticated (Ho 1993); its economic base is shifting from manufacturing to services; its currency is stable and backed up by a respected and predictable monetary authority; its foreign investment is diverse and growing; its labour force is educated and competitive; its economy is mixed and highly integrated.

Long recognised as a centre of free market activity in Asia, Hong Kong is both a product and a beneficiary of global capitalism (Ross and Trachte 1990; Sklair 1991, 1994), a regional and an emerging global centre of finance and trade. Fundamental to global capitalism is not only the international division of labour but also the 'trans-nationalisation of production where through subcontracting, the process of production (or even the same commodity) is globalised' (Dirlik 1994: 348). The globalisation of production and the global marketing of international products are everywhere evident in Hong Kong. Goods and services available in London, New York or Tokyo are as available in Hong Kong, offered with the same flourish, and immediately recognised as part of the world market. While the international division of labour which gives rise to these goods and services is not novel, the extent to which new technologies are adapted, the speed with which they spread, the knowledge which is assumed, and the freedom with which production changes are located and relocated create a qualitatively different environment for an educated labour force and place new demands upon the universities which respond to them.

Nevertheless, at a time of increasing homogenisation of production and a global market, there is also a reaffirmation of local culture and national identity. The reaffirmation of culture is particularly strong in Hong Kong, not only because of the westernisation of society and the intrusion of international capital, but also because of the uncertainties of reunification with China in 1997 and the differing understandings of the Sino-British agreement (Walden 1993). Hong Kong is not unique, however. 'Competing claims of local cultures against the forces of globalisation have forced themselves onto the sociological, cultural and political agendas all over the world' (Sklair 1994: 5). Robertson (1992) sees the conflicts between the global and the local as dynamic tensions which are transforming our way of viewing relationships to national societies, individual identity, the international system, and the very nature of human agency. In the process, culture is not just a recipient of change which is determined by economic circumstance; it is also an influence on the economic order, aided by the conditions of postmodernity, a bringing together of cosmopolitans and locals in world culture (Hannerz 1990), and an insertion of ambivalence about the turns of modernity (Bauman 1990).

HIGHER EDUCATION AND GLOBAL REALITIES

The tension of globalisation and cultural identity are continually reflected in higher education. Ever since John Henry Newman's *The Idea of a University*, institutions of higher education, particularly universities, have been associated with liberal studies, academic freedom and institutional integrity. While these basic features of a university receive widespread support in most societies, especially among those who teach, the dilemma of bringing about a synthesis between globally oriented technologies and the continuity of cultural traditions can only be resolved in particular circumstances. Universities are increasingly likely to be contributors to the advancing technology of globalisation, particularly as they receive funding from government and international corporations. Equally, they are likely to be requested or pressured by civic and political organisations to contribute to an understanding and affirmation of local culture. Then as now they will have to be responsive to the demands of society even while they attempt to preserve freedom and autonomy; then as now they will have to balance the universal pursuit of the sciences with the particular claims of the humanities, of research with social obligation, of academic enquiry with professional competence, of access to the university with selectivity, of technological innovation with the continuity of the arts, of technical assistance with moral commitment, of the business of the university with the university of business (Bok 1982; Pelikan 1992).

In Newman's day, the balance between the global and the cultural was struck in favour of empire and Eurocentric imperialism, but even then there was challenge from within. In the mid-twentieth century, as a result of the challenge of socialism, the rising tide of student power, the strength of anti-colonialism, the frustrations of war and the high point of state welfarism, Eurocentric imperialism on campus gave way to a new cultural sensitivity and a north–south dialogue combined with concerns about social problems and social injustice. But with the opening of British and other western universities to the rest of the world there came too a replacement of empire by a new internationalism in which the influence of transnational corporations, the gradual expansion of trading blocs, the growth of interlocking labour markets, the development of international financial institutions and the search for new forms of governance were taking hold. As a result of the growing tension between the new internationalism and emerging cultural sensitivities, university campuses erupted in the 1960s and 1970s. The meaning of academic freedom, institutional autonomy, and the responsibility of the university to society were widely and intensively debated (Bok 1982). Access to the university and the problem of racial inequality were addressed. Social uses of technological research were questioned. Boycotts and other efforts to avoid unfair labour practices or university linkages with war efforts were implemented. Ethical investing was introduced in many universities.

Today, institutions of higher education continue to undergo fundamental change because of the influence of globalisation (Brown and Scase 1994). The process is as true of higher education in Hong Kong as elsewhere. Within the universities there has already been a fundamental shift from élitism to mass education which is not likely to be reversed. Within private and public workplaces conventional managerial and professional practices based on large scale bureaucracies have been replaced by organisations which require greater flexibility and adaptation. In addition, the rapid diffusion of new technologies and their effective economic and social exploitation is likely to generate new economic opportunities, new forms of work organisation and more varied combinations of work and leisure time (Organisation for Economic Cooperation and Development 1990). Hence universities will be called on to educate a new generation of internationally competitive overseas students, to create a climate in which innovation and change can take place, to engage in lifelong education, to broker linkages between the global and the local, and to integrate economic policies with social and cultural initiatives. Equally, cognitive, motivational, and contextual strategies of teaching (Menges and Svinicki 1991) will be essential to encourage student involvement in learning as well as to foster an understanding of global realities and cultural identity.

CULTURAL IDENTITY AND HIGHER EDUCATION IN HONG KONG

Hong Kong has a long history of affirming its own culture in the face of globalisation and a metanarrative of colonialism. In many ways it is a meeting place of East and West, a focal point where tradition and modernity commingle. Although Chinese in origin, the people of Hong Kong have been for the last 150 years born and raised in a British colony. To the mainland Chinese they are more British in their way of life than they are Chinese; to the British and Europeans they are more Chinese than British; to themselves they are a mix and they are neither; they are instead representative of a new international order, of what Robert Park long ago called the marginal people (Park 1974: 354).

Although migration from the Chinese mainland still has an important influence on the cultural identity of the people of Hong Kong, 'the Hong Kong ethos represents a mixture of traditional Chinese culture and modern cultural traits fostered by the particular nature of the Hong Kong society itself and the changes it has experienced in the past, particularly since the Second World War' (Lau and Kuan 1988: 2). In many respects, therefore, Hong Kong is a 'borrowed place in a borrowed time' (Hughes 1976). The people have a 'sojourn mentality'. Many of the older generation are not long-term residents of the territory, having come as refugees. They frequently go back to visit relatives in the mainland, returning to where they really belong. However, as a society of refugees and immigrants, the Hong Kong people have developed very differently from their counterparts in China, having uprooted themselves from Chinese soil, confronting the face of western colonialism. They are economic leaders in the region. They have come to terms with globalisation by rooting themselves in their own culture and a Confucian educational system.

Hong Kong's cultural identity and economic leadership have roots in its colonial history. One of the ways that the colonial government customarily administered the territory was to have the Chinese rule the Chinese by co-opting members of the upper middle classes as colonial administrators or professionals. So in 1907, when the University of Hong Kong was founded, the medium of instruction was English, and the then governor saw the first university as a 'means of training a new highly educated middle class for Hong Kong' while assuring the use of English language and the furtherance of British influence throughout China (Yau et al. 1993: 65).[1] From the beginning the university was a mock-up of a British institution, subordinated under a colonial administration to legitimate and reinforce colonial hierarchies of rules. By making the reproduction of these hierarchies appear to be based upon a hierarchy of 'gifts', and by converting the hierarchies into academic hierarchies (Bourdieu 1977: 496), the colonial administration firmly established the co-optation of a small Chinese élite while at the same time assuring that the majority of the populace found no place, at least initially, in higher levels of education.

In order to assure the loyalty of the populace the colonial administration also introduced a syllabus called 'civics' throughout the educational system in the late twenties (Morris and Sweeting 1991: 257; Sweeting 1990: 397–407) to curb nationalism and anti-colonialism (Sweeting 1993: 94). After the defeat of the Guomindang nationalist party and the communist takeover of China in 1949, however, the colonial government saw even greater ideological threats to its legitimacy, and the following year introduced a curriculum in which Chinese language and history were played down. At the same time the administration began to highlight the global role of Hong Kong, to stress for the first time the idea of the territory as a cosmopolitan city and its residents as 'citizens of the world'. The new emphasis was a mix of political pragmatism and economic opportunity. The pragmatism came from military and ideological threats in China, and the opportunity from the demand for cheap products in rapidly expanding global markets.

The new emphasis on international trade and global competition created a crisis of cultural identity and nationalist fervour which spilled over into the student movements of the late 1960s and early 1970s. Like students elsewhere, students in Hong Kong demanded more involvement in the affairs of institutions of higher learning, though unlike students elsewhere they were preoccupied with reaffirming their cultural identity, subordinating colonial sentiment in education, and re-examining official linkages with China. Faced with pressure from students and growing nationalist sentiment, the government set up the Chinese University of Hong Kong in 1963.[2] In doing so it recognised several colleges which had moved to Hong Kong in the wake of the communist takeover of China in 1949 (Wang 1982: 195–203). In 1968 the student union of one of the colleges, Chung Chi, called for the recognition of Chinese as one of the official languages of Hong Kong. After long and protracted debate over a three-year period, the demand was finally recognised by the government (Federation of Hong Kong Students 1983: 12), a decision which stands out as one of the more important in the development of higher education within the territory.

Not surprisingly after the nationalist fervour of the 1960s, the administration gradually lowered the educational flag of colonialism, stressing more and more the vocational and professional needs of the Hong Kong population in the face of new global realities. In 1977 a Green Paper anticipated substantial discontent among young people if they were unable to find challenging work in the decade ahead (Hong Kong Government 1977); in 1978 a White Paper called for the restructuring of vocational education to meet new demands of the labour market. In response to both, the government expanded technical institutes and a polytechnic. At the same time, in order to accommodate local cultural sentiment, the University of Hong Kong and the Chinese University of Hong Kong were gradually allowed to expand by 3 per cent per year (Hong Kong Government 1978) and, to offset potential resentment about the limited number of posts available locally, the government encouraged students to study overseas, particularly in the United Kingdom.

It was not until the 1980s, however, that the full expansion of Hong Kong higher education took place after a panel of international educational experts recommended urgent action 'to identify and acquire at least two sites for new institutions' and claimed that the 2 per cent participation rate then prevalent in Hong Kong was far from the actual demand, and strongly recommended 'the expansion of opportunity for study at the degree level, with particular emphasis on degrees in technological subjects and in courses for higher technicians' (Hong Kong Government 1982: 65–7). Faced with growing pressures from many sectors of the society, the administration finally acknowledged, in the latter half of the eighties, the need for a comprehensive and open system of higher education (Hong Kong Education Commission 1986: 126–80).[3] As a result of the new initiatives the participation rate for higher education increased to 7 per cent in 1989–90 (Fan 1990: 12), and 18 per cent by 1995, particularly after the 4 June 1989 incident in Tiananmen Square. The increase helped offset the brain drain from out-migration and reassured the outside world about the future of Hong Kong (Hong Kong Government 1989).[4]

HONG KONG STUDENTS OVERSEAS

Owing to longstanding restrictions on higher education in Hong Kong large numbers of students went overseas, generally for three major reasons: limited educational places in the territory, job discrimination against graduates of local as well as other commonwealth institutions, and political uncertainty. Wu (1992: 47–8) identifies three waves of student migration since World War Two which largely followed the administrative initiatives noted above. The first wave from the late 1940s to the late 1960s saw students leave primarily because of discrimination at home. In general, students from mainland China universities, Hong Kong private colleges and even from the Chinese University of Hong Kong did not have equal opportunity in the job market in Hong Kong with graduates from the University of Hong Kong. Hence they went 'overseas for further studies in order to obtain qualifications recognised within the British Commonwealth or to seek opportunities elsewhere' (Wu 1992: 47).

The second wave was caused by the student and nationalist movements of the 1960s which culminated in the riots of 1967, and by the growth of wealth within the territory. The main push to leave Hong Kong during the second phase came from increasing affluence, but political uncertainty, caused both by pent-up demands for cultural recognition locally and events within China, played a role. The students who left were primarily from relatively well-off families,[5] though unlike their predecessors who went for graduate studies, most second wave students went in pursuit of undergraduate studies. They set a pattern for others to follow in the 1970s, when even higher living standards 'enabled more families to send their children overseas to seek educational opportunities not available in Hong Kong' (Wu 1992: 48). In the third wave, stimulated by political uncertainty due to the impending transfer of sovereignty to China in 1997, overseas education combined with the migration of entire families to create a major outflow of population to North America and Britain. The majority went for university studies but many went for secondary education as well.

It is not possible to generalise about the experiences of Hong Kong students abroad since so little research has been undertaken on the topic. One study at the University of Hull (Leung et al. 1995) suggests that Hong Kong students have faced many of the same challenges as other students from abroad, including initial adjustments to a new environment, financial strain, expectations of high academic attainment, and social isolation; but the study was based primarily on the experience of social work students. To provide additional insight on the aspirations, cultural perceptions and adjustments of Hong Kong students who study abroad, a small survey of academic staff of the City University of Hong Kong was undertaken by the authors for this chapter.[6] Eighty-seven per cent of respondents were second- and third wave students who went to study abroad during the 1970s and the 1980s while in their early twenties. While 60 per cent studied abroad for four years or more, 15 per cent studied for less than a year, the rest typically studying for two or three years. Having for the most part academic careers in mind when they studied abroad, it is not surprising that most (74 per cent) pursued postgraduate programmes, with some pursuing both undergraduate and postgraduate degrees. Interestingly, just under one quarter of respondents (24 per cent) went only for undergraduate programmes abroad and pursued graduate courses back in Hong Kong. This reflects a trend which, as we shall see below, may increase in the future.

Consistent with other students who went abroad to study at this time, respondents gave as their main reasons the limitation in opportunities for studies in Hong Kong, followed by the desire to attend a university with an established reputation in a particular field. The principal reason for choosing an area of study was personal preference rather than opportunity for employment, suggesting that both undergraduate and graduate studies were chosen for intrinsic rather than extrinsic advantage. The intrinsic value of the studies was further reflected in the fact that respondents believed the main value of their studies abroad was an increase of general knowledge, not occupational advantage. On the other hand, when specifically asked whether employment expectations influenced their studies abroad, about one third said that general enhancement of employment in the labour market or of promotion prospects was important.

When asked about their experiences at universities when studying abroad, most claimed to have received basic information on items like accommodation and passports, and orientation to their academic programme, but little that was geared to be helpful in everyday living, including matters like clothing, local shopping, health and social services, arts and entertainment or local transportation. Nor was assistance given to family members. In terms of the teaching environment at the universities, 41 per cent of respondents ranked first the general academic environment of the university where they studied, while the quality of lectures and the quality of libraries were ranked second and third respectively. Ninety per cent claimed that their university was 'stimulating'. When asked specifically about the quality of graduate supervision, the expertise of supervisors was ranked the most important aspect (50 per cent) followed by intellectual stimulation and consistency of advice. In general respondents placed more emphasis on the cognitive than on the cultural aspects of their learning environment. Few identified discrimination, language, or local customs as being problematic even though a third of them experienced derogatory (presumably racial) comments when they were abroad. Fifty-seven per cent of respondents returned to Hong Kong feeling that their experience had helped them better appreciate their own culture; few found it difficult to adjust to Hong Kong when they returned.

TEACHING AND LEARNING THE HONG KONG WAY

In terms of patterns of teaching and learning, western observers frequently state, and sometimes complain, that Hong Kong students, like many of their Asian counterparts, are inclined to use rote-memorisation and formal approaches to education both at home (Murphy 1987) and abroad (Ballard and Clanchy 1984; Bradley and Bradley 1984; Samuelowicz 1987). Interestingly, however, studies have shown that the outcome of formal styles of learning is not necessarily negative. Assessment studies in mathematics and science (Baker 1993; Garden 1987; International Association for the Evaluation of Educational Achievement 1988; Medrich and Griffith 1992) have shown that East Asian students frequently outperform their Western counterparts. Similarly, in terms of language skills and competence Hong Kong students have been found to be above international norms both in their own and in a second language (Johnson and Cheung 1991). This disparity between east and west is particularly significant when we compare western students with students from Confucian-heritage cultures and including Asian-Americans. The latter seem to perform at higher levels than would be expected from their IQ scores (Flynn 1991; Sue and Okazaki 1990). Biggs, an expert on teaching and learning styles, comments:

> There is a high degree of consensus currently amongst researchers into teaching and learning about the conditions for good learning. If they

are right, then learners in Hong Kong schools would show as poor indeed, both in their processes of learning and in the quality of their learning outcomes. The empirical evidence is, however, quite the contrary; along with students from several East- and South-East Asian countries, those in Hong Kong not only keep pace with, but in many aspects outshine their Australasian and American peers in some crucial indices of quality learning.

(Biggs 1994: 20)

The paradox of the Hong Kong learner is something which repeats itself among students coming from other Confucian-heritage cultures as well. In many cases it has been found that these students report a stronger preference for high-level, meaning-based, and deep learning strategies than their western counterparts (Biggs 1990, 1991; Kember and Gow 1991; Watkins et al. 1991). While the terms 'deep' and 'surface' are generic in nature, what they signify to the learner depends very much upon the context and the task as well as the individual's encoding of both (Biggs 1993). To understand the Confucian-heritage culture student, one has to distinguish 'rote learning' (learning in a mechanical way without thought of meaning) from 'repetitive learning' (which uses repetition as a means of ensuring accurate recall). The difference mainly lies in the learner's intentions with respect to meaning. In rote learning, meaning has no place in the learner's intentions; in repetitive learning it may. 'A student who uses repetition to optimise retrieval in an exam is not using a surface approach but making a wise strategic choice' (Biggs 1994: 26). So while westerners may correctly see Asian students as being preoccupied with a high degree of repetitive work they may be wrong in seeing that activity as rote learning and as a surface learning strategy.

An understanding of the paradox of the Confucian-heritage culture student requires one to look closely at the teaching and family environment of the student. With regard to the educational environment, an American educator has observed that in the instruction of art and music, while Western teachers believe in exploration first, then in developing a skill, their Chinese counterparts engage in skill development first, typically involving repetitive learning, then in being creative (Gardner 1989). Teacher–student relations in modern Chinese universities also convey a puzzling ambiguity to western observers. Social relations seem well developed but very hierarchical and formal from the outside, but in reality there is a high degree of interaction, partly because students and teachers both live on campus and partly because of inter-generational respect. Respect for teachers has been fostered over the centuries, thereby creating a kind of reciprocity which is passed on from one generation to the next.

The Chinese family also plays a pivotal role in the education of students which is not easily replicated in the West. While the influence of the family is stronger in younger than later years it is pervasive and carries over into the university. Salili (1994) has found that when comparing the achievement orientation of British and Chinese students, success for the Chinese is highly related to successes in the family and close social groups, while the British see individual achievement and social success quite differently. 'British subjects as a whole saw little or no relationship between individualistic (academic, career, sports, etc.) and affiliative (family social and personal social) goals in importance, whereas for the Chinese there was a close relationship between the two' (Salili 1994: 646). For the Chinese, academic success and failure reflect upon the family, putting great pressure on students to succeed. If students fail, the families lose face, so it is not surprising if studies show that Asian families have higher expectations about their children's educational achievements than those of their Western counterparts (Stevenson et al. 1990). Furthermore, various studies have shown that people in Confucian-heritage cultures attribute success to effort and failure to lack of effort, whereas westerners tend to attribute success to ability and failure to lack of ability (Hess and Azuma 1991; Holloway 1988; Hau and Salili 1991).

Differences in learning styles between students of Confucian-heritage and western countries suggest that in the university as in other levels of education the classroom cannot be seen apart from its cultural context. The perception of the teacher–student relationship as one of tension between authority and proximity is accepted in the East even as it is challenged in the West. The Hong Kong educational system, like other Confucian systems, can be described as a process in which a student views a teacher as a mentor, someone who can provide advice through all stages of learning; the western educational system is a student-centred approach in which a teacher advises a student while respecting individuality and autonomy. The differences in the learning dialogue reflect cultural values, and both teachers and students need to understand each other's respective roles as well as be sensitive to each other's cultural background. At a level of understanding, Confucian-heritage educational cultures may have struck a more harmonious balance between school and society than have most western educational approaches, where what schools demand, and what students 'are prepared to give, are in tension so that artificial motivational systems are rather more necessary in western schools, and the learning pathologies to which they give rise are the more in evidence' (Biggs 1994: 34).

OVERSEAS INSTITUTIONS IN HONG KONG

In addition to studying overseas, students have increasingly had the opportunity of gaining access to higher education through courses offered by overseas institutions of higher education in Hong Kong. The territory has always imported some education in response to demand for subjects related to service industries such as hotel management, business administration, accounting, international trade and financial management. As recently as 1993 it was estimated that the demand for these and similar courses largely exceeded the local supply, and government projections forecast a continuing shortfall in 2001 (Hong Kong Government Education and Manpower Branch 1994). Overseas institutions have stepped into the breach and are beginning to compete with local institutions for students in an expanding array of courses. Faced with declining resources at home and renewed technological opportunities for delivering educational services abroad, they have turned to Hong Kong and other growth areas in Asia where there is a demand for their product. The new global traders of education fall into two groups: those who independently offer programmes of study for residents through distance learning (mainly from the United Kingdom, Australia and the United States), and those which collaborate with local institutions to provide educational opportunities on site (mainly from the United Kingdom, Australia and Canada) (Lee 1996). As Hong Kong approaches a change of sovereignty in 1997, the trend toward the globalisation of educational institutions may well make it the hub of educational exchange between China and the rest of the world. It may also reflect a trend for educational institutions to go in search of international students instead of international students coming to them.

Recent legislative changes in Hong Kong have aided the trend toward global educational products. In the past, the Education Ordinance of Hong Kong stipulated that any organisation which provided educational courses to two or more people on any one day had to be registered with the Director of Education. Recently however, a new law (the Education [Overseas Tertiary Institutions] Exemption Order 1995) has ruled that overseas tertiary institutions can be exempted from the need to register provided that certain conditions are met. The conditions include the following: collaboration with a local tertiary institution; academic recognition by a relevant authority in the home country; maintenance of courses at a level comparable with those offered in the home country; and annual certification and report to the Director of Education (Holford et al. 1995: 74). The law permits a new dimension of collaboration between local and overseas tertiary educational institutions which did not exist before and is congruent with the trend of globalisation. In fact, further down the path of globalisation, a longstanding expert on

continuing education in Hong Kong has recently called for the establishment of a regional body, the Asia Pacific Education Authority, to oversee
the quality of academic programmes offered by various countries in the
region. In addition to educational and advisory roles the authority would
'facilitate international credit transfer in a much more meaningful way
than at present. Such credit transfer arrangements as do exist internationally tend to be only at the institution to institution level' (Lee in
press). As it is in Europe and North America, so is pressure mounting in
Asia for a clear articulation of educational standards, as institutions
compete in the growing international trade in education (Lee 1996).

In addition to the likely growth of joint ventures between local and
foreign educational institutions in Hong Kong, three other policy
changes will affect overseas studies in the future. The first is the decision
in 1994 of the Hong Kong Government to recognise for the first time the
right of university graduates from both mainland China and Taiwan to
apply as civil servants. One consequence of the change on the
educational front is that in the future increasing numbers of Hong Kong
students (particularly those interested in working with government) will
be going back to China rather than to the United Kingdom or other
countries for courses in higher education. The second change is that
universities in China are beginning to offer part-time distance learning
programmes to Hong Kong people who hold full-time jobs in the
territory (Liu 1995: 5), thereby creating competition with established
western universities which have heretofore predominated. The combined effect of the two policies will also enhance the current trend to
localisation (in which senior posts are occupied by qualified Chinese
candidates rather than westerners), thus re-affirming Chinese culture
and values, particularly in the public sector. In addition, a third policy
change (by some universities) to expand graduate programmes and
attract expatriate Chinese students to return to Hong Kong may work in
the same direction. Partly because of the brain drain caused by the
transfer of sovereignty in 1997, and partly out of a desire to become
international institutions in their own right, Hong Kong universities have
inaugurated a policy which may begin to reverse the one-way flow of
educational traffic.

CONCLUSION

Faced with the twin demands of globalisation and cultural identity,
Hong Kong has forged a place in the world which gives shape to its
future as well as its past. Its ability to compete and its mix of the
traditional and the modern are reflected in its educational institutions
and aspirations. In the early stages of development the colonial
administration relied upon expatriates and a small local élite to steer

the affairs of the territory. As economic development advanced, educational institutions expanded, under external and internal pressure, to meet the needs of an increasingly affluent society. Along with economic growth and development, institutions of higher education expanded to meet the demands of a competitive labour market and an emerging middle class. Prior to the 1980s many of Hong Kong's youth went abroad to study because of a lack of spaces at home. In recent years they have continued to go overseas either to further their education or in response to liberalised immigration policies which have allowed them to take up new residences. In the future, they will likely strive to enhance their ability to compete at home and abroad by securing an internationally recognised degree. At the same time, because of the rapid expansion of higher education in the territory in recent years they are likely to be more selective than hitherto in choosing the institutions where they study.

Universities will therefore have to offer more than hospitality and friendly orientations. Even though such activities are important, students are likely to prefer universities where there are sufficient numbers of compatriots to provide a sense of community, where the curriculum reflects a genuine interest in Chinese culture, and where their own style of learning is understood and respected. Hence educators and administrators will be under increased pressure to plan for overseas students on a more systematic basis than in the past. Students from Hong Kong, like their counterparts elsewhere, suffer from a feeling of isolation when they go to study abroad. For most, in addition to the usual minor adjustments of living in another culture there are the demands of learning in a second language; understanding newly acquired technical terminology; the high cost of education abroad; securing financial support from family; adapting to different teaching styles; making friends in a new environment; overcoming or coping with local prejudices; being misunderstood or misrepresented; striving to achieve; being heard; and saving face. While universities cannot plan for all these challenges or protect students from them, they can introduce formal and informal mechanisms to make the initial transition more smooth, to sensitise local students and staff to the significance of cultural differences, to encourage intercultural communication, to promote participation at different levels of institutional decision-making, and to foster a sense of belonging.

How, in the end, universities respond to the learning styles of Hong Kong students and others from Confucian-heritage cultures depends largely on the extent they are aware of and respect different approaches to learning. On the one hand, research on learning styles suggests that students need to be aware of cultural differences and adjust to them; on the other, the achievements of students from Confucian-heritage cultures suggest that staff in western educational institutions may also benefit from revisiting some of the formal approaches to teaching which they have largely repudiated. While Hong Kong and other Asian students may be perceived in western educational institutions as passive and reluctant to participate in critical commentary, there is little in the research to suggest that they would be wise to set aside their learning skills and substitute those of the West. While their traditional learning skills may inhibit them from speaking out in class or challenging their professors, they have helped them compete internationally and score well on standard academic tests.

Hong Kong and other parts of East- and South-East Asia are beginning to compete with established universities abroad in attracting overseas students. The reasons for moving in that direction are threefold. First, to the extent that newly created wealth enables them to develop undergraduate and graduate university spaces equivalent to other developed economies of the world they are able to follow the pattern of older universities. Second, they see the value of diversifying their student body and welcoming students from other cultures to enhance the intellectual and research environment for students who cannot study abroad. Third, they are faced with increased competition from recognised universities and newly emerging private universities which are using increasingly sophisticated marketing strategies to attract a rapidly expanding cohort of university aspirants whose families are able to fund their education. Faced with a potential brain drain, universities in Hong Kong and East Asia recognise that the best defence is to take the offensive by internationalising their own student bodies.

One issue which pervades all cultural differences and makes life easier for students studying abroad is the facilitation of everyday activity on and off campus. As noted in the survey of staff of the City University of Hong Kong who studied overseas, the daily tasks of living and studying are considered as being as important as the complexities and complications of cultural difference. Quality lectures, a good library and an up-to-date computer centre are a significant part of the learning environment; intellectual stimulation and the expertise of a supervisor of graduate studies are integral to the teaching environment; and earning a degree takes precedence over concerns about discrimination or feelings of racism. While this does not mean that respondents consider culture unimportant it serves as a reminder that for most students the purpose of study abroad is largely instrumental, to enable them to compete in the global market, to advance their occupational goals and to enhance their qualifications. In that sense students from Hong Kong, like students elsewhere, participate in education abroad largely in response to market demands and opportunities in their own society. In Hong Kong where competitiveness and individualism overlay traditional Chinese values of filial piety and family responsibility, the potential for the fulfilment of obligation comes from success at home and abroad. Faced with such an overwhelming expectation, and little evidence of threat to the culture of which they are a part, it is perhaps not too surprising that the primary goal of Hong Kong students is global gain.

NOTES

1 A predecessor academic institution to the University of Hong Kong was a college of medicine founded by a few doctors of the London Missionary Society in 1887 and renamed the Hong Kong College of Medicine in 1907. Dr Sun Yat-sen, the founder of China as a republic, was one of its first graduates in 1892. The college was later incorporated into the Faculty of Medicine of the University of Hong Kong (Yau et al. 1993: 65).
2 Post-secondary education was dominated by the University of Hong Kong, particularly for local élites, well into the 1970s. The Chinese University of Hong Kong, by contrast, was a centre of ideological turmoil which was part of the China-Taiwan split after the takeover of China by the Communist Party. In the early stages of the development of the university local academics were often dominated by those educated in Taiwan.
3 It did so by instituting an emergency loan scheme for those already enrolled in recognised first degree courses as well as a longer term scheme of financial assistance for students intending to embark upon higher level education (Hong Kong Government Secretariat 1981: 100–1).
4 At the opening of the 1986–7 Session of the Legislative Council the government announced its intention to proceed with the planning of a third university and announced that a 'well educated community, supported by highly qualified professionals and a skilled labour force, [was] one of the best guarantees of Hong Kong's continued prosperity and well-being' (Hong Kong Government 1986: 16–17).
5 Affluent families were able to send their children abroad for further education, while very few children of the working classes who received scholarships went beyond middle school. Another important factor was the liberalisation of immigration policies in countries like Canada, Australia, New Zealand and to a lesser extent the United States. Hence increasing numbers of students went abroad with their families, with some staying after graduation.
6 The survey was completed 15–31 May 1995. It included staff from four faculties: business, law, science and technology, humanities and social sciences. There were 284 questionnaires distributed and 117 completed (41.2 per cent). The profile of the sample was as follows: 79.5 per cent male and 20.5 per cent female, with 39.3 per cent aged 26–35 and 47.9 per cent aged 36–45. The largest numbers of returns were from the Faculty of Science and Technology and the Faculty of Humanities and Social Sciences at 39.3 per cent each, with the remaining 21.4 per cent from the Faculty of Business and the Faculty of Law. Half of the respondents studied in the United Kingdom with 32.8 per cent in USA, 11.2 per cent in Canada, 3.4 per cent in Australia, and 2.6 per cent elsewhere. 59.9 per cent of respondents studied for 4 years or more, 14.5 per cent for less than one year. Of the 73.5 per cent of respondents who pursued postgraduate degrees (taught or research), 17.9 per cent pursued both undergraduate and postgraduate degrees, and 23.9 per cent pursued only undergraduate degrees.

Chapter 4

Studying in Europe

John Brennan

CONTEXTS

Of the 10 per cent of students at UK universities and colleges who are from overseas, 40 per cent are from member countries of the European Union (Higher Education Statistics Agency 1995). Their numbers reflect the growth of study abroad programmes such as ERASMUS and ECTS sponsored by the European Commission. As such they are the most visible outcome of a macro-policy steer to higher education from outside of the UK. This chapter will consider the purposes of this policy, the responses to it by higher education institutions and the experiences of students and their teachers of its implementation.

According to the European Commission something under 5 per cent of all students in the member states of the European Union study abroad, while Commission policy is to increase this figure to 10 per cent. In actual student numbers this means that 112,733 students participated in ERASMUS programmes in 1993–4, a 30 per cent increase from the previous year (Commission of the European Communities 1994) – the equivalent of the total number of students in a medium-sized country such as Scotland.

The scale of these programmes must also be seen in relation to the enormous expansion of higher education in all European countries in the last few years. The growth of European student mobility has more than kept pace with this overall expansion; and this points to a distinctive feature of student mobility in Europe: it is a characteristic of mass rather than élite higher education.

While study abroad has always been an option for the wealthy few, the large-scale development of grant-supported EC programmes is a genuine mass phenomenon. It is not the preserve of a small number of élite institutions but reaches deep into the large and diversified higher education systems of Europe; while participating students are drawn from a wide range of social and educational backgrounds (Maiworm et al. 1991).

As far as UK higher education institutions are concerned, students from mainland Europe naturally come from very different higher education systems and traditions. Unlike students from the former British colonies, with their experiences of A-levels, grammar schools and other manifestations of an imperially transplanted education system, European students have quite different educational experiences and expectations from the home students alongside whom they are studying. In so far as it is justifiable to speak of Continental European and Anglo-Saxon traditions of higher education (van Vught 1993), UK higher education stands apart from most other European higher education systems. It follows that as students from Europe spend only a minority of their higher education studying abroad they must be sufficiently flexible and adaptable to move in and out of different traditions and cultures.

However, as all European systems of higher education undergo major changes, some commentators point to clear signs of convergence in certain respects (van Vught and Westerheijden 1993). In particular, massification, diversity and control now relate closely to the pursuit of quality.

In most systems of higher education, and particularly in the United Kingdom, exclusiveness has been the traditional form of quality assurance in higher education, with entry restricted, socially and educationally, not just for students but for their teachers. Today exclusiveness has relaxed, and in all higher education systems in the western world there are more students and more people teaching them than was the case even 10 or 15 years ago. This shift from élite to mass higher education lessens dramatically the reliance that can be placed on exclusiveness of entry as the prime mechanism of quality assurance. The educational backgrounds of students are more varied, as are the qualifications and experience of the staff who teach them, and the financial cost and visibility of higher education have increased exponentially.

The growth of higher education has in most systems led to increased diversity of content, delivery mechanisms and models of assessment in order to cater for students with increasingly varied backgrounds, needs and ambitions. This has led to a growth of fields of study undertaken outside of the frameworks of established academic disciplines – frameworks which have traditionally provided widely accepted criteria of academic standards. Without the criteria of quality provided by these frameworks there is a suspicion for some that 'anything goes'. Frequently tradition is equated with quality and innovation is viewed with suspicion; new forms of higher education need justifying in ways that familiar forms do not.

Increased diversity entails increased choices, and users of higher education have many more options open to them than hitherto. If their choices are to be informed ones they require more information about their options, and this has led, particularly in countries which accord primacy to the operation of market forces, to the growing importance of the provision of information to inform consumer choice. This need is clearly greater still with study abroad programmes.

The political and economic basis of the growth in higher education, which includes creating a more highly skilled labour force and contributing to economic growth, ensures that governments are increasingly interested in it. In mass higher education, extrinsic functions of this kind become more important than such intrinsic ones as knowledge creation and transmission in shaping governmental higher education policy. Thus greater external accountability is required of higher education and greater emphasis placed on value for money, while traditional autonomies are replaced by systems of evaluation and quality control. The inner life of higher education can no longer be safely left to academics.

The growth of what has been called the 'evaluative state' (Neave 1988), including a rise in managerialism and the development of externally set objectives, forms part of the backcloth to study abroad in Europe, and it is against this broader socio-political context that the micro-level processes of student exchange, curriculum, teaching and assessment must be analysed.

To summarise, therefore, study abroad in Europe is:

- a manifestation of social and educational policy at the European level;
- an aspect of a transnational trend towards massification and diversification of higher education;
- encompasses a range of educational traditions and cultures;
- subjected to increasingly stringent forms of external evaluation and accountability demands.

THE POLICY FRAMEWORK

The ERASMUS programme was introduced in June 1987 and its objectives were to achieve a significant increase in student and staff mobility between higher education institutions, to promote broad and lasting inter-institutional cooperation and to contribute to the economic and social development of higher education graduates with direct experience of intra-European cooperation (Wilson 1994). These objectives were social more than specifically educational in that they did not concern themselves with what students were intended to learn as a result of their study abroad experiences. More recent statements signal a significant change of emphasis.

In 1991 the European Commission stressed the importance of higher education developing a European dimension by means of student mobility, cooperation between institutions, Europeanisation of the curriculum, the central importance of language, the training of teachers, the recognition of qualifications and periods of study, the international role of higher education, information and policy analysis, and dialogue with the higher education sector (Commission of the European Communities 1991). These notions constituted the framework of a comprehensive policy statement on higher education encompassing labour markets, demography, mobility, research, regional development, social policy, culture and European integration.

More recently, the SOCRATES programme, which subsumes ERAS-MUS, sets out three ERASMUS-type activities: promoting the European dimension in higher education institutions, setting up European university networks and, in third place only, funding student mobility grants (Commission of the European Communities 1993b: 31). Thus while mobility and recognition issues remain important elements of promoting the European dimension, the emphasis has moved from mobility as such to a broader set of educational activities 'designed to bring a European dimension to all areas of study for the benefit of each and every student', involving for example:

> the incorporation into curricula of elements designed to enhance understanding of the cultural, political, economic and social characteristics of other member states as well as elements relating to European integration, especially through the creation of multi- or inter-disciplinary modules.
>
> (Commission of the European Communities 1993b: 33)

The proposed European University Networks are intended to help facilitate this by engaging in the evaluation of curricula for specific disciplines, the design of joint programmes and specialised courses, scientific analysis and reflection on a specific area of studies, and information services for network members.

Not only, however, is study abroad in Europe part of an increasingly explicit statement of educational policy by its principal sponsor the European Commission, but the statement finds echoes in the policy statements of other international bodies. UNESCO, for example, proclaims that 'the response of higher education to a changing world should be guided by three watchwords: relevance, quality and internationalisation' (United Nations Educational, Scientific and Cultural Organisation 1995: 7). It elaborates the third of these as follows:

> The internationalisation of higher education is first of all a reflection of the universal character of learning and research. It is reinforced by

the current processes of economic and political integration as well as by the growing need for intercultural understanding. The number of students, teachers and researchers who work, live and communicate in an international context attests to this trend. The considerable expansion of various types of networking and other linking arrangements among institutions, academics and students is facilitated by the steady advance of information and communication technologies.

(United Nations Educational, Scientific and Cultural Organisation
1995: 10)

While it is of course hardly surprising that international organisations call for an internationalisation of higher education, the arguments are themselves persuasive. Other authors have, for example, called for universities to embrace an educational philosophy with 'no ideological, national and cultural boundaries' (Calleja 1995: 41) and to help 'make the whole of Europe a natural area of activity for as many people as possible' (Daniel 1993: 30). From these perspectives international education moves from being an additional or marginal aspect of higher education to one of its central elements.

Notwithstanding its increasing emphasis on the principle of subsidiarity in its relationships with the EU, the UK Government has broadly endorsed the above policy steers. Thus its response to the EC Memorandum on Higher Education claimed that 'the UK Government's aim is to embed the European dimension in the daily practice of all higher education institutions' (Department for Education 1992); and in a speech in London in 1993, the then Minister of State noted that 'it is only common sense to prepare young people for increasing trade and leisure links with Europe' (Boswell 1994: 13), warning against academic tourism and stressing that quality must take top priority in any new higher education programme.

THE QUALITY FRAMEWORK

Recent and current debates in the United Kingdom about higher education quality are aspects of an international theme (van Vught 1993). Conferences have discussed, international bodies have set up projects, national governments have established quality agencies; and although the aims of these activities have frequently been obscure, they have generated discussion about, and focused attention on the quality of higher education.

Conceptions of quality have nonetheless been elusive. A growing literature on the subject, much of it drawing on developments in manufacturing industry, has attempted clarification and, in particular, exhortation. For example one publication has described quality as variously 'exceptional', 'perfection', 'fitness for purpose', 'value for money' and 'transformation', the author preferring the latter option which he sees as 'empowering students to help them achieve to the best of their abilities' (Harvey 1995: 153–4). Barnett, on the other hand, has proposed a categorisation of quality evaluation based on the dimensions of power and enlightenment, the former divided into collegial and bureaucratic forms and the latter either emancipatory or technicist (Barnett 1994: 175).

Notwithstanding the ranges of definitions and purposes to be found in the quality literature, there appear in practice to be two main approaches to assessing quality.[1] The first, norm-referenced, approach, based on collegial peer review (external or internal) largely draws on the conventions of the academic community – or more correctly subject communities – and tends to be implicit and intrinsic in its approach to quality. The second, criterion-referenced, approach, using performance indicators plus a more managerialist version of peer review, draws on institutional goals and checklist criteria of national agencies in a manner both more explicit and more extrinsic, giving greater weight to stakeholders outside of the academic community. Effectively the debate about quality is a debate about power, the relative autonomy of higher education institutions and the distribution of power within them.

In practice both approaches coexist in most institutions and most European countries, though with significant differences of emphasis and varying degrees of clarity. Most European countries now have national quality bodies which, *inter alia*, publish reports on the quality of provision. Everywhere institutions and programmes are being assessed, even if the criteria used and the consequences of the assessment are different and frequently far from clear.

What then are the implications for study abroad of these developments in quality assessment? Virtually all quality assessment systems claim to be about achieving accountability and improvement (Vroeijen-stijn 1994), but when assessing study abroad there are difficulties in achieving either.

Not least is the question of who is doing the assessing. Most bilateral student exchange schemes will be subject to at least four assessment systems, those of the two institutions concerned and those of the two national quality bodies. In the United Kingdom the existence of parallel systems of assessment and audit adds an additional element; and most quality assessment systems in Europe will probably come to have both institutional and subject-level elements, the former concentrating on institutional policies, procedures and resources, the latter assessing more directly the quality of education provided. And to these institutional and national systems must be added the evaluation activities of the

Commission itself and of bodies such as the European Rectors Conference.

In this multiplicity of assessment it is unlikely that common criteria will be used even when it is clear what the criteria are. The collegial approach to quality assessment faces problems stemming from institutional and educational diversity, including ensuring a shared understanding of conventions between assessors and assessed, and avoiding the use of inappropriate criteria. As these problems occur even at national level, given the increasingly heterogeneous nature of national educational systems (Trow 1994), they are likely to be even more evident in a transnational context; and it is clear that where criteria of quality are not shared external assessment leads to compliance rather than improvement.

Within more explicit managerial assessment systems, problems arise in goal identification, not least against whose goals quality is to be assessed: the European Commission's educational policy framework; the policies and practices of national quality agencies; the missions of institutions; the goals of programme planners; the intentions of individual academics; and the wishes and aspirations of students. The question of whose goals take priority is one of power rather than quality.

However, rather than concluding that quality assessment is unlikely to offer anything of value to study abroad, these complexities may cause proper attention to be focused on the question of what study abroad is actually for. What should be the goals of study abroad and how best are they to be achieved? As we have seen, the European Commission has been getting more explicit about this. It has moved from a position where cross-European collaboration was a worthy end in itself to one where it is a means to the achievement of other goals. This being so, the Commission's recent statement (Commission of the European Communities 1994) provides useful contours for institutional debate.

Commission policy objectives can be summarised as achieving an occupationally mobile European citizenry, and embracing economic, political and cultural considerations. But is such an objective to be achieved simply by studying abroad for a period or does it imply the provision of specially designed educational experiences? At the institutional level the question is whether the intention is to ensure that students studying abroad are equipped to fit into the requirements of different national higher education systems, or whether it is to encourage institutions to accommodate European purposes, as held either by the European Commission or by the students. To do the former, improvements in student support systems may be sufficient; to address the latter fundamental institutional change may be needed.

In considering the case for the second of these approaches, it should not be assumed that harmonisation of higher education is being advocated. One of the things which study abroad and external quality assessment have in common is an assumption that critical exposure to alternative ways of doing things may of itself lead to development and improvement. Thus in considering institutional changes to accommodate the needs of study abroad students – whether by internationalising the curriculum or modifying teaching, assessment and pastoral care – institutions may be improving the educational experiences of all their students.

How far any of this is likely may be considered by looking at some recent studies which have examined 'quality differences' across Europe. These have been of two sorts: EC-sponsored evaluations of ERASMUS programmes themselves and special studies supported by particular national governments who have had concerns about the comparative quality of their graduates.

EVALUATIONS OF ERASMUS

Since 1989 the European Commission has supported projects which analyse the experiences of students on ERASMUS programmes. The purposes of these projects have been three-fold: to provide information for future students opting for study abroad in Europe, to provide feedback for higher education institutions on their activities in study abroad, and to provide a basis for the evaluation of the ERASMUS programme as a whole by the Commission and national governments. The projects have incidentally achieved a fourth purpose by providing us with unrivalled information about the differences between European higher education systems as experienced by their students. The messages from these studies are clear as far as UK higher education is concerned. However, first we should consider what the studies tell us about study abroad itself.

Study abroad is a social as well as an educational experience, and students may encounter problems in either respect. An early study identified nine problems rated relatively serious by students, including predominantly social matters (too much contact with people from home country, accommodation, finance) as well as explicitly educational issues (differences in teaching and learning styles and taking examinations in a foreign language) (Teichler 1991). Students tended to rate their academic progress abroad positively (55 per cent as better than at their home institution) although academic recognition by their home institution was a problem in around 50 per cent of cases. Overall almost all ERASMUS students regarded their experiences as 'academically and culturally worthwhile'. Areas where improvements were suggested included the quality of preparation by the home institution, the extent and quality of advice and support provided by the host institution and the academic recognition granted for the study abroad period (Maiworm et al. 1991).

Since greater differences were found in student experiences between countries than between institutions or disciplines, it is proper to investigate the experiences of ERASMUS students studying in the United Kingdom and of UK students studying elsewhere. The United Kingdom is well represented in the ERASMUS programme. British students make up 18–19 per cent of ERASMUS students even though they comprise only 14 per cent of all students at institutions of higher education in EU countries (Teichler 1994); and, conversely, the United Kingdom is a popular destination for ERASMUS students, with 27–8 per cent going to UK institutions. Hence UK institutions import three overseas students for every two they export (Teichler 1994). UK students participating in ERASMUS are younger than the ERASMUS average (having a mean age of 21.4 against 22.6 for the system as a whole), and a high proportion study business studies (31 per cent compared with 24 per cent) (Teichler 1994).

On the face of it, students coming to the United Kingdom receive a better deal than UK students studying elsewhere:

> ERASMUS students going to the UK and to the Republic of Ireland stated by far the least problems, and British and Irish ERASMUS students going to other countries clearly cite the most problems. We certainly might conclude that the general teaching and learning as well as administrative environment at British and Irish universities is viewed quite favourably both by home and host students.
>
> (Teichler 1994: 23)

Students coming to the United Kingdom have greater proficiency in English than UK students have in the language of their host country (Teichler 1994) though it is the perception of local ERASMUS coordinators as well as the students that as far as directly academic issues are concerned UK students encounter more problems in studying abroad than do foreign students studying in the UK. UK graduates who have taken part in ERASMUS programmes are less likely to work abroad than other ERASMUS students (14 per cent compared to 18 per cent overall), and are more likely to be dissatisfied with the jobs they have obtained relative to their qualifications (34 per cent compared to 24 per cent) (Teichler and Maiworm 1994).

Overall the UK experience of ERASMUS is less favourable than the average both in terms of UK students studying abroad and students from elsewhere in Europe studying in the UK. Positive features are the appreciation of teaching, communication and administration styles of UK institutions by incoming students, though on the other hand European students studying in the UK tend to find the courses 'less demanding' than those experienced elsewhere. UK students encounter more administrative and academic problems abroad, have more language problems, and assess academic progress less favourably than average ERASMUS students.

ERASMUS students as a whole view study abroad favourably on both social and educational grounds. After graduation such study is associated with more international professional activity than would be expected of graduates generally, although opinions and attitudes towards host countries do not generally change significantly as a result of studying there.

COMPARING QUALITIES

The existence of Anglo-Saxon and Continental European traditions of higher education has already been noted. In practice, however, each national system of higher education has certain distinctive features, and it is partly because there are differences in the experience of being a student in different countries that study abroad can be so valuable. The problem is in distinguishing differences likely to have a positive educational impact on the student from those likely to impede educational development. There seems little point in exchanging the experience of a well run stimulating course at home for a badly run low quality one abroad.

Higher education institutions in the UK are seen both by students from other countries and by home students to be characterised by

a strong emphasis on independent work and out-of-class communication between teaching staff and students, by the important role of written examinations and evaluation of papers submitted, and by little use of publications in foreign languages.

(Teichler 1994: 22)

In contrast, French universities are said to place strong emphasis on the acquisition of facts, regular class attendance and dependence on teachers, to allow students little choice or autonomy, and for there to be little out-of-class communication with teachers. German universities on the other hand appear to place great emphasis on students' freedom and independence and are less concerned about regular class attendance than about the understanding of theories, concepts and paradigms (Teichler 1994).

Differences in pedagogy are one thing but differences in educational levels and standards are another. According to the ERASMUS evaluations, UK students overall rated their academic progress less positively than the ERASMUS average. The perception of teaching staff in the UK and elsewhere was that UK students were more likely to find the academic level of courses abroad too high, whereas ERASMUS students coming to the United Kingdom had few problems of this kind. Incoming UK students were rated lower academically by teaching staff than students of other EC countries. UK teachers on the other hand found incoming students the equals of home students, whereas teachers in other countries rated them as slightly inferior (Maiworm, Steube and Teichler 1991). Hence, while it would be premature to conclude on the basis of these findings that teaching and learning at institutions of higher education in the United Kingdom is on average below EC level, the above-stated observations both by those coordinating the ERASMUS programme and by the students participating in the ERASMUS programme are certainly not in tune with the traditional notion of a very high quality of teaching and learning at institutions of higher education in the United Kingdom (Teichler 1994: 26).

Other evidence is equally incriminating. A number of recent studies have compared programme quality in business studies, economics and various branches of engineering in Sweden, France, Germany, the Netherlands, Finland, the United Kingdom, Belgium and Switzerland (see Brennan 1993). These studies have all used a form of international peer review, bringing together academics in relevant disciplines to examine programme documentation and discuss it with representatives of the programmes concerned. The formal purposes of the studies have not been to make rankings – whether of programmes, institutions or countries – and they have all conceived of quality as multi-dimensional and related to national and disciplinary contexts. Nonetheless the studies paint a consistent picture of the relative academic standing of UK degree courses. Thus a study of electrical engineering courses in six countries concluded:

> the Committee has the impression that the English Engineering programmes of 4 years are below the level of the Master of Engineering programmes in West European (mainland) universities.
> (Swedish National Board of Universities and Colleges 1992)

A study sponsored by the Dutch Association of Universities reached similar conclusions, and a later study explicitly excluded UK first degrees in engineering on the grounds that they were not comparable to their continental European counterparts. A study of economics in the United Kingdom, Germany and the Netherlands found less attention to and lower levels of student achievement in statistical and quantitative methods in the UK, together with indications of learning outcomes being related to differences between the three countries in the length of programmes and in teaching and assessment methods (Brennan et al. 1993). A review of these studies, explicitly excluding the longer Scottish first degree, concluded that overall:

English [*sic*] first degrees provide a quick way to obtaining a degree qualification. But there is at least some evidence to suggest that they are not fully equivalent to their continental counterparts in either the range of their curriculum or in the levels of their students' achievements. This may partly be to do with the length of study, but also partly to do with the relative youth of the students and the characteristics of their secondary education.

(Brennan 1993: 27)

There are, of course, important differences in context and tradition to be taken into account in interpreting the results of such studies. Nevertheless, these studies, together with the ERASMUS evaluations, suggest that UK higher education is less demanding than is the case in mainland Europe.

THE ASSESSMENT OF QUALITY AND STUDYING IN EUROPE

As we have noted, across much of Europe the assessment of higher education quality is increasingly explicit, multi-dimensional and public. This is relevant to study abroad in three respects: it may help higher education institutions improve their study abroad arrangements, institutions will be required to account for the quality of their study abroad arrangements, and the experience of studying abroad can itself inform quality assurance processes for purposes both of accountability and improvement.

How might external quality assurance assist study abroad? Publishing reports on the quality of provision in different institutions may help institutions find suitable partners, students find suitable courses, and employers find suitable graduates. This at least is the theory: to inform choice and help create an educational market. This assumes of course that the reports are informative and deemed to have value, and that they are widely disseminated and read. At present none of these assumptions holds, though such reports are in future increasingly likely to find their way into the public domain, serving as a source of information about good practice and problems encountered and, presumably, influencing behaviour. A high proportion of reports of the quality assessments undertaken by the UK funding councils have addressed study abroad, as have a number of the audit reports of the Higher Education Quality Council. Also, quite apart from the reporting arrangements, the dual processes of self- and external assessment of programmes usefully expose both problems and achievements.

Study abroad arrangements will increasingly come under external scrutiny, not just by UK assessment bodies but also by bodies to whom partner institutions are accountable. We have already noted that the

European Commission and the European Rectors Conference are undertaking quality assessments, while in many countries, though not currently the UK, the European context of quality assessment is evidenced by the inclusion of foreign academics on assessment panels.

The most important way in which study abroad programmes are relevant to quality assessment lies in their potential to stimulate debate on quality improvement. They provide a rich source of information about alternative ways of doing things and, notwithstanding all the caveats about context, provide indicators of relative effectiveness. At a time of increasingly rapid change and diversification in higher education, knowledge of how things are done elsewhere is especially valuable. It is in this sense ironic that European study abroad programmes have given academic staff opportunities to study other courses in ways that hardly exist within the home country.

CONCLUSIONS: THE EUROPEAN DIMENSION AND LEARNING FROM OTHERS

Study abroad programmes are but one aspect of a Europeanisation of UK higher education manifested in an increasingly explicit policy framework at European level, competition for resources to support activities connected with these policies, and a transnational institutional collaboration which is better developed than inter-institutional collaboration within countries. Almost any higher education institution of any size now has a European office, and they are rarely short of work.

In looking at quality dimensions of study abroad in Europe, the key principle is that we have much to learn from others. While it is of course important that we find better ways to help foreign students obtain the maximum benefit from their experiences of studying in the UK, it is at least equally important to ensure that our universities and colleges obtain the maximum benefit from their experiences of teaching these students by increasing their understanding of the different educational traditions which they represent.

The goals of study abroad programmes are only partly to do with the experiences of the students who participate in them. They are also about internationalising institutions of higher education in new ways, introducing a European dimension into the experience of higher education of both students and staff, and creating the framework for a flexible European system of institutions and programmes. In all this, 'quality' is a linking concept between the agendas of policy-makers and wider publics. It operates at national and international levels, particularly in terms of accountability, and addresses the experiences of students and their teachers in countless lecture halls, libraries and laboratories across Europe in terms of improvement. It would, to put it no higher, be as well for those concerned with the latter function to be aware of the agendas of those concerned with the former.

NOTE

1 The term 'quality assessment' is used throughout this paper in its international generic sense and not to refer to the specific arrangements operated by the national funding bodies in the UK.

Chapter 5

Communication for learning across cultures

Martin Cortazzi and Lixian Jin

It is generally accepted that learning to communicate is important in higher education: most departments see both written and oral communication as being key competencies in subject learning. With overseas students this is commonly seen as a need (where necessary) for developing advanced language skills, often linked with study skills and issues concerning learning in Britain (e.g. seminar skills, IT skills, assessment procedures). A third element – beyond *communication* and *learning* – is often underestimated. This is the element of *culture*.

The teaching and learning situation in British higher education is necessarily one which involves the need to develop inter-cultural competencies: not only is the indigenous student population highly multi-cultural but the presence of large numbers of overseas students greatly enriches this cultural diversity. There is therefore a need for staff and students to develop inter-cultural skills, both *learning to communicate across cultures* and *communicating for learning across cultures*.

This chapter focuses on issues of overseas students' learning which revolve around inter-cultural communication. Culture is seen in terms of principles of expectations and interpretations which are often taken for granted and therefore overlooked. The chapter surveys some ways in which hidden assumptions about culture infuse communication and learning. These cultural influences are conceptualised in terms of *academic cultures, cultures of communication* and *cultures of learning*, as shown in Figure 5.1. Briefly, *academic culture* refers to the cultural norms and expectations involved in academic activity. A *culture of communication* refers to expected ways of communicating and of interpreting others' communication in a cultural group. A *culture of learning* refers to cultural beliefs and values about teaching and learning, expectations about classroom behaviour and what constitutes 'good' work. These three key terms are elaborated below.

A key feature of the interaction between culture, communication and learning is that participants do not only carry cultural behaviour and concepts into the classroom but that they also use the specific framework

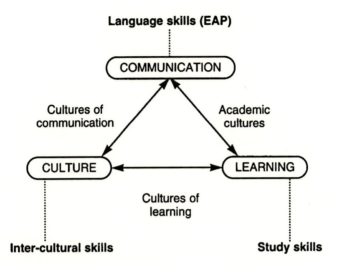

Figure 5.1 Cultural infusions in communication and learning
(EAP = English for Academic Purposes)

of their cultures to interpret and assess other peoples' words, actions, and academic performance.

ACADEMIC CULTURES

Academic cultures are the systems of beliefs, expectations and cultural practices about how to perform academically. For skilled practitioners – such as academic staff – many aspects seem obvious but are rarely made explicit. One reason for this is that culture 'works' precisely because participants do not have to think about making it work, one simply does what is expected. It is, perhaps, only with novices or those who clearly expect something else (some overseas students) that we need to give attention to academic culture.

Galtung (1981) outlines some different approaches to culture and intellectual style in a discussion of four styles: Saxonic, Teutonic, Gallic and Nipponic. Saxonic culture, he says, encourages debate in relatively more socially equal relationships and favours empirical approaches to research. Teutonic culture is based more on 'master–disciple' relationships, using deductive approaches which encourage students to follow logical implications rigorously. Gallic culture is also horizontal in terms of relationships but favours non-deductive approaches, encouraging persuasive eloquence. Nipponic culture is based on hierarchical relations in which debate is dialectical and primarily social rather than intellectual. Clearly, Galtung's list does not include all academic cultures and we would add Sinic or Chinese academic culture, as outlined below.

In British higher education, academic culture has been explored at various levels. Becher (1989) proposed that different disciplines have different academic cultures, maintaining that there are identifiable patterns within the relationship between the 'knowledge focus' and 'knowledge communities' of each discipline. In effect, each discipline may have its own professional culture, as Evans (1988, 1993) has illustrated in studies of foreign language and English departments.

These analyses draw attention to some key features which are likely to be new or different for overseas students. There may be cultural gaps between what is valued and expected in a British academic culture and the expectations students bring with them based on their educational experience elsewhere, as shown in Box 5.1.

Box 5.1 shows the expectations held by British staff compared with those of Chinese students (or Chinese staff). It is drawn up on the basis of questionnaire and interview data from 101 mainland Chinese students and 37 of their British supervisors. Box 5.1 should be interpreted in the light of three qualifying remarks. First, the expectations shown may not always be realised, but they do seem to be goals. Second, as with all cultural issues, not every individual will conform to group trends. Third, the expectations are shown as polarities rather than as binary opposites: both sides may value both aspects to some extent yet there is a clear emphasis in the direction shown. Particular circumstances may alter this emphasis.

British academic culture has an individual orientation. There is a degree of equality between individuals so that 'horizontal' relationships are emphasised. Students are expected to develop as individuals with their own opinions; independence of mind, creativity and originality are valued. In contrast, the academic culture of the Chinese (and many other non-western groups) emphasises relationships. The collective consciousness of the group is important. Hierarchical relations obtain strongly

British academic expectations	Academic expectations held by Chinese and other groups
Individual orientation	Collective consciousness
Horizontal relations	Hierarchical relations
Active involvement	Passive participation
Verbal explicitness	Contextualised communication
Speaker/writer responsibility	Listener/reader responsibility
Independence of mind	Dependence on authority
Creativity, originality	Mastery, transmission
Discussion, argument, challenge	Agreement, harmony, face
Seeking alternatives	Single solution
Critical evaluation	Assumed acceptance

Box 5.1 Academic culture gaps between the expectations of British university staff and those of some overseas studends (after Jim 1992; Jim and Cotazzi 1993)

between those who are older, senior or in authority, and those who are younger, junior or subordinate. It follows that a learner's duty is to understand and master what those in authority say, as transmission, before any independence of mind or creativity in a field can be expected. It is believed that this is an effective and relatively short way to achieve the creative stage. Students will hesitate before offering opinions until they sense what the group feels or the direction that the teacher expects them to pursue. Where British tutors may expect active involvement and verbal explicitness from students, Chinese students prefer to listen to the teacher, as an expert. They may seem 'passive' to tutors but they are active in their minds. When they do speak, their meaning may seem vague or elusive since it is contextualised, presuming that much can be taken for granted and that *both* listener/reader and speaker/writer are responsible for communication. This means, in fact, that for Chinese (and Japanese or other groups) the listener is given credit for being able to work out implications; being too explicit may actually be considered insulting since it presumes the listener cannot understand otherwise. British tutors may expect group discussion, with some argument and challenge of viewpoints in an effort to seek alternative interpretations or evaluate approaches critically. Chinese students, however, strive for agreement and harmony in a group since to disagree may be to risk loss of face. A single 'right' solution for a pragmatic purpose is sought which, when acknowledged by experts, can be accepted as correct without the need for further evaluation.

These expectations of academic cultures are realised in day-to-day interaction through talk, or writing, i.e. they are exchanged through cultures of communication.

CULTURES OF COMMUNICATION

Students coming from different cultural backgrounds will often use different styles of communication in English, even when they have attained very high language competence. Cultural ways of speaking and writing are transferred from other languages into English, especially those ways which are taken for granted. Whereas grammar and vocabulary are obvious areas which may need attention, other aspects of cultures of communication may be overlooked, for example uses of intonation, pauses, eye contact, body language, rhetorical patterns and ways of presenting information (Smith 1987; Saville-Troike 1989; Gudykunst 1994).

The real challenge with such differences in cultures of communication is that they often lead to wrong assessments of those who use them. For example, if students from the Middle East use the heavy intonation, relatively loud voices and rhetorical exaggeration which are acceptable (or desirable) in their native Arabic they may be seen by British tutors and students (quite wrongly) as overbearing or aggressive.

Another example is the use of pauses in turn-taking. Participants in a discussion know by the length of a pause that a speaker has finished and that they can take a turn. However, the timing of such pauses can vary across cultures. Among many Greek students the pauses between turns are minimal; speakers alternate rapidly and overlaps between one speaker and the next are accepted as showing solidarity between speakers who understand each other. In contrast, among Scandinavian students, particularly Finns, such pauses are often one or two seconds longer as participants show respect for others' independence and perhaps think carefully about what they want to say. A problem may arise when the two groups talk to each other: both groups unwittingly use their own culture of communication in English, not only to express themselves but also to interpret others' talk and to judge others as speakers. Greek students report that they feel long silences, which leads them to wonder if they have said something wrong or (given that Scandinavians are often highly competent in English) whether they have made a linguistic mistake. As a result the Greeks feel insecure (unnecessarily). The Scandinavians meanwhile feel that the Greeks keep interrupting them since their uptake of turns is so much quicker. They feel (wrongly) that the Greek students are aggressive. British tutors, using a pause and turn-taking system which lies between that of the Greeks and Scandinavians, may also draw such wrong conclusions.

Apparently simple words like 'yes' and 'no' can function quite differently in some cultures of communication. Among Japanese students, for example, many may say 'yes' simply to indicate that they hear and understand (but not necessarily to show agreement) while 'no' is very rarely used to express disagreement since this directness is thought to cause offence or loss of face (Christopher 1984: 155; Random 1987: 24). Rather than saying 'no', many Japanese prefer vague expressions which leave other possibilities open: 'Perhaps', 'I'm not sure', 'It is very difficult'. To say 'no' directly would seem, in Japan, as if this is a negative comment to the person rather than to his or her idea, opinion or request. Thus some Japanese students are hurt when others disagree publicly with their ideas. Some students from Taiwan adopt a similar cultural style of communication.

Pausing and answering 'yes' or 'no' can be affected by other factors, such as the need for extra time to understand a previous utterance when using English as a second language. Repeating something can give this essential extra time for mental processing (and repetition can itself sometimes be a signal of understanding), though such factors are easily forgotten when tutors, naturally enough, focus on content. This is illustrated from a tutor's comment in a research interview about a Chinese student:

> There are long silences and I don't know whether they are silences of understanding...or whether they are silences of misunderstanding, that he can't make a voice to show that he understands, because he doesn't. There are these long pauses and I break these pauses by saying, 'I'll say that again, just so I can be sure you've understood and if you don't understand please tell me.' So I will say it again and then there'll be another long pause and I'll say 'Did you understand that?' and he never replies 'yes' or 'no', never. So I say again 'Did you understand?' and the reply is always a repetition of something I've just said. He never says he doesn't understand and he never says he does.... He clearly understands more than we realise, but nobody is quite sure how much.
>
> (Jin 1992: 334)

The tutor's perplexity is compounded by the student's cultural dilemma: if he says he does not understand, the student loses face and also the implication is that the tutor did not explain properly, which for the student implies that the tutor, as an authority, will lose face. The student, out of respect for the tutor, does not wish this to happen.

Rhetorical patterns of cultural ways of communicating information in discourse can also cause problems. A good example is the preference for *deductive* or *inductive* discourse patterns, i.e. whether the main idea is introduced first, followed by background information and supporting arguments, or vice versa. Depending on the precise context, British tutors will probably prefer the former, for example in introductory paragraphs, whereas Chinese students (and others from South- and East Asia) will more naturally use the latter (Young 1994; Scollon and Scollon 1995). This is generally true in both speech and writing.

Chinese speakers feel the need to establish common ground and build up rapport so they give relevant background information before they lead the hearer up to the main point. This shows why the topic is important and prepares the hearer to accept the main point which may only get a brief mention – after all, it will be clear to the listener familiar with this discourse pattern where the argument is coming from and what the obvious conclusion is. In the same way, in writing the whole is outlined before parts, reasons are given before results, causes are shown before effects (because...so...) and background is foregrounded.

British tutors, in contrast, expect an early signal of where the argument is going to, otherwise the writing would be considered 'unclear' or 'waffling'. Tutors expect students to get to the main point quickly, often they anticipate a clear overview to show the direction of the discourse right at the beginning, especially in answering a question in an exam or formal situation. Background information or supporting evidence can follow; since the hearer or reader already has a good idea of the main point it will be clear how this background is relevant.

Each of these contrasting patterns is valid but either can be wrongly perceived. The main point may be missed by someone who expects it to be somewhere else. Perhaps more seriously, both tutors and students may judge each others' competence on the basis of how they present information. Some British tutors see the Asian preference as 'drifting', 'waffling', 'beating around the bush', 'not getting to the point'. Some Asians see the British pattern as 'a give-away' since 'there is no reason to listen or read once the main point is known', whereas 'the main point cannot be appreciated without necessary background so we give background first, then tutors will know what we know'. Both sides could be helped if they were aware of the British expectation that the background *comes from* the main point and that a clear initial outline of an argument is expected, while for many Asian students the background *leads up to* the main point in a reader–writer collaborative scheme of communication where both are responsible for negotiated meanings.

In academic writing or seminar presentations the choice of such patterns goes beyond mere cultural differences: since students are assumed to be communicating what they have learnt their discourse patterns are interpreted and assessed as learning, not as culture. A verified case showing what may occur in a Chinese postgraduate student's assignment in Education which was assessed as 37 per cent, with many margin comments such as 'Where's the point?', 'Is this relevant?', 'I don't see the connection', and nearer to the end of each section, 'Oh, here you are, this is your main point!' The student was deeply upset, believing she had worked hard, had included all the relevant information and covered all the points in the argument. A British peer read the work and agreed, but pointed out how the main idea or topic sentence was at the end of each paragraph, hence the tutor's comments. They photocopied the original, cut up and rearranged the topic sentences and resubmitted a revamped photocopy. This was then assessed as 54 per cent.

While there is no evidence to indicate the frequency of the impact of these discourse patterns on assessment, we have collected in interviews with overseas students many comments revealing that for them it was extremely helpful to be given explicit guidance about British academic expectations.

The following comment from a Chinese postgraduate shows that some students do achieve a useful cultural insight into academic discourse. The comment shows how specific contexts can lead to variations in different disciplines. It also shows diverse cultural reactions to such differences.

In the science reports written by westerners, they normally give an introduction which reviews the research done by others, very wordy. When they discuss the new techniques or new methodology, they put in quite a lot of irrelevant quotations from others and their previous writing. In the end, they again give reviews and prospects and implications of this research. So their papers are quite long with a lot of work mentioned.

But our Chinese writing is different. We just introduce this new method or technique, our thinking on this research, how it is used or processed, what effect it has to this project and to the whole technical world, how it can solve the problem. This is because people who read this journal have already known about the history of the research and where the problem is. What they need to know is how to solve this problem. They won't read those review parts. They just jump to the new part they want to know. So our way would save readers' time and the space of the journal.

When I talked about this to my British colleagues, some just smiled, some just said 'No, no!' I always argue that 'your British government documents or rules are normally short and concise'. But my professors always said that 'your Chinese government report or commentary is always long and wordy'. I said 'You're right, your government just tells you that you must do this or you mustn't do that. They don't tell you why. That's why it is concise. But our government has to explain why we can't do this, why we can do that. That's why it becomes long.'

Our writing styles are just opposite to British ones. About politics, we often quote ancestors' and important persons' words, review what has happened now and give a prospect of the future. But these do not exist so often in our science writings.

(Jin 1992)

CULTURES OF LEARNING

Academic cultures and cultures of communication come together in cultures of learning. Whereas an academic culture depends on the norms, values and expectations of academics (and therefore includes research and professional activities such as staff meetings or conferences), a culture of learning depends on the norms, values and expectations of teachers and learners relative to classroom activity. It is impossible to give serious consideration to inter-cultural issues involving overseas students without some notion that fundamental presuppositions about how to learn, how to teach, what constitutes 'good' work, how to participate in learning contexts, etc., can vary from culture to culture. It is not simply that overseas students encounter different ways of teaching and different expectations about learning; rather such encounters are juxtaposed with the cultures of learning they bring with them. All too often, both British tutors and the students themselves are not aware of what is involved.

Two examples may help to sketch the territory before a more systematic outline is presented. Following a lecture about social science research methods, a Saudi Arabian student asked, 'Which method is the best?' The professor explained that the three approaches he had outlined all had advantages and disadvantages and the answer to the student's question depended on the appropriateness of any particular method to help answer a particular research question. He gave detailed examples. This comprehensive answer (from the professor's viewpoint) was not enough to satisfy the student who then asked 'Which method do the staff use here?' Again, the professor repeated the gist of the previous answer, adding that staff used a range of methods. Still not satisfied, the student finally asked, 'Which method do you use yourself?' The student, who was able and intelligent, later explained that his basic presupposition was that there is a best method, a best solution and a single ultimate answer, stemming from ideas of ultimate (religious) truth (see Perry 1988, for examples of similar beliefs from American students). At the time of hearing he believed the professor was hiding the answer but wanted students to find it themselves. Only later, after much discussion and reading, was he able to separate religious truth from research methods in social science.

In a second example of mismatches in cultures of learning, some East European postgraduate students have difficulty understanding the British concept of an essay, particularly essay-type answers in exams. The reason is that, until recently, many Russian and East European university exams were oral. They involved students giving oral presentations on topics selected randomly from a published list, which required extensive memorisation as preparation. The British tendency to dismiss this as 'rote-learning' could undermine these students' confidence in what they have been trained to do (successfully) in a particular culture of learning. The students' abilities in oral presentation could, of course, be harnessed in British seminar contexts and their ability to memorise need not be devalued, though complementary skills in analysis and critical evaluation will be required in the UK.

As a third example, we summarise aspects of a Chinese culture of learning based on a long-term investigation using a range of data: interviews, questionnaires, classroom observations and video recordings, and student essays (Jin and Cortazzi 1993, 1995, 1996; Cortazzi and Jin 1996). Clearly, not every Chinese student will follow this culture of learning, though they will probably recognise its influence. This longstanding Chinese culture of learning derives in large part from Confucian traditions (Chen 1990) but it can be seen as influential in contemporary China (Louie 1984) and in East Asia in general (Yum 1988), combined with modern trends.

As shown in Box 5.2, knowledge is central to learning: the university teacher is expected to have deep knowledge, as an authority and expert. This knowledge will be transmitted to students, who expect to listen and work hard to internalise it. Students consider that deep reflection and consideration of topics in their minds is part of learning. This fundamentally cognitive approach is, however, practised in a social context. This context is viewed very differently from British ideas about active participation in discussion groups. The Chinese see learning as depending on the teacher for knowledge, and also for care, concern and help since the teacher–student relationship is reciprocal: students respect and obey the teacher, the teacher teaches and cares for students like a parent. Traditional notions of filial piety are thus extended to teachers in a relationship of mutual responsibility for learning. Chinese students may be disappointed or disillusioned if they observe British teachers who do not seem, in their eyes, to carry out their part in this reciprocal relationship. The social context includes peers, who have a strong role in supporting learning in a collective, as much out of class as within it. This does not particularly include group work or discussion in class since the aim is to achieve group harmony in common effort, not to air opinions or to disagree with peers, and certainly not to disagree with a respected teacher. The social context includes an important moral dimension: a good teacher is a moral example for students to follow and he or she will

Student view of teacher roles	Teacher view of teacher roles
• be an authority, expert • be a model: knowing that, how to • be a parent, friend • *know students' problems* • *give answers, clear guidance: teach us what to do*	• be a facilitator, organiser • be a model of how to find out • be a friendly critic

Student view of student roles	Teacher view of student roles
• develop receptivity, collective harmony, apprenticeship, deductive learning • respect teacher: learn by listening and reflection • learn methods, technical advances • focus on product, result	• develop independence, individuality, creativity, inductive learning • participate: engage in dialogue • develop critical thinking • focus on process of learning, research skills • *ask if there are problems* • *find own answers* • *should know what to do or work it out*

Box 5.2 *Different perceptions of teacher and student roles in higher education: Chinese students and British teachers*

not only teach the 'subject' in hand but will teach students about 'life'.

Where western teachers sometimes see Chinese students as 'passive' they should realise that the Chinese culture of learning includes the need to listen to think and reflect, to respect and obey the teacher and, probably, not to volunteer comments unless asked, in order not to interrupt the teacher. Learning is an apprenticeship, listening to and following a master–teacher. Learning involves heavy memorisation – this is often brushed aside as 'rote-learning' or 'parrot learning' by western teachers. But this is to miss the Chinese point, which is that understanding may not be immediate but may come in enlightenment later after a period of hard work. Thus what is memorised may be understood now (through close attention and repetition) but understanding might also come later after memorisation. Memorising is thus only a stage in learning, not the goal. As in an apprenticeship, creativity or originality may come later, after mastery, but cannot be expected immediately, when students feel they do not 'know' enough to say or do something original. Meanwhile it is better to quote past masters and authorities. Memorising their words and ideas is a concession to collected past experience.

Such cultures of learning can have a dramatic effect on the student–teacher interaction which is at the heart of communication for learning.

STUDENT–TEACHER INTERACTION

Many of the aspects discussed so far are summarised in Box 5.2, which shows overseas students' expectations (particularly of Chinese students but also of other East- and South Asian and some Middle Eastern students) contrasted with likely expectations of British lecturers. Such contrasts emerge in interaction. They are especially important because they affect participants' perceptions of each other.

These perceptions, as Box 5.2 shows (italicised items), can be asymmetrical. Many British lecturers expect students to ask for help if they have problems. Expressing anxiety, difficulties or lack of understanding seems to be a normal part of learning. In contrast, Chinese students expect that teachers, like parents, will show sufficient care and concern to be aware of students' problems and to offer help unasked. The students believe that to ask for help is to give a burden to others so they will be reluctant to give the teacher their problem. The result is that lecturers may think that such overseas students do not need help since they do not express a need for it, while the students (who do have problems) wonder whether the teacher really cares for them since he or she does not give help. This impasse is parallel to the situation of research students and supervisors: many supervisors believe that at advanced postgraduate levels students should think of their basic research questions for themselves, should know what to do or should work out research problems for themselves as part of their development as researchers. However, the research students' academic culture and culture of learning gives the supervisor, as teacher and example, a much more leading role in actually teaching and giving specific guidance for each step. In consequence of these asymmetrical expectations, British supervisors may conclude that the students have little initiative, are not ready for research, or require more supervision time than they have available. The students may conclude that, since the supervisor does not give full guidance, he or she does not really know the field and is not a competent supervisor.

The situation can be compounded by different cultures of communication: from the students' viewpoint, a direct question to elicit help might be interpreted negatively by the lecturer, as indirect criticism of not having explained something before. Students may therefore use the indirect strategy of hinting about their problem, in the hope that the lecturer will then offer help. However, British staff, less used to such an implicit style of communication, may not treat it seriously or may miss the point altogether.

A culture of communication can also affect course evaluation. It is not uncommon for course leaders to elicit student feedback through discussion groups which reflect on the course, give critical comment and suggestions, then report back. Some overseas students do not see the point of this: for them, the discussion wastes potential teaching time; the teacher (as a 'master', 'parent' or 'friend') should be sensitive to how the course is going without asking students. In a group of mixed nationalities, some Asians will not express opinions which seem to run counter to what others in the group are saying. These students also find it difficult to express any negative comments forcefully, lest the teacher loses face, so their remarks may be considerably toned down. For such reasons their views may not be represented in a report-back session. Some Asian students have commented that their solution is to talk individually to the course leader after the session. Such a private word, perhaps to praise or criticise aspects of the course, is however not given full value by the listener who has apparently brushed it aside as being 'unofficial' or 'merely being polite'. The listener may not realise that those 'private' words are exactly what students want to express, that they come forward with great courage and believe that these words with their special effort will be highly valued. Lack of sensitivity on other students' and the lecturer's part thus effectively disenfranchises some students. Their comments are simply not picked up. Consequences may include that overseas students feel their opinions are not valued; their opinions are not properly channelled back to university staff so that they may not know which part of the course is appreciated or considered unsatisfactory by these groups of overseas students. This may lead to further misunderstanding, such as racism (concluding that the views of these students are not dealt with because they are looked down upon), which may affect their self-confidence and may prevent them from sharing their views with other students or tutors for at least the time of the course.

LEARNING ACROSS CULTURES

A number of issues have been raised in this chapter related to academic cultures, cultures of communication and cultures of learning. These issues could be seen, perhaps, as problems – to be solved by giving students more information about British ways. However, these issues are not simply matters of communication but of cultural infusions in communication for learning. As has been shown, in many instances the key to understanding these issues is to see the cultural element in terms of participants' expectations and their interpretations. This might suggest that there is an opportunity here for *learning across cultures*, a skill which is arguably a basic competence in the contemporary academic world, where almost every teaching and learning context has become internationalised.

Learning across cultures means considering overseas (and British) students as bearers of cultures. Since cultures carry with them principles and systems of interpretation, the potential solution of simply asking overseas students to assimilate to British ways is unlikely to be successful since these aspects of culture are deep-rooted and change may be seen as a threat to identity.

The basic need is for participants in higher education to be aware of the kinds of cultural variation in communication and learning which can lead to different understandings. This means that both teachers and students need awareness of how to interpret others' words and to be sensitive to ways in which their own words might be interpreted.

The situation of communicating for learning across cultures thus invites *cultural synergy* (Jin 1992; Jin and Cortazzi 1995). This could be defined as the mutual effort of both teachers and students to understand each other's academic cultures, cultures of communication and cultures of learning. This would include the effort to understand others' principles of interpretation. The point about cultural synergy is that neither side loses – both gain.

When students raise their awareness of how their talk or writing might be (mis)understood by British tutors, on the basis of appreciating the three kinds of cultures outlined here (cultures of communication, learning, and academic cultures), they will learn to see communication in terms of choices between ways of saying things to people who interpret on the basis of cultural principles. They will inevitably move towards British academic ways, but without losing their own. When they see tutors making efforts to understand them in their own terms they will realise there is no threat to their cultural identity but rather the opportunity to enlarge their cultural repertoire of strategies.

For tutors, the notion of cultural synergy is an opportunity for professional development, to learn across cultures. The tutor's efforts to learn to understand overseas students in their own terms implies some movement towards them. Like the students, tutors do not need to surrender their own (British) academic ways, but can only gain by understanding others' ways. Arguably, to understand alternative approaches and interpretations is at the heart of academic endeavour (in one's own subject area). Cultural synergy means applying this open reflective attitude to the teaching–learning relationship. It is part of this relationship that teachers are also learners. In cultural synergy, students become teachers, helping tutors to understand their interpretations.

Learning across cultures through cultural synergy is therefore of mutual benefit for both students and teachers. In this reciprocal relationship between cultures, the whole is more than the sum of the parts. Everybody learns.

GUIDELINES FOR TEACHERS (AND STUDENTS) IN HIGHER EDUCATION

The discussion in this chapter raises implications for practical teaching, including:

1 Be aware that academic cultures vary: teaching (and learning) among culturally diverse groups enables us to see some ways in which this variation works.
2 Be aware that there are cultural aspects of communication and learning: these may affect teachers' and students' understanding of each other's communication and work.
3 Beware of transferring conclusions about cultural variation to representatives of those cultures: the culture is not the person; not every individual conforms to all cultural trends; cultural generalisations themselves vary in how they are realised according to the context.
4 Try to reflect on how communication for learning is being used by students (and teachers): What presuppositions and cultural styles are involved?
5 Ask students (and teachers) about their expectations of learning: what do they expect about teachers' and students' roles, 'good' work, written assignments, seminars, tutorials, etc. Discuss good examples.
6 Observe how students talk and listen to each other (and to teachers): which cultural aspects affect communication? Ask other participants later about any unclear aspects. A list of points to observe are: *intonation,*

pausing, silence, turn taking, ways of asking, ways of showing respect, agreeing and disagreeing, where the main point occurs in discourse, how opinions are shared, attitudes to authority, role of memorisation, being creative and original, degrees of explicitness, being critical, and critical evaluation.

7 Practise cultural synergy: try to understand students' (and teachers') cultures of communication and learning, and their academic cultures. Help them to understand counterpart cultures (including your own). What new teaching (and learning) strategies do you need to develop to take account of their cultural expectations?

Chapter 6

Gender matters
Access, welfare, teaching and learning

Caroline Wright

INTRODUCTION

There can be little doubt that a concern with the quality of teaching and learning for overseas students in higher education (HE) must encompass a concern with gender. Over two decades of scholarship in the general education field has stressed the need to take gender into account. It is widely recognised as an important axis around which educational experiences may be structured, and one which must be pivotal to any initiatives promoting equal opportunities in education. This makes it all the more unfortunate that so little has been written on gender in relation to overseas students in HE. By identifying gender issues of relevance to practitioners and policy-makers concerned with overseas students, as well as to students themselves, this chapter seeks to begin attending to such an omission.

The first part of the chapter explores the emergence of gender as an important issue in education, relating it to earlier debates around social class. It then examines the neglect of gender in the HE literature as a whole, and the fact that it barely arises at all in the section of the literature concerning overseas students. The scope of this work is also indicated, together with some discussion of the relationship between a focus on gender and a focus on women. Thereafter, attention is turned to three substantive issues pertaining to gender and overseas students in HE: access, welfare, and teaching and learning. Each is examined in turn, on the basis of the specific material available, the insights that might be drawn from the wider discipline of gender studies, and the author's own observations and experience. Suggestions are made for a more gender-sensitive approach to the education of overseas students, and for a more radical perspective on equal opportunities than currently characterises many HE institutions.

EDUCATION AND THE QUESTION OF GENDER

Contemporary debates about gender and education owe much to the feminist scholarship which flourished during the 1970s and 1980s. The particular lines of enquiry pursued have also related, however, to the rich seam of scholarship on educational inequality laid down in the 1970s. As sociologists and educationists engaged with the concepts of social structure which preoccupied so many scholars at the time, they laid the foundations for a substantial re-theorising of the relationship between education and the individual.

The extent to which educational experiences and outcomes were differentiated by social class became a central debate in the 1970s (Bernstein 1975; Bowles and Gintis 1976; Illich 1973), challenging what has since been referred to as the 'myth of meritocracy' (Stanworth 1981: 9). Hitherto, this myth served to obscure the relationships between class and education; unhappy educational experiences and/or poor educational attainment were assumed to result from intellectual deficiency and/or inadequate motivation, and the kind of education provided was rarely seen as having any bearing on the matter. Rapidly, however, the values and norms explicit or implicit in the establishment and practice of formal education were being related to educational achievement and to life chances. It was argued that the culture of education favoured the middle classes, helping to secure their high achievement and thus to perpetuate their relatively privileged position in society, while it disempowered those from working-class backgrounds, contributing to their poorer achievement and so reproducing their lower status throughout life.

Such accounts have, of course, in common with structuralist accounts in general, since been subject to substantial critique. Too crude is the concept that education helps to determine the stratification of society, too blind to individual agency and the diversities of educational practice. Too functionalist are the links made between education and capitalism – between the educational failure of the masses and capitalists' requirements for a large pool of compliant, relatively unskilled workers – too prone to collapsing into a conspiracy thesis. Notwithstanding such problems, however, these debates set important agendas which are still being worked through today. By opening up for scrutiny the content and culture of education, and by recognising the need to disaggregate educational experiences, the old debates on class are there in the wings more often than the contemporary scholarship on stage in the 1990s might acknowledge.

As more sophisticated concerns with social class emerged in the late 1970s (for example Willis 1977), other statuses came under scrutiny in relation to education. Gender, race, age and sexuality have all come to the fore in the literature, more or less in that chronological order. A particularly striking feature is that in all cases debates have been initiated in the context of primary and secondary education, with the tertiary sector being attended to only later, if at all. Thomas (1990: 7) relates this lag to 'the reluctance of academics critically to examine their own institutions'. Whatever the reason, work relating to gender and HE (Acker and Piper 1984; Lewis and Habeshaw 1990; Thomas 1990) only emerged some five or ten years after the first work on gender and schooling (Delamont 1980; Stanworth 1981; Spender and Sarah 1980; Spender 1982), while some of the contemporary concerns with sexuality and schooling (Mac an Ghaill 1994; Skeggs 1991; Wolpe 1988) have, as far as I am aware, not yet reached the HE literature.

A second feature of the education literature is a tendency to embark on the consideration of issues like gender, race, age and sexuality in terms of the educational experiences of those whose status in society is subordinate. So, for example, attention is paid not to gender *per se* but to women students, not to the dynamics of race/ethnicity but to non-white students, not to sexuality as a whole but to lesbian and gay students. The aim is to map inequalities of educational experience and outcome, and in so doing a valuable contribution has been made. Taking women as an example, they have been 'written in' to accounts which had presumed learners to be male, and the extent to which their educational experiences and attainment differs from men's has been highlighted. However, although this kind of compensatory project is arguably a necessary starting point, contemporary empirical and theoretical preoccupations suggest new lines of enquiry privileging the relational aspects of educational inequality. The focus on women and femininity is giving way to a burgeoning interest in men and masculinities, and in the relationship between hegemonic constructions of masculinity and experiences of education, both female and male. Empirically, this shift has been fuelled by recent reversals in women's historically lower educational achievement. With women now out-performing males at all levels of education up to HE, a new concern to explain male under-achievement has been generated (BBC 1994). Theoretically, such a shift relates to the (re)conceptualising of gender as a relationship rather than as a variable, as a process rather than a state (Maharaj 1995; Connell 1995: 44), such that it makes no sense to consider men or women, masculinity or femininity, in isolation from one another.

GENDER AND OVERSEAS STUDENTS

If gender has finally come of age in the literature on the tertiary education sector (Thomas 1990; Blackmore and Kenway 1993), following an initial concern with women borrowed from the literature on schooling

(Acker and Piper 1984; Martin et al. 1981) it is noticeable by its absence from the sub-set of work that attends to overseas students. The under-developed state of this field, coupled with the all too frequent tendency of commentators to see gender issues as supplementary questions to be tackled only when the general work has been done, make this gap unsurprising, if lamentable. What literature exists on overseas students tends to be preoccupied either with cost-benefit analyses of overseas student recruitment (Robins 1963; Williams 1981; Woodhall 1981) or with collecting the perspectives of overseas students on their educational experiences (Morris 1967; Hughes 1990; Kinnell 1990). The former approach is tellingly one-sided in its instrumentality, considering the costs and benefits to the UK economy and UK institutions but not to the students themselves, and, although the overseas student cohort is generally disaggregated by subject and by country of origin, gender is typically ignored. The latter body of work is at least student-centred, but there is little or no consideration of the extent to which the educational experiences and attitudes of overseas students are differentiated by gender.

In fact, the overseas student literature has barely even got to grips with women students, paying attention to whom, I argued above, might be the precursor to a concern with gender. The one notable example of work concentrating on women, Goldsmith and Shawcross' ground-breaking work *It Ain't Half Sexist, Mum: Women as Overseas Students in the UK*, is now over ten years old and, despite the strong case put forward by the authors for further research, has not been followed up. In consequence, their observation that 'surveys tend to treat overseas students as "genderless", or rather as being typically single, young and male' (Goldsmith and Shawcross 1985: 5), remains valid all too often. For example, the otherwise thoughtful and insightful review of overseas student perspectives on learning edited by Kinnell (1990) does not even make clear how many of the overseas students sampled were female and how many were male. Moreover, since Lewins' (1990) contribution to the volume discusses both the chauvinism of male students towards female university staff (p. 93) and the loneliness of isolated student wives (p. 92), wittingly or otherwise the assumption that overseas students are male is perpetuated.

An obvious rejoinder to any charge that the overseas student literature has implicitly or explicitly focused on male students is that this reflects the fact that women are but a minority of overseas students. This is indeed the case, as the following section on access demonstrates. Yet, ignoring the experiences and perspectives of those students who are female, however few, is not justified, especially since the proportion of female students from overseas is increasing. Indeed the views of female students may be under-represented in surveys of overseas students precisely because gender issues are not taken into account. UKCOSA report having had difficulties persuading female overseas students to express their views (Sherlock 1995) and it is conceivable that the socialisation of women and their perceived status within the HE institution, together with the cultural norms that restrict the participation of certain groups of women in public life, render them less likely to respond than men.

My analytical preference for work on gender rather than on women is probably clear by now. However, while so much important research is still to be done documenting and analysing the HE experiences of women overseas students, we might expect to find men remaining in the analytical background. So it is in this chapter which, despite a title encompassing gender, is principally concerned with women overseas students. Male overseas students are not wholly absent from the text – a concern with the number of overseas students who are female necessarily says something about the number who are male, for example – but there is little emphasis on constructions of masculinity or on the role that HE plays in the creation and recreation of gendered categories. Indeed, my use of the word 'gender' is to say more about the long-term direction I would like to see research going in than to reflect what already exists.

A QUESTION OF ACCESS

Access is an obvious starting point when considering gender issues relating to overseas students, and the evidence is that women continue to be under-represented, and men over-represented, in the overseas student cohort. Indeed, this does not come as any great surprise, given that most of the history of HE has involved the non-representation or under-representation of women. The deficit of women, however, seems to be more persistent among overseas students than in the student population as a whole.

It was not until the latter half of the nineteenth century that women were admitted to universities in the UK, and even then they were there only on sufferance, in separate colleges and having to fight for the right to be accepted on the same terms as men (Dyhouse 1984), amidst 'scientific' claims that 'prolonged education would lead to mental and physiological derangement in women students' (Burstyn 1984: 65). As the twentieth century wore on, women's access to HE improved but slowly; in 1966–7 they were still only 27 per cent of all university undergraduates (Watts 1972: 48). Since then progress has been more marked, women making up 41 per cent of full-time undergraduate entrants in 1976–7 (calculated from Farrant 1981: 71), 43.1 per cent of all undergraduates in 1987–8 (Thomas 1990: 3), and 47.1 per cent of all full-time undergraduates in 1993–4 (calculated from UGC 1994: 14–15). However, the gender gap among overseas students has remained more substantial. As late as 1982–3, women were still only 25.8 per cent of all overseas enrolments in the HE sector, although by 1992–3 they had increased their share to 40 per cent (calculated from Department for Education 1994: Table 3) and a year later, 1993–4, to 41 per cent (calculated from UGC 1994: 14–15).

Although welcome, this recent increase in the proportion of overseas students who are female should be no cause for complacency. Indeed, the disaggregated picture is rather less healthy. A more substantial deficit of women persists at the postgraduate level than at the undergraduate level, women comprising only 22.2 per cent of all overseas postgraduates in the HE sector in 1982–3, 33.8 per cent in 1992–3 (calculated from Department for Education 1994: Table 3) and 34.7 per cent in 1993–4 (calculated from UGC 1994: 16–17). This deficit is in keeping with, although more acute than, that concerning all postgraduate students, 40 per cent of whom were female in 1993–4 (calculated from ibid.: 16–17).

The gender gap also varies substantially according to the geographical origin of overseas students, as Table 6.1 illustrates.

The first thing to note is that the deficit of females is less marked among students from elsewhere in Europe than from the rest of the world. Also worth highlighting is that there is actually a deficit of male students from seven countries, all, with the exceptions of Japan and Thailand, in Europe or North America. However, the most striking aspect of Table 6.1 is the magnitude of the deficit of women from certain countries and regions. The vast majority of students coming from the Middle East who were enrolled in UK HE institutions in 1992–3 were male, with women making up fewer than 15 per cent of students from Libya, Saudi Arabia and Iran. South Asia also shows a substantial deficit, women comprising only 15 per cent of students from Pakistan and less than 30 per cent from India, Bangladesh and Sri Lanka, as does Africa, with women making up less than 30 per cent of students from Zambia, Botswana, Tanzania, Ghana and Zimbabwe.

This deficit of females among the overseas student population is of concern for a number of reasons. Obviously it raises questions of equity. 'Women constitute the largest disadvantaged social group in the world, and it is especially important that they have access to education to build their own self-awareness, confidence, and to equip them to challenge the discrimination they face and to develop their own skills' (Goldsmith and Shawcross 1985: 5). There are also issues of efficiency involved, since women will be an under-utilised resource if they are not given every opportunity to enhance their capacities. At the same time, the overseas student question is not just about what British higher education can offer to others, but about what is gained through the diversity of cultural

ORIGIN	WOMEN	MEN	% WOMEN
Other EC	14812	18206	44.9%
Other overseas	22578	37506	37.6%
Malaysia	3431	4892	41.2%
Hong Kong	2416	4103	36.6%
Germany	3149	3841	45.9%
France	3170	3087	50.6%
United States	2862	2236	56.1%
Ireland	1985	2514	44.1%
Singapore	1223	2099	36.8%
Spain	1351	1381	49.4%
Japan	1157	883	56.7%
Italy	1057	1050	50.2%
Greece	1977	3960	33.3%
Cyprus	730	1156	38.7%
Norway	806	1052	43.4%
China	379	1041	26.7%
Netherlands	664	698	48.8%
Kenya	496	776	39.0%
Canada	574	698	45.1%
Belgium	530	612	46.4%
Pakistan	167	938	15.1%
India	316	779	29.0%
Taiwan	444	594	42.8%
Israel	249	702	26.2%
Nigeria	289	581	33.2%
Turkey	243	597	28.9%
Brazil	332	538	38.2%
Portugal	310	420	42.5%
Denmark	390	340	53.4%
Thailand	304	297	50.6%
Brunei	263	429	38.0%
Sri Lanka	193	476	28.8%
Iran	98	558	14.9%
Oman	77	404	16.0%
Sweden	330	248	57.1%
Zambia	135	448	23.2%
South Korea	114	458	19.9%
Saudi Arabia	63	497	11.2%
Australia	243	346	41.2%
Botswana	171	406	29.6%
South Africa	191	386	33.1%
Switzerland	260	293	47.0%
Indonesia	128	362	26.1%
Tanzania	130	354	26.8%
Libya	39	467	10.7%
Zimbabwe	130	319	29.0%
Mauritius	172	270	38.9%
Bangladesh	117	299	28.1%
Ghana	92	322	22.2%
Mexico	118	301	28.2%
Bahrain	49	171	22.3%
Kuwait	128	257	33.2%
Others	3100	5600	35.6%

Table 6.1 Full-time students from overseas* in UK higher education, 1992–3, by sex and origin
* From the top 50 sending counties:
Source: Calculated from Department for Education 1994: Table 6

backgrounds that overseas students embody (Williams 1981: 11), and women are an important dimension of this diversity.

A systematic examination of the barriers to the participation of overseas women in HE in the UK is required, in an effort both to understand and to redress their under-representation. In the absence of such a study we must surmise as best we can from the evidence available. A recent British Council document seeking to increase women's presence in the overseas student body refers to cultural and educational barriers to women's study overseas, including their primary responsibilities for childcare and domestic work around the world, social and cultural taboos against women travelling alone, preconceived ideas about women's unsuitability for HE, and lower female enrolment rates in formal education (Peace et al. 1994: 7). Poverty may also be an important factor – the 1985 survey by Goldsmith and Shawcross referred to earlier notes that 'women from lower socio-economic classes worldwide are less likely to have access to higher education overseas than are women from more affluent classes', and highlights a dramatic under-representation of women on scholarship schemes (Goldsmith and Shawcross 1985: 17).

Improving women's access to funding may be within the remit of UK bodies to an extent that changing the home cultures of prospective students is not. The British Council manages over 20 per cent of the awards through which overseas students fund their studies in Britain (Hughes 1990: 50) and has recently launched an initiative to enhance women's share of the Technical Cooperation Training awards it manages, which are funded by the Overseas Development Administration (Peace et al. 1994). In 1993–4 women received only 27 per cent of new awards, there were no women recipients at all from five of the 56 countries represented (Oman, Senegal, Uruguay, Fiji and Vanuatu) and women were one-fifth or less of the recipients from eighteen others, principally in Africa (ibid. 1994: Annex 3). Recommendations to redress the balance include the following: setting targets for women recipients; working with the ministry nominating recipients to stress the importance of a gender balance; flexibility over the age limit for awards (to avoid disadvantaging women whose career progression is slower compared to men because of time spent child-rearing); and outreach work briefing and supporting female students.

A final aspect of access that is worth examination is that of subject choice. Figures for UK-domiciled students indicate substantial gender skewing, whereby the arts are designated a 'woman's field' and the sciences a 'man's field'. In 1993–4 the ratio of female to male full-time home undergraduates was 1:6 in engineering and technology, 2:1 in languages studies, and 1:3 in mathematics and computing science (UGC 1994: 8). It is pertinent to ask whether such skewing is also a feature of overseas enrolment, but up-to-date statistics giving a gender breakdown have proved elusive. Substantial subject skewing has clearly existed in the past – in 1978–9 women comprised only 13 per cent of all overseas enrolments in technical subjects but were 52 per cent of such enrolments in the arts (Goldsmith and Shawcross 1985: 18). Interestingly, however, disaggregation by origin suggests that gender-stereotyping in subject choice was more endemic among students from the industrialised north than among students from the developing world, a larger proportion of the latter being enrolled for technical subjects (Goldsmith and Shawcross 1985: 21).

WELFARE ISSUES

Two factors combine to make the consideration of gender and welfare needs problematic. On the one hand, much that is known about the welfare of overseas students originates from samples with 70 per cent or more male respondents (Blaug and Woodhall 1981: 241; Hughes 1990: 44). Although this may have reflected the national proportion of male overseas students at the time of the surveys, there is also very limited disaggregation of the data by gender. On the other hand, overseas students are a highly diverse group, making it difficult to generalise about their welfare needs and the gender dimensions thereof. In much of this section, therefore, I seek only to raise issues which might be of relevance, and which those involved in the HE of overseas students might reflect on.

Obviously many of the welfare needs of overseas students identified in the literature apply to both men and women. Specialist advisory and support services, suitable accommodation secured in advance of arrival, and opportunities to build up social networks have an important part to play in the welfare of all overseas students, to which list might be added adequate childcare facilities for those students with children. However, gender divisions and gender norms serve to make the requirements of female students particularly distinct. The question of accommodation is a case in point.

The literature has paid much attention to the need to provide family accommodation for overseas students (Goldsmith and Shawcross 1985: 22; Kinnell 1990: 23; Lewins 1990: 92; Hughes 1990). In addition it is also important to offer single/unaccompanied overseas students the opportunity of same-sex accommodation, and the chance to select accommodation likely to be quiet and conducive to serious study. The accommodation provided for undergraduate home students, especially first-years away from home for the first time, will suit some overseas students but, in my experience, will be a very uncomfortable environment for others. This is particularly the case for women, since restrictions concerning contact with the opposite sex are generally applied more rigidly to women than to men (Hughes 1990: 37). The aim of the accommodation office should be to inform students in advance about their options and permit choice, rather than to prescribe or to make assumptions about accommodation needs in relation to gender.

On a related point, the typical social activities that a department lays on for students may be culturally unacceptable for some women (and men), because they involve mixed groups and are focused around alcohol. Since these may be the very environments in which many British students relax and friendships are formed (Goldsmith and Shawcross 1985: 25), overseas students can feel excluded and isolated. Moreover, 'if their cultural background inhibits them from seeking the comfort of light and warmth in public places such as pubs, bars, dances and parties, where other students can take refuge' (Goldsmith and Shawcross 1985: 25), women students will find it especially difficult to adjust to low-standard student accommodation.

The almost-global assumption that women take primary responsi-bility for housework and childcare has very important consequences for the welfare of women students from overseas, as it does for many women home students. Married male overseas students, particularly those coming from so far afield that they remain in the UK for the whole duration of their studies, are often accompanied by their wife, who takes responsibility for domestic work and childcare and leaves them free to concentrate on their studies. It has been much more difficult for women students to bring their husband to the UK (and less likely that he would take responsibility for cooking and cleaning even if they could do so). In the past, immigration law stipulated that a man from overseas who was in Britain to study had the right to bring his wife and any children under eighteen with him, but a woman did not, on the grounds that she was not the 'household head' (Goldsmith and Shawcross 1985: 6). This legislative inequality was amended in early 1995, such that women students may also be accompanied by their spouse as a dependant (UKCOSA 1995a: 11), although there are very stringent criteria.

Children raise particular dilemmas for women overseas students. Should finances permit, women may want to bring children with them for the duration of their studies. However, this imposes a double burden of work and responsibility, in the university and at home, to an extent that is not true for male students accompanied by children. Finding suitable accommodation for children and convenient and affordable childcare facilities, as well as coming to grips with local schools and the National Health Service, are all time-consuming activities that generally fall more to women than to men. Moreover, as a recent study of UK mature women students with children has shown, there is often an element of conflict and tension for women students with families as well as over-work, since the socially constructed value base of the two institutions, the home and the university, advocate women's whole-hearted involvement in one to the exclusion of the other (Edwards 1993: 13). While male involvement in the public sphere is typically considered an essential part of his contribution to the private sphere, 'women cannot meet public world obligations without being accused of neglecting their duties in the private domain' (Edwards 1993: 63). Precisely because of this, women also face difficulties if they are not accompanied by their children, their own sense of loss and worry being compounded by the censure they may face from others. As a result of these problems, and since the age of reproduction typically coincides with that for HE, many women face a dilemma: children or HE (Goldsmith and Shawcross 1985: 22). For those attempting to juggle both, it is important that academic staff remain sensitive to their multi-faceted lives, the practical and financial burden of childcare arrangements, and the problem of childcare in school holidays.

It should be clear from the above that meeting the welfare needs of overseas students involves an awareness of both gender and culture, and a sensitivity to the ways in which they interact. Those working in universities need to take responsibility for informing themselves about issues of cultural diversity, and, as a recent UKCOSA video, *Partners in Discovery*, stresses, 'to see the development of cultural sensitivity to be personally rewarding as well as professionally essential' (UKCOSA: 1995b). In so doing, an awareness should be fostered that Britain itself is a nation of diverse cultures, such that many overseas students share a common cultural heritage with British nationals from ethnic minorities.

It is also important to provide overseas students with guidelines on British culture and gender relations, whilst recognising that these are not homogeneous. Several researchers have highlighted the problem of a lack of respect for female authority on the part of male overseas students (Lewins 1990: 93; Hughes 1990: 78), but tend to portray this as some kind of endemic 'male chauvinism' rather than identifying a need for (re)education about gender. The British Council (1995) has begun to tackle such issues, in its guide for overseas students and visitors. A short section on sexual equality emphasises women's important role in the workforce in Britain, their freedom of movement in the public sphere, and their legal entitlement to be accorded equal respect and status with men (ibid.: 64). This might be extended to include definitions of sexual harassment, with individual universities providing details about their policies, and information about the norms of social and sexual relationships in Britain (for example, the general acceptability of interchange between the sexes, such that a proximity of relations cannot be interpreted as sexual interest). The intention should be to inform and to provoke thought and discussion rather than to dictate.

Meeting welfare needs involves responding to the issues that different groups of overseas students identify for themselves and to the complaints that they make about existing provision. Interestingly, there is some evidence that women are less likely to know how to complain and to effect complaints than men (Hughes 1990: 56). Welfare is also about supporting the efforts that overseas students make to improve their experiences of HE in Britain. Student societies based around nationality and/or religious belief are now common, particularly in larger institutions, and play a valuable role in making the university environment more hospitable. However, it is important to bear in mind that, as with any group, membership is not homogeneous and power will almost certainly be unevenly distributed. In this respect, any university funding must take account of who represents the group, their power base within the group and their agenda *vis-à-vis* other group members. Particular caution is necessary in respect of fundamentalist groups, no matter what religion they are connected to, since they may be characterised by an agenda to use religion as a basis to shore up the patriarchal family and extend social control over women (Cockburn 1995). In their rush to recognise cultural diversity, universities may be keen to fund such groups, and to be seen doing so, but to support them without considering the way in which they are stratified may, however unwittingly, contribute to women's inequality.

QUALITY TEACHING AND LEARNING

A concern with gender and overseas students is not simply a concern with the proportions of women and men who gain access to HE, important as that is, or their welfare, but must encompass the 'quality' of the teaching and learning environment they enter. Indeed, an obvious dimension of the 'quality' issue so preoccupying the university sector is the extent to which the diverse needs of students are met and opportunities to develop skills and enhance knowledge provided. In tackling these questions, and faced with the (by now familiar) absence of gender issues in the literature on the teaching and learning of overseas students, I shall extrapolate from the general literature on HE as well as that on primary and secondary education. I have also found it useful to situate the discussion in the context of the discourse of equal opportunities (EO), so often the practical and conceptual framework through which universities attend to issues of gender and diversity.

Commentators typically distinguish between liberal and radical interpretations of EO. The liberal model relies heavily on the concept of the 'level playing field' and concentrates on removing barriers to learning, such as the sex-stereotyped expectations of teachers and pupils, so that all can compete freely and fairly for reward (Coppock et al. 1995: 49; Taylor 1993). In contrast, the radical model of EO is concerned to transform the system of education, in recognition that the liberal language of merit and ability 'may just perpetuate the advantages of those who have historically had easiest access to academic study' (De Groot 1995: 2). Particular attention is paid to the way in which power is built and renewed within educational institutions (Taylor 1993), to the male monopolisation of knowledge and culture inherent in the curriculum and to the sexual politics of daily life (Coppock et al. 1995: 56). A radical version of EO is certainly not about equal treatment; indeed it is emphasised that equal treatment can result in inequality of outcome. This is because it cannot be assumed that all students start from the same point, that they all have the same goals, that they will all learn in the same way, or that they all have the same levels of confidence (Piper 1984: 17; Randall 1987: 162).

Aspects of both the liberal and radical agendas are relevant in considering how the university teaching environment might be sensitive to the gender dynamics of overseas student learning, as well as in setting agendas for much-needed research. For example, a liberal-inspired reflection by practitioners about the extent to which their treatment of and attitudes towards male and female students differs is to be encouraged (in a spirit of enlightenment rather than condemnation), and research into this issue is sorely needed. Certainly in schools it is clear that boys are treated as more significant, more likely to succeed, more worthy of attention than girls and, perhaps in consequence, their names are learnt more easily by the teacher (Randall 1987: 162; Stanworth 1987: 199–200; Spender 1984: 136). How this relates to academic performance at school has become a complex question, given the recent out-performance of girls by boys. At the university level, however, males have held on to their advantage, and a particularly uneven distribution of first-class degrees makes questions about teacher expectations and attitudes in respect of female students particularly pertinent (Sutherland 1995: 15). It is to be hoped that in the future academic performance will be disaggregated by area of domicile as well as gender, so that research can also explore the relative treatment of students on the basis of origin.

Drawing from the radical agenda, it is important to redress the lack of attention that is paid to the culture and content of the HE curriculum (Williams et al. 1989: 25). Once again, the HE education literature lags behind that on schools, where an early preoccupation with the class-based content of the curriculum shifted to include scrutiny of its gender content (Spender 1982; Weiner and Arnot 1987; Wolpe 1988) and more recently a concern with race/ethnicity has come to the fore (Mirza 1992). Where the content of an HE course 'reflects and reinforces patriarchal, middle-class and white norms and values' (Edwards 1993: 4) it is clearly neither value-free nor in the interests of overseas students, particularly women. Ideologies of masculine superiority and of white British superiority transmitted through the curriculum serve both to oppress students who do not fit these identities and to exclude them from definitions of and the production of knowledge (Acker 1984: 25). Instead, attention must be paid to ensuring that the curriculum is sensitive to broader structural relations of patriarchy, capitalism and neo-colonialism (Coppock et al. 1995: 67), and that it recognises and validates knowledge, culture and experience from beyond the mainstream (Williams et al. 1989: 25). Lewis and Habeshaw (1990) provide a very comprehensive checklist, give numerous examples of good practice in teaching and also cover issues of assessment. The particular experiences and knowledge of overseas students can be deployed as a teaching resource, although it is important to avoid what Blake (1995: 29) calls the 'black expert syndrome' – assuming that one individual can speak for a whole nation or culture, or indeed a sex.

Interest in the EO policies of universities is burgeoning, and two recent reviews of practice (Williams et al. 1989; CUCO 1994) illustrate how rapidly the field is growing. But it is important that policies become deeds as well as words, and that EO is integrated across the policy spectrum. Weiner (1993: 122) has called for the evaluation of teaching to include an assessment of its impact on under-represented groups, and it would certainly be useful to see the inclusiveness of the curriculum become an element in the auditing of HE teaching quality. Indeed, wider consideration of the extent to which different groups of students experience the university in different ways – as a reassuringly familiar place or a disconcertingly alien one – would greatly enhance our understanding of the learning process. While women postgraduate research students feel the lack of female colleagues (Taylorson 1984: 151), black women at any level may feel invisible given the dearth of black women colleagues (Blake 1995: 28), and Goldsmith and Shawcross recommend more active recruitment of black and overseas academic staff in Universities, to provide more diverse role models for students (Goldsmith and Shawcross 1985: 31).

It is also important to recognise that students all begin at different points, that the prior educational experiences of overseas students are cross-cut by gender and nationality, and that in consequence it is not adequate to treat all students in the same way or to make the same assumptions about them. For example, overseas students often show great deference to teachers (Kinnell 1990: 3), and it cannot be guaranteed that they will ask for help when needed, in spite of blanket invitations to do so (Channell 1990: 71), nor understand the European mode of taking responsibility for one's own learning. This is particularly the case for female students from cultures which lay great store by feminine deference, and expect women not to speak until spoken to and not to take the initiative. Moreover, the anxieties faced by all students in a new environment (Kinnell 1990: 20) may be especially acute for women, who tend to under-estimate their abilities (Piper 1984: 9; Stanworth 1987: 208) and may also have had little experience of independent living as a result of norms of paternalism. Thus while workshops on study skills may be an important provision for all overseas students, they may be particularly vital for some women students. It should go without saying, however, that in making these points I am relying on conjecture to an extent; research is urgently needed to document the learning experiences of overseas students, in all its diversity, just as it has been called for in relation to another minority group on the campus: mature women (Hayes and Flannery 1995).

Considering the teaching and learning needs of overseas students in the context of the radical approach to EO has the advantage of avoiding the tendency to conceive of overseas students as a problem group with 'special needs'. I would argue that, in fact, all students have special needs, although because the special needs of white, middle-class heterosexual males have been built into the development of HE institutions, such that they are automatically and seamlessly taken care of, they are much less visible. Meeting the needs of all students is, in part, about recognising who is already privileged. As one black British student expressed it, 'I came to realise that...university was a big game reserve with protected and unprotected species. I was not a protected species' (Blake 1995: 30). Thus advocating policies to better serve overseas students is not about preferential treatment or special pleading, but involves a reorientation of priorities and resources to help expand the protected status that men and whites have long enjoyed (Roberts 1984: 210).

CONCLUSION

One thing that all British universities have in common in the 1990s is the drive to recruit overseas students, as part of an ongoing effort to diversify income sources. In so doing, the HE sector has a responsibility to ensure that the needs of such students are met, and a small but growing literature, both official (CVCP/CDP 1992; Shawcross et al. 1987; Education Counselling Service/British Council, undated), and academic (Kinnell 1990; Hughes 1990) addresses this question. As I have shown in this chapter, however, this literature is typically gender-blind, and as such out of step with the educational literature in general. In reviewing the importance of gender in three distinct, but interrelated areas, access, welfare, and teaching and learning, it is to be hoped that I have stimulated reflections on current practices in HE and the ways they might be improved, as well as begun to map out an agenda for future research. Indeed, the process of gendering policies relating to overseas students needs to go hand-in-hand with research. It is research which will, for example, make funding bodies and admissions officers aware of the gender gaps in overseas student access, and inform their reflections as to how their own practices might facilitate women's participation in HE.

At the same time, I have tried to avoid over-generalising about the needs and experiences of overseas students, and to emphasise that I am providing a set of questions to be asked about existing practices and provision rather than a blanket set of policies to be implemented. As the literature on overseas students develops it would do well to build on Goldsmith and Shawcross' (1985) pioneering study but also to transcend it, with an emphasis on gender rather than women and on gender in conjunction with a range of other factors, such as class, race, ethnicity, age, sexuality, etc. This kind of integrated approach is beginning to emerge in the literature on schooling, with Mac an Ghaill (1994) exploring issues of gender and sexuality in secondary school, and Mirza (1992) examining the comprehensive school experiences of those who are young, female and black. Such multi-faceted approaches are sorely needed in the literatuure on overseas students, where issues of race, ethnicity, religious affiliation and nationality are particularly pertinent. The emerging literature on black access in the UK provides some useful pointers, notably Ayuru's (1995) examination of gender and the politics of black access to HE institutions, but is of course restricted to home students.

Above all I want to stress that taking gender into account in respect of overseas students means resisting any account of women's disadvantage which is premised on their inherent qualities *qua* women. Instead, it involves a sensitivity to the structural factors within the university system and within the wider society which may simultaneously constrain the capacity of overseas student women as a group and enhance those of overseas student men as a group. Bodies like the British Council and UKCOSA have begun to pay serious attention to this question. It is to be hoped that their efforts can be sustained, as well as reinforced from within the higher education sector itself by both academic research and new policy agendas.

My concern is to provide food for thought for those concerned with teaching overseas students and those concerned with their recruitment, in the hope of promoting more reflective and gender-aware practice. In so doing, I seek to resist a tendency noted in much of the existing literature on overseas students to perceive them as a problem-group, requiring extra resources to meet 'special' needs. I find such an approach unhelpful not because additional resources are not required and not because many overseas students do not face real difficulties, but because as a conceptual framework it makes the student the problem and HE institutions the solution. Experiences of racism, culture-shock, poverty, inappropriate provision, etc., have as much to do with British society as they do with individual overseas students. Indeed it is the interface between them that must be examined, and tendencies to construct the student as the problem need to be resisted. At the same time, improving the experiences of overseas students is not just about a new policy-and-resources initiative imposed from the top, but requires real and sustained dialogue between all groups in the HE sector, as well as a recognition of the active steps overseas students have always taken to help themselves.

Chapter 7

The purpose of study, attitudes to study and staff–student relationships

John Barker

The aim of this chapter is to draw upon available empirical evidence in order to examine three issues which are central to the learning experience of overseas students. In the first place, why are they studying? Is there any degree of commonality in the objectives they are aiming to achieve through studying? If there is, this may have implications for higher education institutions in terms of the subjects and courses offered. Second, are there any significant features of the attitudes, values and motivation which overseas students bring to the lecture or tutorial room, an awareness of which might cause academic staff to modify their approach? Finally, in terms of relationships, what do they expect of their lecturers and tutors and what do we expect of them? How far apart are these expectations and what can we do about this?

THE PURPOSE OF STUDY

Is there any evidence which might indicate whether overseas students have any common purposes in studying? There does not seem to be a great deal but what there is tends in a broad but particular direction. Lewis (1984), in his study of overseas students at York University, differentiates between undergraduate and postgraduate students in this respect. Undergraduates tended to 'see entry to university as part of a natural progression of education' (Lewis 1984: 95). Postgraduates, on the other hand, tended to be 'more functionally concerned with future job implications of their studies' (ibid.: 96); they usually came for specialist knowledge and the prestige of a British qualification would probably lead to enhanced job prospects. Furnham and Bochner (1986), while admittedly asking a different question, 'Why do students go abroad to study?' conclude that

> there is no doubt that the overwhelming majority of foreign students are primarily interested in getting a degree and/or professional training rather than learning a second culture or achieving personal

growth. Uppermost in their minds are concerns about the tangible pay-offs a sojourn might provide in the shape of career advancement, prestige and upward mobility.

(Furnham and Bochner 1986: 38)

These findings are supported by Allen and Higgins (1994), who asked the question 'Why study in the UK?' The reason most frequently given (67 per cent of respondents) was because the English language was spoken. Allen and Higgins did not investigate why English was important to the respondents but it is surely significant that, in their survey of subjects being studied, only 1.8 per cent were studying languages *per se*. The next reason most frequently given was that UK qualifications were recognised by their home governments or by companies in their home countries. Worth noting from their survey, particularly in the context of this book, is that the standard and quality of education in the UK and the good international reputation of UK education were the next reasons in order of frequency, views which were also identified by Lewis when students were asked about their expectations of their courses. It is also worth noting that when students were asked why they would definitely recommend the particular institution they were attending, Allen and Higgins found that 'the perceived standing of the institution in terms of its reputation and the quality of the education provided were the most frequently mentioned reasons' (Allen and Higgins 1994: 90). Elsey (1990) reaches similar conclusions. The acquisition of knowledge and academic achievement were seen as a means to an end, that is updating a speciality, improving professional performance or enhancing career prospects. The students' expectations were 'firmly fastened to the vocational relevance of their studies for work roles back in their own country' (Elsey 1990: 52). The development of English language skills was also high on the list. A different perspective is provided by Hofstede (1994). His study reinforces the conclusions reached by the previously quoted sources yet at the same time raises serious doubts about their usefulness as they stand. The conclusions from his researches, quoted here and elsewhere in this chapter, are highly relevant both to a consideration of the content and teaching methods of courses and for an understanding of the cultural differences present in staff–student relationships as observed by many researchers. In examining the differences between *individualist* and *collectivist* societies, Hofstede has the following to say concerning the purpose of education. The *individualist* society 'aims at preparing the individual for a place in a society of other individuals. This means learning to cope with new, unknown, unforeseen situations.... The purpose of learning is less to know how to do, as to know how to learn. The assumption is that learning in life never ends' (Hofstede 1994: 63). In the *collectivist* society there is a stress on adaptation to the skills and virtues necessary to be an acceptable group member. This leads to a premium on the products of tradition. Learning is more often seen as a one-time process, reserved for the young only, who have to learn how to do things in order to participate in society.

(Hofstede 1994: 63)

The difference extends to the role of academic qualifications:

In the individualist society the diploma not only improves the holder's economic worth but also his or her self-respect: it provides a sense of achievement. In the collectivist society a diploma is an honor to the holder and his or her ingroup which entitles the holder to associate with members of higher-status groups.... The social acceptance that comes with the diploma is more important than the individual self-respect that comes with mastering a subject.

(Hofstede 1994: 63)

Hofstede identifies Great Britain as a highly individualist society. Our concept of lifelong learning is therefore not surprising. Other individualist countries include the USA, Australia, New Zealand and Denmark. Indonesia, South Korea, Singapore and Hong Kong, for example, are identified as collectivist societies. For them, education tends to be about learning how to do. Given the potential for conflict on this one issue, the purpose of education, we should be very cautious in making recommendations about 'overseas' students. Hence the serious doubts mentioned earlier about the usefulness, as they stand, of many of the conclusions reached about them.

For those, however, for whom the purpose of study is 'learning how to do', i.e. many of the students referred to in the above and other sources, the content of their course is of the greatest importance. Here we run into a problem identified by a number of researchers, ethnocentrism – in thought processes, approach to the subject and the material itself.

Bligh et al. (1981), in discussing western courses when transplanted to developing countries, point out that 'what is learned will vary according to language and culture. Consequently... they are not only often inappropriate, but are perceived quite differently by both teachers and students from those in its country of origin' (ibid. 1981: 95–6). They go on to say that

there is a strong danger that a course which is based upon content and standards drawn from another culture with vastly different needs and priorities, will only serve to divorce the thinking of the educated élite from the rest of the country's inhabitants.

(Bligh et al. 1981: 96)

There is no reason to suppose that the potential results should be any different when the students are transplanted to the courses.

Lewis identifies the same problem and gives examples from education and economics. It is worth quoting one of these in full as it defines the problem clearly.

> Similarly, the study of the economics of developed, industrialised countries with a substantial and strong monetary system carries with it, in such countries, many assumptions with which it is taken for granted that many readers of the relevant texts will be familiar. Such assumptions will cover vocabulary, as well as the parameters and concepts through which the analysis is developed. These may not have much concrete meaning to a student from a third world country where different assumptions operate.
>
> (Lewis 1984: 103–4)

Lewis goes on to state that the situation was not so marked for science students, since 'There is a universality to the content and concepts of science' (Lewis 1984: 104), or for postgraduate research students who could be expected to have mastered the principles of their chosen subject and were now specialising. The most disturbing conclusion emerging from this part of Lewis' research is that the academic staff interviewed seemed wholly unaware of any ethnocentrism in their teaching. They considered students' problems to be at the surface level of the language, 'concerned with vocabulary, spelling, grammar and syntax. There was no mention of the cultural assumptions built into the structure of knowledge put over in their courses' (ibid.: 105).

Lewis' findings are supported by Elsey who reports that overseas students on taught courses acutely felt 'the almost complete absence of anything other than an ethnocentric British view in some areas of study' (Elsey 1990: 51). He found a similar situation with research students, who were caused problems by their supervisors' tendencies to view their work from a British perspective only.

Hofstede, in his discussion of intercultural encounters in schools, provides further support, particularly of Lewis' theme of 'the "hidden curriculum" of the language of discourse' (Hofstede 1994: 104), when he comments 'Information is more than words: it is words which fit into a cultural framework' (ibid.: 217). He goes on to conclude that 'Much of what students from poor countries learn at universities in rich countries is hardly relevant in their home country situation. What is the interest for a future manager in an Indian company of mathematical modelling of the US stock market?' (ibid.: 217). Hofstede's argument applies to the appropriateness not only of the technology we teach but also of the organisational systems which control that technology. He poses the question 'To what extent do theories developed in one country and reflecting the cultural boundaries of that country apply to other countries? Do American management theories apply in Japan? In India?' (Hofstede 1980: 50). These questions reinforce the uneasiness which many teachers of management have long felt at the unthinking application of American management theories in British companies and schools of management. If the still largely American-sourced theories on such issues as motivation, reward systems, leadership and delegation do not successfully transfer wholesale to British culture, what is the tutor doing if he or she teaches them as 'facts' to students and managers from France and Germany, to say nothing of Bangladesh, Sri Lanka or Nigeria?

The important point to emerge from the evidence is that we should be very careful about thinking in terms of 'overseas' students. They come from such a variety of cultural backgrounds that there may be circumstances where they have not much more in common than that they are students and literally come from overseas. Accepting this caveat, it does appear that for many of them the purpose of study is 'advancement', whether this is economic or social, through acquiring specialist knowledge and skills, including language and gaining qualifications which are valued by employers. There tends to be a practical purpose for studying. In this case, the matter of ethnocentrism is a critical one. I agree with Lewis that here we encounter 'the pervasiveness of background experience and its influence on attitudes and expectations' (Lewis 1984: 104) and that what he describes as 'the "hidden curriculum" of the language of discourse' can cause major problems for students. I part company from him, however, where he defines this factor as 'the shades of meaning which are taken for granted by native speakers, and which are part of the social experience of growing up and learning the language and the embedded concepts it represents' (ibid.: 104). The issue of ethnocentrism is still tied to language instead of to the fundamental levels of values and beliefs, which may, for instance, be revealed even in the use of the term 'overseas students'. I cannot, therefore, agree with Lewis' final conclusion that 'Only practice, through extensive contact with indigenous speakers can ameliorate this problem' (ibid.: 104). Taken at the level of language, the process of attempting to clarify cultural differences solely through such contact and practice is too time-consuming. Many of our overseas students are here for one year only. Moreover, there is no guarantee that the underlying issues will be either identified or addressed; cultural differences may actually be reinforced, leaving the participants, in the words of Carl Rogers, 'missing each other in psychological space'.

ATTITUDES TOWARD STUDY

What does the evidence tell us about the attitudes of overseas students towards study, their motivation and the pressures they face?

Elsey claims that 'Overseas students have a pressing need, perhaps above all else, to return home with the inner satisfaction and the outward measure of successful academic achievement' (Elsey 1990: 46). 'It was clear that overseas students were very motivated to succeed and make the most of their opportunities' (ibid.: 52), including the acquisition of English language skills. When overseas students were asked about their academic concerns, the fear of failure loomed largest. As he points out 'many overseas students have placed themselves in a high-risk position, with the fear of failure looming large in most minds' (ibid.: 47). This fear is compounded by the often high cost of their course. As Elsey succinctly expresses it, 'a great deal of money has changed hands' (ibid.: 47). This money (from my own experience) has often been provided by parents or by the extended family in the home country. No wonder failure 'looms large'. We need to be cautious, however, about assuming fear of failure as a universal motivator. Elsey was referring to a survey of academic hopes and fears among newly arrived overseas students at Loughborough and Nottingham universities. He does not give a breakdown of the countries from which they came. Hofstede points out that failing in school can be a disaster in a 'masculine' culture such as Germany or Japan. In a 'feminine' culture, such as the Netherlands or Denmark, however, failure in school is a relatively minor matter.

Coupled with fear of failure, Elsey uses the phrase 'losing face' as being of great concern to newly arrived overseas students. This phrase is frequently used in connection with overseas students, usually from Asiatic countries, with a general assumption that we all know what it means. It is useful to examine its meaning because of its implications.

David Yau-fai Ho (1976), a Hong Kong social scientist, describes it thus:

> Face is the respectability and/or deference which a person can claim for himself from others, by virtue of the relative position he occupies in his social network and the degree to which he is judged to have functioned adequately in that position as well as acceptably in his general conduct; the face extended to a person by others is a function of the degree of congruence between judgements of his total condition in life, including his actions as well as those of people closely associated with him, and the social expectations that others have placed upon him.
>
> (Ho 1976: 883)

Ho emphasises the power of 'face' as a motivator. 'The desire to gain face, to avoid losing face, and to save face when it is threatened is a powerful social motive' (Ho 1976: 883); seeming, however, to modify this somewhat when he says 'Whether face is gained or not does not in itself bring into question one's social aptitude, decency, or adequacy, but whether face is lost or not does' (ibid.: 872).

Those who work with overseas students also need to bear in mind his observation that

> The distinction which I have made between face on the one hand and personality and personal prestige on the other is a basic one with great theoretical import. It reflects two fundamentally different orientations in viewing human behaviour: the Western orientation, with its preoccupation with the individual, and the Chinese orientation, which places the accent on the reciprocity of obligations, dependence, and esteem protection.
>
> (Ho 1976: 883)

Hofstede, who also identifies 'face' as a characteristic of collectivist cultures, explores the implications for the classroom:

> In the collectivist classroom the virtues of harmony and the maintenance of 'face' reign supreme. Confrontations and conflicts should be avoided, or at least formulated so as not to hurt anyone; even students should not lose face if this can be avoided.... At all times the teacher is dealing with the student as part of an ingroup, never as an isolated individual.
>
> (Hofstede 1980: 62)

In the individualist classroom, 'confrontations and open discussion of conflicts is often considered salutary, and face-consciousness is weak or non-existent' (ibid.: 63).

What can we make of this evidence? Are there any significant attitudes and motivators which overseas students share? There seems to be sufficient evidence to suggest that, when they arrive in the UK, overseas students bring with them particularly positive attitudes to study, perhaps because so many of them are taking specialist or vocationally oriented courses, perhaps also because many of them, being postgraduates, are therefore somewhat older and more sure about what they want to do. It is reasonable to say that, in general, they have a clear purpose for studying, their approach is focused and they know how they are going to use their academic experience subsequently. There also seems to be sufficient evidence to conclude that they are usually highly motivated to make the most of their course of study, thereby succeeding in gaining the qualifications which lead to 'advancement', in whatever form they seek it. There is a general willingness to put in long hours of study. On the negative side, it is evident that a number of students are driven at least partially by fear of failure and losing face and by family, social and financial pressures and obligations. Beyond this the evidence has no clear implications because it is impossible to think in generic terms of 'overseas students'. Motivation encompasses a complex set of individual human behaviours, even when working within a single culture. Culturally related theories of motivation cannot be regarded as anything more than generalisations, certainly not as offering specific directives in an individual case. How many different nationalities and cultures are represented in individual classrooms? Consider also that the theories of motivation which we commonly draw upon are western, Anglo-Saxon, largely American and even middle-class American in their cultural roots. They are based on the attitudes, values, beliefs and assumptions of that culture. The further away from middle-class America we go, the less relevant they become.

A useful way forward, I suggest, is based upon the information found in any good management textbook, in the section 'Motivating Your Staff'. The advice is to get to know your staff individually, find out what motivates them and then act appropriately whenever possible. For 'staff' substitute 'overseas students'.

Another issue can appropriately be considered under the heading of 'Attitudes' and might serve as an illustration of the complexity of cultural issues – collusion between students on assignments, or more simply, copying. In our individualist, British culture, copying is an offence and dealt with as such, through the loss of marks for that piece of work or even disqualification. We intend that the individual should feel guilt at infringing the rules. To a student from a collectivist culture, however, there is nothing morally wrong with collusion. It does not contravene the moral code; indeed it may be construed as cooperation. In such a culture resources, including intellectual ones, are to be shared; opinions expressed are those of the group, not the individual.

Some years ago, as a visiting lecturer, I was teaching the principles of management to a group composed entirely of mature, overseas students taking a diploma course in management at a British college. When the coursework was handed in for assessment, I became virtually certain that collusion had taken place. Several pieces of coursework were almost identical, even down to the illustrations and actual words used. The students involved were all from the same, Asian, country. I reported the matter to the course director, who, as it happened was from another, Asian, country. He investigated further and established that collusion had indeed taken place. The assignment had been first written by the most senior manager in the group, to whom the others reported in the department back in their home country. The assignment was then circulated among the other managers as a model answer. I was outraged; this was cheating. My instinctive reaction was to punish the students involved by awarding no marks to them for the assignment. The course director advised instead an explanation to the students of our norms of behaviour in this matter, followed by a request to conform to them in the future but no further action in this instance. I eventually agreed on the basis that our rules might not have been clearly spelled out to the students in the first place. Was I 'right' to do this?

STAFF–STUDENT RELATIONSHIPS

There has been considerable investigation into the relationships between staff and overseas students. This survey of the available information is representative, not comprehensive. Singh (1963, quoted in Furnham and Bochner 1963: 120), identifies teacher–student relationships as a source of difficulties, particularly regarding status. Currie and Leggatt (1965: 142–3), in a study of approximately 4,000 East African students studying in the UK, found that 22 per cent felt that the advice available to them on personal matters was inadequate, 25 per cent of the students said that they had never had a conversation with a member of staff outside teaching periods and 17 per cent found members of the academic staff either too aloof or too busy to be easily approachable.

Lewis makes some very useful points when discussing the approachability of staff and gives two delightfully contrasting viewpoints of the same situation. It is worth quoting these in full as they illustrate the influence of different cultural backgrounds on students' expectations and highlight the dangers of regarding 'overseas students' as a coherent group.

> For example, a Greek and an American student, at the same stage of reading for the same degree in the same department commented, respectively: 'I found the staff very helpful and not like the "baronial" professors at home who are very high and don't talk to students' (G); and 'I was most disappointed with the lack of concern for students shown by the faculty. I was almost being begged to learn when I was in the States' (A).
>
> (Lewis 1984: 98)

Lewis speaks of the problems which overseas students faced in adjusting to a different type of student–lecturer relationship than was expected or had previously been experienced and stresses the effect which previous educational experiences had on perceptions. 'Where students had experienced learning in contexts which were very one-sided, and where they were not accustomed to being treated in sociable terms by faculty staff, it is not surprising that their settling in periods were rather difficult' (Lewis 1984: 103).

Lewis makes the important point that language difficulties can be seen wrongly as the cause of problems in relationships, the real cause lying in the expectations produced by previous experiences – that is, cultural differences. A quotation from an Italian postgraduate is illuminating: 'We used language as an alibi. There were other difficulties of communication, but we blamed language' (Lewis 1984: 100). Lewis also found that academic staff could differ substantially in their interpretation of common experiences. Staff were, for instance, concerned that 'overseas students seemed rather withdrawn in the relatively informal settings of seminars and tutorials' (ibid.: 105) and any sign of non-participation in group learning situations was also 'taken as an indicator of linguistic difficulty' (ibid.: 106). Lewis reasonably interprets this as, at worst, staff insensitivity, entailing 'the misinterpretation of withdrawal as indicating linguistic incompetence rather than social insecurity' (ibid.: 106) and, at best, as indicating 'some lack of concern with the social dimensions of the student experience' (ibid.: 106).

In his examination of the student perspective, Elsey reports that 'the nature of the relationship between academic tutor and student was clearly seen as of pivotal importance' (Elsey 1990: 50). There was a 'recurring theme of regarding the tutor as "guide, philosopher and friend" ' (ibid.: 50). The expectation of students was that 'the individual tutorial would somehow meet needs and would be echoed by a sensitive and caring tutor' (ibid.: 50) . Their principal needs were for 'good quality rapport with their academic tutors, especially for a sympathetic listening ear and personal support' (ibid.: 51). Elsey found the same expectations and needs to an even greater degree among research students, who had in their minds a picture of the ideal supervisor providing, 'considerable structured guidance, especially at the early stages of a research project, complete with comprehensive feedback through regular tutorial discussions' (ibid.: 55). The reality was sometimes different. Criticism was made of the lack of or limited personal attention and guidance given by some academic staff. This view was echoed by some research students, who felt that their supervisors did not try to see situations from the students' point of view. A common problem was actually getting to see their supervisors regularly.

Channell (1990) examines the issues in considerable detail. Her conclusions are essentially the same as Elsey's. Most students saw the student–tutor relationship as a key one and both needed and desired a higher level of tutor contact than they got. In this matter students tended to see the onus of initiating contact to be with the tutor, on the first and subsequent occasions. 'It was pointed out that due to their former mode of education in a hierarchical structure, many overseas students would find it very difficult to approach a tutor despite blanket invitations to do so at the beginning of the course' (Channell 1990: 71). In this context, Channell also points out that 'many overseas students felt inhibitions which prevented them from seeing a tutor for fear of losing face' (ibid.:

72), a fear which is echoed by a student quoted in Allen and Higgins' survey: 'It is hard, if I complain he will think I am no good' (Allen and Higgins 1994: 70). Her second conclusion is that students often found the system of learning in British higher education much less structured than they would have liked. Many students said that they were often left uncertain in the first place about what they were expected to do and that subsequently there was not enough contact with academic staff or sufficient direction and guidance from them. Channell finally concludes that overseas students generally felt misunderstood by tutors. She does not, however, indicate why she reaches this view. I suggest that their feelings of being misunderstood were largely caused by an inability or unwillingness on the part of staff to see a situation from the overseas student's point of view, coupled with other factors such as cultural stereotyping and difficulties with the use of names. Channell also describes the students' view of the ideal research supervisor as one who is 'both a counsellor and a teacher' (Channell 1990: 74) and makes the additional observation that 'it seemed that some research students were less concerned about the amount of time supervisors gave them than about the quality of help when they did get supervision' (ibid.: 77).

Turning to the views of university academic staff, Elsey makes some telling points. First, students' expectations for high quality interpersonal relationships conflicted with 'the real-world concerns of academics' (Elsey 1990: 57), specifically the 'research and publications track-record, which lies at the heart of career promotion and status' (ibid.: 57). Second, some staff felt pressurised by overseas students' needs for time and attention. A common view of overseas students was that they were 'a burden in the teaching and learning domain' (ibid.: 58). He comes to the depressing conclusion that

> Basically the hard truth is that there seems to be little bonus in teaching overseas students or taking a real interest in their personal lives. Certainly there was no career advantage in being an effective teacher or supervisor of those whose needs were greatest.
>
> (Elsey 1990: 60)

This is hardly the best attitude of mind upon which to build effective staff–student relationships.

In looking at the relationships from a person-to-person angle, Channell concludes that tutors generally 'see overseas students as voraciously demanding of their time' (Channell 1990: 79), even when given willingly. One of the many quotations illustrates the point admirably: 'Set boundaries on what you can and will do for them. Demands and expectations otherwise become limitless' (ibid.: 73). Overseas students were also seen as over-dependent. A comment from an engineering admissions tutor epitomises this view: 'they have a "you tell me what you want and I'll do it" approach' (ibid.: 66). Associated with this is the tendency of overseas students, as perceived by tutors, to put staff on a pedestal, a feeling which is expressed in a variety of forms throughout Channell's investigation. This links directly with her conclusion, that tutors 'are aware that their role is to encourage independence but don't always know how to do it, that is, by giving the right kind of feedback' (ibid.: 79). Perhaps she is a little generous to staff in reaching this conclusion. A study of her evidence and in particular the comments of staff and students suggests that some staff either do not have the inclination or believe they do not have the time to establish personal relationships and then provide the guidance and feedback which are necessary to bring about independence.

In Channell's view, feedback is clearly a key element in a successful student–tutor relationship and it is worth exploring here in some detail. The researchers were interested in the quantity, type and perceived usefulness of academic feedback. As in other areas of this investigation they obtained a mixed response; many students were satisfied on all counts with the feedback they received but many were not. Constructive feedback on work standards was considered essential, in order that students could judge how they were progressing and identify areas on which to concentrate. However, 'Several mentioned the depression they had suffered when work was returned with neither comments, suggestions, nor invitations to discuss it' (Channell 1990: 77) and 'Several students commented in interviews that difficulties they had experienced with academic work were not picked up quickly enough or at all' (ibid.: 77). Students expected staff to be interested in their work and to criticise it, with suggestions for improvement and for further study. The impression, which many of them had, was that staff did not take their work seriously and did not value it. Students felt they were expected to complete work as hurdles to be jumped and to get on with the next assignment.

What then can be made of the evidence? Channell gives a clear summary of the starting point:

> It became clear when we compared our student and our tutor data that the two groups bring to the relationship two very different sets of expectations of each other. These expectations, on either side, are conditioned by the previous cultural experience of the two groups. Hence we were able to identify mismatches in expectation, leading to misinterpretation of the other's behaviour, as a cause of difficulty in the student–tutor relationship.
>
> (Channell 1990: 63)

The basis of the mismatch is, as Elsey and Channell both point out, to do with on the one hand, British higher education's emphasis on self-reliance and self-directed study, with minimal control by staff, as exemplified in the phrase 'reading for a degree' and on the other hand, the needs and expectations of many overseas students for substantial teaching and tutorial support. The mismatch then continues from different understandings of the purposes of university education, to the roles of lecturers and tutors and to the responsibilities of the students themselves. It is compounded by the ever-worsening staff–student ratio, the reward system for staff in higher education and, potentially, by any over-enthusiastic selling of British higher education abroad and inadequate orientation and preparation of overseas students for study in Britain.

The situation is, however, more complex than tutors and students having different expectations, in that the central issue is the consequence of cultural differences at both the institutional and the interpersonal level. Hofstede, for example, throws light upon the issue in a number of ways. In examining the consequences of attitudes towards 'Power Distance' in society, he comments regarding education:

> In the large power distance situation the parent–child inequality is perpetuated by a teacher–student inequality which caters to the need for dependence well established in the student's mind. Teachers are treated with respect. . . . The educational process is teacher-centred: teachers outline the intellectual paths to be followed. In the classroom there is supposed to be a strict order with the teacher initiating all communication. Students in class speak up only when invited to; teachers are never publicly contradicted or criticised. . . . The educational process is highly personalized: especially in more advanced subjects at universities what is transferred is not seen as an impersonal 'truth' but as the personal wisdom of the teacher. The teacher is a 'guru'.
> (Hofstede 1994: 34)

Thus we can see the cultural origins of so many of the attitudes revealed by Channell and her co-researchers and begin to realise how deeply embedded these must be by the age of eighteen or more. In contrast

> in the small power distance situation teachers are supposed to treat the students as basic equals and expected to be treated as equals by the students. . . . The educational process is student-centred, with a premium on student initiative: students are expected to find their own intellectual paths. Students make uninvited interventions in class, they are supposed to ask questions when they do not understand something. They argue with teachers, express disagreement and criticisms in front of the teachers. . . . The educational process is rather impersonal; what is transferred comprises 'truth' or 'facts' which exist

independently of this particular teacher. Effective learning in such a system depends very much on whether the supposed two-way communication between students and teacher is, indeed, established. The entire system is based on the students' well-developed need for independence.

(Hofstede 1994: 34)

In the Power Distance Index Great Britain ranks 42nd equal out of 53 countries and regions in its willingness to accept unequal power distribution. It is therefore not surprising to find in a relatively low power-distance society such as Great Britain the characteristics of higher education as described by Elsey and Channell. Moreover, since these characteristics are a manifestation in one aspect of society of the fundamental values and beliefs which underpin the society as a whole, the immense difficulty in changing them must be appreciated.

The theme may be taken further by examining the behavioural consequences of attitudes towards 'uncertainty avoidance' in society. Hofstede makes the following points concerning education: 'Students from strong uncertainty avoidance countries expect their teachers to be the experts who have all the answers. Teachers who use cryptic academic language are respected. . . . Students in these countries will not, as a rule, confess to intellectual disagreement with their teachers' (Hofstede 1994: 119–20). 'Students [are] comfortable in structured learning situations and concerned with the right answers' (ibid.: 125). Contrast that with 'Students from weak uncertainty-avoidance countries accept a teacher who says "I don't know". Their respect goes to teachers who use plain language. . . . Intellectual disagreement in academic matters in these cultures can be seen as a stimulating exercise' (ibid.: 120). 'Students [are] comfortable with open-ended learning situations and concerned with good discussions' (ibid.: 125).

Hofstede illustrates this difference in practice when he describes the difficulties he faced in choosing how much structure to build into his teaching on an international teachers (of management) programme.

Most Germans, for example, favour structured learning situations with precise objectives, detailed assignments, and strict timetables. They like situations in which there is one correct answer which they can find. They expect to be rewarded for accuracy. Their preferences are typical for strong uncertainty-avoidance countries. Most British participants on the other hand despise too much structure. They like open-ended learning situations with vague objectives, broad assignments, and no timetables at all. The suggestion that there could be only one correct answer is taboo with them. They expect to be rewarded for originality. Their reactions are typical for countries with weak uncertainty avoidance.

(Hofstede 1994: 119)

In the Uncertainty Avoidance Index, Germany ranked 29th out of 53 in its aversion to uncertain or unknown situations and Great Britain 47th equal. In comparison, France was ranked 10th equal and Singapore the least averse to uncertainty. Herein lies an example of the danger and, to a degree, pointlessness of considering 'overseas students' as a group and making recommendations on that basis. Elsey, for example, holds up the practices of university adult education tutors as a model of effective teaching and learning, since they encourage adult learners to take responsibility for their learning, while the teacher's role becomes that of a facilitator. Here, 'Emphasis is placed on experiential learning', since this 'comes closer to natural processes of learning and is made real by encouraging the practices of group discussion, active and critical questioning, negotiated and contract-based, self-directed learning' (Elsey 1990: 48). This statement represents the beliefs and values of a member of a low power-distance and low uncertainty-avoidance society, namely Great Britain, and is broadly appropriate in that society. But to then argue that such practices are also the best ones to use in the teaching of 'overseas students' in general is to ignore the great diversity of the cultures from which they come and the matter of the appropriateness of the method for the learner.

A note of warning should be sounded. Hofstede states that he is not comparing individuals but what he calls 'central tendencies' (Hofstede 1994: 253) in the evidence from each country in his survey. He points out that there were very few individual respondents' answers which exactly matched the mean score and he warns against making assumptions about individuals on the basis of central tendencies in the data for their countries. As he says, 'If we want to find out about Mr Suzuki and Ms Smith we had better make our judgement after meeting and getting to know them' (ibid.: 253). What the central tendencies are useful for is describing the social systems from which the individual students come and which shape, to a greater or lesser degree, their expectations of others. Taken on this basis, Hofstede's work illustrates vividly the complex diversity of cultural influences and individual expectations which we commit ourselves to satisfying when we admit 'overseas' students to our institutions.

CONCLUDING COMMENTS

Such is the diversity of overseas students' cultural backgrounds that it is probably idealistic to propose that we all learn more about each other's cultures. Moreover, it is unreasonable to expect either academic staff or students to change significantly the attitudes and values with which they have grown up. In this connection, the overseas-student–university relationship needs to be put into a proper perspective. It is not purely a 'customer–supplier' relationship. It is true that the university takes money in return for the provision of services and therefore has a responsibility for the quantity and quality of those services. On the other hand, students have to meet certain academic standards in order to gain access to the services and ultimately acquire the qualification which may be regarded as the 'end product'. The relationship is one of mutual responsibility.

An overwhelming impression one gains from reading the empirical sources is of a gulf; it does not arise from institutional policy or personal malice but from lack of awareness that there are alternative ways of looking at things. There is a need for all concerned to make some move towards accepting that there are other cultures and values than their own and to understand the implications for the processes of teaching and learning. In this way it may be possible to resolve some of the methodological and pedagogical issues which have practical implications for the provision of quality teaching and learning.

To be realistic, in view of the pressures on time and the complexity of the cultural issues, creating awareness is probably as far as we can reasonably aim to go. How might we achieve it? Certainly it has to be built into the formal structure of student teaching and staff development; otherwise it runs the risk of not being taken seriously. It should be at the core of any student orientation programme. It could be built into study skills and departmental induction programmes. It should included in induction programmes for probationary academic staff. My own experiences have been very positive. In running a study skills programme for overseas students taking an MSc course in construction, we begin with an examination of what culture is and how it influences teaching and learning in British universities. This gives the students an opportunity to modify their expectations and also provides them with a cognitive framework for the skills sessions which follow. Similarly, when teaching a management of human resources module to students from several EC countries attending an MSc course in European construction engineering, we begin with an examination of 'culture'. This serves to provide a frame of reference in which to study the theory and practice of management and also to explore reactions towards the methods of teaching, learning and assessment which we will be using in the module. In both instances I use Hofstede's work as the basis. The students find the work illuminating and immediately relevant to their needs.

Part II

Practice: supporting learning

Chapter 8

The induction of international students to academic life in the United Kingdom

Murray Macrae

PREVIEW

This chapter discusses the induction of international students to university education in the UK. Its emphasis is upon preparation for academic life.

In response to the activities and advice of the United Kingdom Council for Overseas Student Affairs (UKCOSA 1987, 1989, 1992), most UK universities aim to ensure the physical welfare of new student arrivals in Britain. However, it is equally important that they also provide an orientation to academia. There are some initial actions that international students and their tutors might consider in order to improve the process of becoming acculturated to academic life prior to and soon after arrival in the UK. In particular there is much more that universities could do to assist international students with language orientation, obtaining maximum benefit from university study facilities and learning the process of studentship so that they might more quickly take advantage from their courses and research opportunities.

INTRODUCTION

International students are taken to be undergraduates or postgraduates who normally reside outside the UK but who undertake tertiary level education there. Home students are those who have been normally resident within the UK before going to university.

For home students, the period of induction normally covers the first few weeks following their entry to university. The induction of international students, however, may commence up to a year before they begin their course and is likely to extend well beyond the traditional freshers' week. For undergraduate international students the settling-in period may last for the first semester or longer; postgraduates may require at least the first term.

During induction, international students are obliged to accommodate a much greater number of changes than home students. There are many specific welfare factors which have to be dealt with before serious studies can begin. Typically they will include:

- satisfying immigration and visa requirements;
- managing changes in diet and accommodation;
- understanding and arranging care under the National Health Service;
- adjusting to a new environment which includes not only a campus, a city and a new country but also a fairly demanding climate;
- overcoming homesickness and loneliness;
- settling into a new community, many members of whom will appear unapproachable and some of whom may be racist.

All of the above will interfere with the learning process to varying extents and at various times and they have to be catered for. However, thanks to the activities and advice of UKCOSA (see for example UKCOSA 1987, 1989, 1992; Shotnes 1985), it is now generally the case that British institutions of higher learning have developed fairly effective orientation programmes which provide personal advice, guidance and help to international students when they first arrive. Therefore, although the effect upon learning of factors of the kind listed above will always be a serious consideration, the personal welfare of international students is not the primary concern of this chapter.

It is assumed that international students primarily travel to Britain in order to benefit from courses and study opportunities which are not available in their own countries. In addition, as Makepeace (1989) suggests, there may also be a desire to obtain internationally recognised qualifications in order to enhance future personal prospects. Whatever the case, university departments which accept international students do so on the understanding that what they provide can be assimilated by the students in such a way that they will benefit from the teaching, tuition and research opportunities which are available. If universities are to be effective then the academic welfare of international students must be as much to the fore as their personal welfare. Indeed, as Fenwick and Moss (1985) stress, student welfare must embrace support for the learning process as well as assisting with hygiene factors such as those listed above.

It is therefore necessary to consider ways in which the academic welfare of international students can be improved during the period of induction. The meaning, significance and value of pre-course assessments of English language ability are first discussed. Ways in which international students should be introduced to the use of university learning resources (laboratories, libraries, computers) are then considered. The chapter concludes with some discussion on the academic support that universities, tutors and supervisors can offer during the important initial phase of student life in the UK.

IDENTIFYING THE LANGUAGE NEEDS OF INTERNATIONAL STUDENTS

Virtually all teaching and research in higher education in Britain is conducted in the medium of English. This is likely to be a matter of some concern for the majority (about 88 per cent) of international students, for whom English is at best their second language. Ideally, to maximise the benefits of studying in Britain, international students should ensure that they are competent in English before they embark on their courses.

In order to raise their language competence, students who plan to study in Britain often invest in pre-sessional English courses. Many do so, at considerable personal cost, on their own initiative; others are advised by their sponsors or by the institutions to which they are applying. A consequence of this has been a growth in the number of language courses, often located within specialist schools or centres, which aim to cater for the language requirements of students aspiring to tertiary level studies. It is estimated (Jordan 1977; Williams et al. 1986) that about one-third of international students would benefit from attending pre-sessional language courses. To judge whether attendance at such courses is advisable, the level of English competence of applicants should be known and understood by both the applicants and those who select them. The following information may be useful for applicants, selectors and those responsible for the induction of international students to tertiary education.

The meaning and value of IELTS and TOEFL test scores

Ideally, competence in English should be measured *before* students begin their studies and, where possible, any necessary interventions should be carried out in order to improve English language *in advance of* the commencement of courses.

Of the many instruments designed to measure English language competence, the IELTS and TOEFL tests are the two most commonly available.

IELTS

The *International English Language Testing System* (IELTS) is British in origin and is monitored by the University of Cambridge Local Examinations Syndicate (UCLES). The IELTS test contains open and closed items which measure ability in the four principle study modes: listening, academic reading, academic writing, and speaking (IELTS 1985). Outcomes provide profiles of ability for each of the four modes on a nine-point scale (marked to the nearest half point). The four marks are then compiled to give a single IELTS score or band. Table 8.1 gives overall descriptors and capability statements for each band.

Table 8.1 The Meaning of IELTS scores (based on IELTS 1995)

Band	User type	Description	Academic capability
9	Expert	Has fully operational command of English: appropriate accurate and fluent with complete understanding.	Will cope with linguistically demanding academic courses (e.g. medicine, law, linguistics, journalism, library studies); also those in Bands 5 and 6 below.
8	Very good	Has fully operational command of English with only occasional unsystematic inaccuracies and inappropriacies. Misunderstandings may occur in unfamiliar situations. Handles complex detailed argument well.	Should cope as Band 1 above.
7	Good	Has operational command of English with occasional inaccuracies, inappropriacies and misunderstandings in some situations. Generally handles complex language well and understands detailed reasoning.	Likely to cope as Band 1 above.
6	Competent	Has generally effective command of English despite some inaccuracies, inappropriacies and misunderstandings. Can use and understand fairly complex language, particularly in familiar situations.	Will cope with linguistically less demanding academic courses (e.g. agriculture, mathematics, technology, computer-based studies, telecommunications) and with linguistically demanding training courses (e.g. air-traffic control, engineering, pure and applied sciences, industrial safety); also those in Band 5 below.

Band	User type	Description	Academic capability
5	Modest	Has partial command of English, coping with overall meaning in most situations, though is likely to make many mistakes. Should be able to handle basic communications in own field.	Will cope with linguistically less demanding training courses (e.g. animal husbandry, catering, fire services).
4	Limited	Basic competence limited to familiar situations. Frequent breakdowns in communications occur.	Unlikely to cope linguistically with any higher education courses.
3	Extremely limited	Conveys and understands only general meaning in very familiar situations. Frequent breakdowns in communication occur.	Unlikely to cope linguistically with any higher education courses.
2	Intermittent	No real communication is possible except for the most basic information using isolated words or short formulae in familiar situations and to meet immediate needs. Has great difficulty understanding spoken and written English.	Will not cope linguistically with higher education courses.
1	Non-user	Has no ability to use English beyond a few isolated words.	Will not cope linguistically.

TOEFL

The *Test of English as Foreign Language* (TOEFL) is a widely used international instrument which has been developed in and is monitored by the Educational Testing Service in Princeton, USA. A TOEFL score is in the form of a single mark out of about 700 based on scores obtained on closed (multiple-choice) items in the following modes: listening comprehension, grammar, vocabulary, and reading comprehension.

Comparing IELTS with TOEFL

Generally, language tutors in UK regard the IELTS test as providing a 'much more reliable measure [than TOEFL] of a student's command of academic English' (Green 1995: 1). For this reason IELTS tends to be preferred by selectors in British universities. Nevertheless either set of scores will give an indication of an international student's level of English language skills and whether he or she should receive pre-sessional tuition. Table 8.2 shows, roughly, how IELTS and TOEFL scores compare.

Table 8.2 IELTS and TOEFL: equivalent scores

IELTS	3.5	4.0	4.5	5.0	5.5	6.0	6.5	7.0	7.5	8.0	8.5	9.0
TOEFL	425	450	475	500	525	550	575	600	625	650	675	700

Contextualising language scores

When selecting students, it is necessary to consider IELTS and TOEFL scores within the context of a variety of factors such as the applicant's age, motivation and educational, cultural and first-language background. For example, if a course places emphasis on reading and writing, then a low score in listening comprehension may be acceptable (note that the IELTS test distinguishes between these skills, whereas TOEFL does not).

Another consideration is the environment in which the student is being tutored. If, as undergraduates, overseas students are placed with first-language students, then they may need a high IELTS/TOEFL score, say a minimum of 6.5/575. If, however, a group of postgraduates are working with others within an international centre with the support of tutors who are widely experienced in teaching second-language students, then lower scores, such as 6.0/550, may be acceptable at entry.

Language policy

Departments and centres in institutions of higher education normally develop their own policies with regard to providing applicants with advice on language competence and the possible need for tuition. Box 8.1 is an example of the policy of a university-based *Centre for International Studies in Education* which provides taught courses leading to advanced diplomas and masters degrees to graduate teachers.

The advice in Box 8.1 is empirical and is based on the collective experience of the Centre's tutors and the nature of their taught courses. Policy with regard to the admission of students to courses which contain advanced linguistic components may be somewhat tighter. For example,

UNIVERSITY OF NEWCASTLE
CENTRE FOR INTERNATIONAL STUDIES IN EDUCATION

English Language Competence

Advice to Applicants

All courses are conducted in the medium of English. You are examined by essays and a dissertation which are expected to be presented in acceptable English. To benefit from your course your English language ability must be adequate for you to study at an advanced level.

If English is not your first language then, where possible, you should take an IELTS or TOEFL test before applying. Please include a copy of your result with your application.

The following table gives our advice with regard to particular ranges of IELTS/TOEFL scores.

IELTS	TOEFL	Advice
6.5 & over	575 & over	Your English is likely to satisfy course requirements.
5.5–6.0	525–574	You will probably cope but may require some assistance. You would benefit from a 1–3 month pre-sessional English course.
4.5–5.0	475–524	We recommend you attend a 6-month pre-sessional English course.
below 4.5	below 475	We recommend you attend a 9–12 month pre-sessional English course.

A score of at least 6.0 (IELTS) or 550 (TOEFL) will be an advantage when applying for admission. However, even if you score higher, you will benefit from attending a pre-sessional English course.

CISE tutors are experienced in working with students for whom English is a second (or third, etc.) language. However, you have a responsibility to yourself and your sponsors to make sure that your English is good enough for you to benefit from your course.

Box 8.1 English language advice to postgraduate applicants who are likely to receive strong tutorial support

English Proficiency

Recommendation to Applicants

Applicants should *either* provide evidence of having achieved a minimum IELTS 6.5 (TOEFL 575) by the commencement of the course *or* attend an appropriate English language course prior to registration.

Recommendations for length of English language course are given below.

IELTS	TOEFL	Comment
up to 4	up to 450	Limited communication on simple topics. 12-month English course is essential.
5	500	Survival level; inadequate for university study. 6 to 9-month pre-sessional English course essential.
6	550	Minimum level for university study in technical subjects (natural sciences, applied sciences, mathematics). 3 to 6-month pre-sessional English course strongly recommended.
7	590	Minimum level for university study in subjects with advanced linguistic requirements (English language, literature, lingustics, law, business studies). Course not essential, but 1-month course would be advantageous.
8,9	600–700	Equivalent to native speaker apart from accent. Courses unnecessary.

Box 8.2 General recommendations on English proficiency to university applicants

IELTS/TOEFL scores of 6.5/575 or 7.0/600 may be required as a condition of entry; failing that, students will be advised to attend pre-sessional courses in English. Box 8.2 is an example of the general advice that a university may send to applicants.

It is estimated that an effective pre-sessional course of four to six months can increase an IELTS score by as much as one point. An improvement of this magnitude may well bring about a significant improvement to the academic welfare of many international students, especially postgraduates attending one-year courses, such as a taught masters degree, where there is a relatively short time in which to become linguistically acclimatised. It is a matter for selectors of international students to be aware of those institutions which provide effective pre-sessional courses and students should not hesitate to ask them for advice. For both, the British Council can supply information, either directly at its various offices throughout the world or through its publications (e.g. British Council 1995).

THE INDUCTION OF INTERNATIONAL STUDENTS TO STUDY FACILITIES

University facilities for learning and research

Apart from tutorial inputs and the provision of lecture rooms, laboratory, library and computer access are three of the most important academic support facilities that universities place at their students' disposal. Their provision accounts for a large part of the tuition fee. The efficient use of these facilities is essential if the period spent at university is to be effective in both academic and value-for-money terms.

The general quality of UK university laboratory, library and computing provision is extremely high; moreover these facilities are subject to continual review and update. It is quite likely, however, that their degree of sophistication may initially be confusing to international students. Reasons for this often stem from an increasing dependency on modern technology where the effective use of mechanical and electronic facilities assumes a technological background that is often missing, and where there is sometimes an aversion towards reading, understanding and following technical instructions and manuals (a difficulty which some tutors share with their students!).

Learning how to use and benefit from laboratories, libraries and computers must be regarded as an integral part of the academic induction process.

Using laboratories

Although laboratory practicals are a key feature of British university courses in medicine, the natural sciences and engineering, they may not be so prominent in the minds or collective experience of many international students. Such students may have received their education in countries where practical work is prohibitively expensive or where the prevailing philosophy is that academics should engage in theory and leave practical considerations to others. In Britain, however, practical work is regarded as a central component of training in scientific method and enquiry. It is therefore necessary for tutors, demonstrators, technicians and safety officers in departments which include laboratories, to ensure that international students understand and appreciate the laboratory ethos. During the early stages, many are likely to require special assistance. Demonstrators and technicians may have a significant, and hitherto unrecognised, role to play in this connection.

Using the library

On matriculation, students are normally issued with a means of enabling them to register with their university library. University libraries are generally extremely well stocked and, as well as books and journals, they contain electrical and electronic reference materials such as sound and video recordings and CD-ROM disks. The computerisation of libraries means that retrieval is facilitated, but only if the user takes the trouble to learn and use the system.

In order not to be overwhelmed on first entering their university library, it is important for international students to realise that the differences between those libraries they may have encountered in the past and the ones they will meet at university are really only associated with scale, quality of provision and type of retrieval system. They should also remember that they exist to provide a service to their clients: the students and staff of the university community.

Many universities run induction courses for students and it is essential that international students attend and attempt to obtain full benefit from them. In addition, most universities provide written advice on the use of their particular libraries. Primrose (1991) contains an example of the kind of general advice on library use that a university might offer. Tutors can assist during induction by setting an early assignment which obliges their students to visit and use the library.

Using computers

Most students in British universities have direct access to centrally served computer terminals which, in addition to their use as stand-alone workstations, are linked to the library and the internet. Computer facilities are virtually always available for postgraduates; for undergraduates, computers are generally available in the ratio of about one workstation for every five to eight students. Figure 8.1 summarises some of the computer services which students can expect to obtain.

The services shown in Figure 8.1 will only be beneficial if students are reasonably 'computerate'. Unfortunately, for the novice, becoming

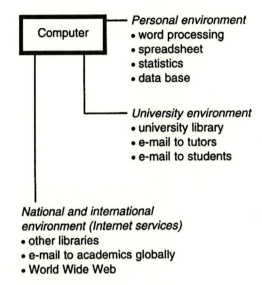

Figure 8.1 Computer services

computerate often presents a huge obstacle. As a result there is frequently a reluctance to get to grips with both the hardware and software. This reluctance is more marked amongst older students and, to some extent, amongst certain international students. Some of the issues surrounding the use of computers are discussed below. In each case an issue is raised and the response is given in italics.

- For newcomers there is a lack of familiarity with the hardware and the jargon of computers. As with many other new situations there is a period of initiation to go through followed by a fairly steep learning curve.

  This is to be expected, especially in cases where students come from non-technical backgrounds. However, all students should be strongly urged 'to take the plunge'. For example, terms like e-mail, internet and World Wide Web as used in Figure 8.1 will seem mysterious to the uninitiated and will remain so until they are actually used in context. Thereafter, as with most jargon, the mystery soon disappears. Initiation should therefore be embraced, not avoided.

- For most people, conceptual difficulties often arise with computers, which come to be regarded as mysterious boxes.

  This obstacle is overcome as soon as users realise that there is no need for them to understand what goes on inside the box. Conceptually, using a computer is rather like using a telephone or a cassette recorder.

- To be able to communicate with the computer, users must learn to manage computer operating systems. Unfortunately they may have to cope with a number of different operating systems.

  There is no escaping this. For day-to-day use, most universities offer a choice of PC or Macintosh. Whereas Macintosh is undoubtedly the more user-friendly system, the PC (Personal Computer) operating system is used on about 85 per cent of computers worldwide and is getting better. Unless they have Macintosh systems at home, it is recommended that international students use PC systems.

- There are many software packages to comprehend and learn.

  Universities will generally offer a range of popular software packages for word-processing, spreadsheets, statistics and data bases. These are usually supported by nearby instruction sheets or self-learning guides. Tutors should advise beginners with regard to selection of software, using their familiarity with those packages which are most relevant to their own academic interests and those of their students. Tutors can also help students by setting an early assignment which necessitates the use of a particular piece of software: e.g. some data to process, a partially written essay to complete in a given format.

- Many novices also have to learn keyboard skills, i.e. typing.

  Three years of being an undergraduate may provide sufficient time for a student to become a reasonably good touch typist. This would be ideal and there are computer packages which teach typing. For students with time restrictions, then modified two- or three-finger typing may be the only sensible possibility. In either event, there is no substitute for 'hands on' experience and practice at a keyboard. Again, tutors can assist the learning process by insisting on word-processed submissions from the very beginning.

- New users are often afraid that they may damage computers through ignorance or carelessness.

  This is very unlikely, since computer workstations are controlled through central servers which automatically safeguard the software and the operating systems. It is virtually impossible to damage a computer workstation by careless use. However it is possible to lose files if they are not properly saved.

- Computers and software are subject to continual revision and improvement.

  All users must be able to cope with change. Mercifully such changes are usually incremental: in other words, that which has been learned in the past will usually remain useful in future.

Although the above points contain quite legitimate concerns, they must be overcome if international students are to obtain the maximum academic benefit from the resources which universities provide. For their part, tutors should urge students to log onto the computer system and begin to use the software *from day one*.

There are some strategies which may assist international students to overcome their initial reluctance to engage with computers:

- It is often very effective if tutors ask a more experienced student (e.g. a second year student or a previous computer user) to assist newcomers. In most cases, a student who is an experienced computer user is quite keen to show a less experienced colleague how to get started. Peer assistance of this kind is mutually beneficial, the teacher learning as much if not more that the taught.
- As mentioned earlier, tutors should consider setting small but appropriate academic tasks which will require students to use computers. These could take various forms: to insert a 500-word abstract into a document which is previously given to the student on disk; to present some numerical data in a variety of graphical forms; to write the tutor an e-mail message, perhaps requesting a tutorial; to search for a particular abstract on a CD-ROM and print it off; to tabulate numerical or written data; to scan a photograph, a map or a complex line drawing and incorporate it into a piece of descriptive text.

The best advice a tutor can give a student is not to delay becoming a computer user. Experience indicates that this aim is perfectly achievable during the academic induction process, provided students learn by actually working at the computer (not *about* the computer).

SUPERVISION OF INTERNATIONAL STUDENTS

Academic orientation

Apart from problems with language and the use of facilities, international students frequently find difficulty in adjusting to new academic modes. For example, the following appear to present particular problems:

- being unable to participate fully in seminars;
- developing academic self-discipline;
- acquiring adequate feedback on performance;
- coping with the variety of assignments that are expected;
- understanding examination methods and developing appropriate techniques.

Makepeace (1989), reporting on his own research and that of others (notably Church 1982), indicates that the above problems, *inter alia*, are frequently mentioned by international students as causing initial concern during their orientation to academic work. The aspects above all form part of the overall adjustment that international students are obliged to make to a different system of education. Allied to these problems is the general helplessness of the new arrival which often manifests itself in illness and uncertainty regarding who to turn to for help. As Makepeace advises, in such circumstances staff 'may often have to make the first move' (Makepeace 1989: 22).

Universities should therefore ensure that, in addition to providing for student welfare, their introductory programmes should include *academic* orientation. Such a programme could be in the form of a service unit which lasts for the first semester. Typically, it would include the following:

- The educational system of the UK
  Students should understand where they are located within the system of their country of sojourn. This section would include information and brief discussion on British primary, secondary and tertiary education systems.
- Library skills
  To include finding, using and acknowledging printed and electronic source materials; effective reading.
- Study skills
  To include taking effective notes; planning, preparation and presentation of assignments; report writing; essay writing; dissertation preparation; proposal preparation.
- Studentship
  To include discussion of the purpose of lectures, seminars and tutorials; laboratory ethos and safety; the role of the tutor; the role of the supervisor.
- Assignments and examinations
  To include varieties of assignments; criteria of good work; criteria of poor work; planning revision.

This unit could be provided by a service department of the university (perhaps located within a department of education or a language centre) with specialist inputs from arts and sciences faculties.

Relationships between international students and supervisors

Brown and Atkins (1988: 129) warn that 'supervising overseas students may require more time, effort and skill than supervising home British students'. These extra demands often create problems for international students and their supervisors. Part of the problem arises out of the adjustments which are required of *both* groups. Whereas students normally perceive that the lecturer's main responsibility is to teach and supervise, lecturers are very much aware of the considerable drain that teaching and tutoring can make upon the time and energy that is available for them to fulfil research, committee and administrative functions. This can lead to a mismatch of expectations surrounding academic roles and responsibilities.

Table 8.3, which is based partly on two surveys by UKCOSA (1985, 1989), juxtaposes some of the principle differences between the expectations of international students and their supervisors.

It should be noted in Table 8.3 that the two sets of views are presented in a deliberately exaggerated polarised way; in reality the position of an

Table 8.3 Some academic activities: expectations of international students and supervisors

Academic activity	International student's expectation	Supervisor's expectation
Learning	Teacher-led with teacher telling student what to learn; rote learning regarded as acceptable.	The student takes on the major responsibility for own learning; develops and uses ability to think and work independently.
Lectures	Should contain the complete course; all the facts and the right answers should be provided.	Should sensitise students to key issues and stimulate them to develop their own ideas through self-study.
Teaching style in seminars	Didactic, product-oriented; the teacher provides unquestionable knowledge, views, etc.; students listen, accept and take passive role.	Problem-solving, process-oriented; the teacher raising argument and discussion; students talk, question and play active part.
Tutorials and role of tutor	Extremely important; a strong personal friendly relationship with tutor; tutor is someone to cling to; individual tuition; tutor to provide closely structured guidance and feedback on work, to set clear standards and, last but not least, to make sure students 'get through'.	Tutorial work not a serious priority (low university status compared with research); nothing in it for the tutor; tutors should deal with academic rather than personal matters; group tutorials often more efficient; tutor is not supposed to 'drive' students or give undue help.
Course work	Right answers should be learned and reproduced on demand.	Problem solving and original approaches are more valued than regurgitation of lecture notes.
Examinations and dissertations	An opportunity to play it safe by assembling and regurgitating lecture notes, books and articles which have been read; copying and plagiarism are legitimate since the outcomes contain correct information.	Critical argument, discussion, evidence, evaluation and originality are highly valued; no 'right answers', particularly in arts and social sciences; plagiarism and fabrication of results are virtually a crime.

individual student or supervisor is likely to lie somewhere between the two sets of extremes.

In order to avoid disappointment it is necessary that each group, whether international students or supervisors, is aware of and understands the responsibilities of the other. This process may be assisted if the position regarding mutual responsibilities between supervisor and student is clarified during the induction period and adhered to strictly thereafter. However, even taking such precautions is by no means a guarantee that misunderstandings will be avoided or that responsibilities will somehow become reduced, particularly with students engaged on research.

As Brown and Atkins (1988: 129) observe, 'It would seem therefore that in accepting an overseas research student [tutors] are often accepting greater responsibility for supervision'.

To accept greater responsibility of this kind often calls for a particular kind of academic altruism which is certainly not accounted for in the current indicators of performance in UK universities. This possibly gives rise to some lecturers who rationalise that the time and ingenuity spent in supervising international students might be put to better use in research, publication, and being seen on the right committees. However, those who do undertake this responsibility play a significant part in raising the international profile of universities: by raising the quality of teaching and learning, particularly during the induction period, they are playing an important role in fostering the growth of transfer within the international academic community.

Chapter 9

Through a glass darkly
Problems of studying at advanced level through the medium of English

Nadine K. Cammish

Malcolm Bradbury, in his novel *Eating People is Wrong* (1959), portrays Mr Eborebelosa, an African student studying at a British university, as a comic figure who 'disliked meeting people and had been closeting himself in lavatories to avoid it' (Bradbury 1959: 35). Treece, his tutor, says to him:

> 'Life here may be difficult, but you can't go on retiring into lavatories indefinitely. You must come out into the real world and face these problems sensibly and maturely.'
>
> (Bradbury 1959: 28)

Bradbury's Mr Eborebelosa was perhaps considered funny by some readers when the novel was first published, but in the 1990s, Bradbury's depiction of him seems not only unkind but patronisingly racist. The problems anyone has to face in pursuing studies in a country other than one's own really can at first seem to be overwhelming and for many students, language is a core problem. Coping with living in a different culture and learning through the medium of a second or foreign language can indeed feel as though one is 'seeing through a glass darkly'; this can be either daunting as Mr Eborebelosa obviously found it, or an exciting and challenging experience. Much depends not only on the individual students but on the teachers by whom they are taught.

In commenting on the problems of children in school having to be educated through a language medium which is not their mother tongue, Spolsky says 'It must be obvious to all that incomprehensible education is immoral' (Spolsky 1977: 20). Obviously, overseas students studying at British higher education institutions make their own individual efforts to overcome their linguistic problems but the effort should not be one-sided. Tutors and lecturers are morally obliged both to make themselves understood and to enable their overseas students to express their own thoughts and ideas in speech and writing. If university and college teachers constantly monitor their own use of language with a heightened awareness of the extent to which they are communicating successfully and if they develop strategies to enable students, in their turn, to communicate better, then it is not only those who are not native speakers of English who benefit but all students, whatever their background.

Problems in studying at advanced level through the medium of English may depend very much on the type of experience of learning English the overseas students have had. For some, English is a *foreign language*, learned as a school subject. Attitudes, motivation, methodology, techniques and teacher expertise vary widely from country to country and within each country. Some students may have been taught with what might be classified as a 'communicative approach' and will be confident and adept linguistically at a conversational level, capable of 'surviving' in the foreign language situation. Their surface fluency may be deceptive, however; if they have had little experience of learning about another subject through the medium of English, aural comprehension skills, for example, may not be sufficiently developed for coping with extended periods of listening such as in lectures and the students may tire easily. Conversely, they may have experienced a rather more traditional type of language teaching which concentrates on developing reading and writing skills; problems may therefore arise when they have to interact orally as for example in small group sessions. Social and cultural factors may also be involved here as we shall see later. For other students it may be a problem of range of vocabulary, especially perhaps the technical vocabulary, abbreviations and acronyms used in a particular subject area. The specialised lexis can be acquired quickly but teachers should not assume it is there in the first place.

The materials used for teaching English as a foreign language in the students' home countries may also affect their preparedness for tackling their studies in Britain. Students from Western Europe not only already share in the Graeco-Roman and Judaeo-Christian cultural strains which underlie British culture and tradition but have also been taught English from textbooks which attempt to mirror the contemporary British way of life and to teach the language and its registers in that context. This is particularly true in the case of German textbooks for English (see for example Buttjes and Byram 1990). However, as Cem and Margaret Alptekin (1984) point out, some countries outside Europe are not happy about the idea, held particularly by some expatriate EFL teachers, that language and culture are indivisible and have to be taught together. Although these countries want their young people to learn English for *instrumental* reasons, they do not want them to acquire at the same time the cultural baggage which may come with it.

In addition, for younger learners in other countries there are strong educational reasons for the localisation of teaching materials to enable children to use the foreign language to talk about their own world and their own experience. As Hutchinson (1970) says of a pupil learning French as a foreign language in an African context:

> How can he be expected to begin to think in French, if he is not given the means and vocabulary to express his own thoughts, his own needs, the ideas which come from his own daily life?
>
> (Hutchinson 1970: 80)

One thinks particularly of Searle's (1972) moving description of a small boy on a Caribbean island: outside the sun shines down on the tropical vegetation and inside the classroom the boy has to study a text entitled *How we nearly froze to death: the story of an Outward Bound adventure in Scotland*. The situation is, as Searle says, 'culturally absurd' – 'He is mystified, alienated from his own world, his own island' (Searle 1972: 33–4).

It was this problem which fuelled the widespread movements to localise teaching materials in the sixties and seventies, affecting both foreign language and second language text books (see for example Cammish 1980). Materials were produced which were 'culturally and experientially appropriate' (Alptekin 1984: 16).

In addition to this argument for localisation, as we have seen, it is for learners of all ages that some countries reject the western ideas that seem to be part of any 'language plus culture' package. The cultural norms and values may be not only alien but unacceptable on religious, moral or political grounds and hence considered to constitute a threat to national identity (Alptekin 1984). Language-teaching materials are produced therefore which often reflect only the traditions and cultural values of the learners' own country. Where this has been the experience of students who ultimately come to study in Britain, their knowledge of English may be good in terms of linguistic competence, that is they may be very capable in terms of producing well-formed, grammatically accurate language. Their communicative competence in terms of situationally and socially appropriate language, however, may not be adequate for effective interaction with native-speakers in a British cultural setting unless the native-speakers are aware of and sympathetic to the problem. Moreover, listening and reading skills which may be effective when dealing with 'culture-free' material, can be seriously challenged by the native-speaker's casual and unthinking use of allusions and references which are culture-specific. Everyday references can be bewildering for some overseas students. One lecturer, in discussing selective education, referred to separating the sheep from the goats. He was asked by a puzzled student what farming had to do with educational organisation. On another occasion, a Chinese student from Xian was heard to ask plaintively: 'But who *are* Adam and Eve?' The richness of the metaphors and allusions of a language may delight the foreign student who is a linguist or who has integrative motivation in learning it; for the student whose motivation is instrumental, who sees the language as an international *lingua franca* and a language of technology, such things are perhaps an irritant. In any case, as Rivers (1983) points out:

> We must not violate the private and deeply emotional identification of our students by insisting that they value what we value and share our culturally acquired attitudes.
>
> (Rivers 1983: 149)

Simply understanding another culture and the ability to cope effectively with its demands are sufficient to ensure good communication and good interpersonal relationships.

Another group of overseas students are those who have learned English not as a foreign but as a *second language*: at least part of their education has usually been conducted through the medium of English. Some may be illiterate in their mother tongue because in primary school they achieved literacy via English; others may have switched to English medium only in the secondary school or in higher education. The 1953 UNESCO report, a highly influential document, stated categorically:

> It is axiomatic that the best medium for teaching a child is his mother tongue. Psychologically, it is the system of meaningful signs that in his mind works automatically for expression and understanding. Sociologically it is a means of identification among the members of the community to which he belongs. Educationally, he learns more quickly through it than through an unfamiliar linguistic medium.
>
> (UNESCO 1953: 11)

Pupils who have the disadvantage of learning through the medium of a language which is not their mother tongue have what the UNESCO Report describes as a 'double burden' (UNESCO 1953: 48): they have to deal both with the input of new information and ideas and with their presentation in an unfamiliar language. Le Page describes their education as being 'sealed off in a kind of linguistic polythene bag' from their everyday lives at home (Le Page 1964: 24). That these pupils succeed nevertheless is greatly to their credit.

Some of the survival techniques they employed as children in school may however still affect them as learners at university level. They may have used rote-learning to disguise lack of understanding or an inadequate standard of written English and may again fall back on this technique when tackling examinations, learning whole examination answers by heart, even though they no longer need to do so. Students from countries where rote-learning is a traditional part of education or religious training may be particularly good at this and may take time to adapt to the different academic culture prevalent in British universities.

A group of South-East Asian students interviewed about this confessed to carefully preparing essay answers in advance and then, by prodigious feats of memory, reproducing them in the examination, solely because they were frightened that under examination conditions, their English would be inadequate.

The phenomenon of 'World Englishes' is another factor which affects the linguistic aspects of students' work. In what have been described as the 'Outer Circle' countries (i.e. those such as India, Nigeria, etc., where English was first introduced as a colonial language for administrative purposes) as opposed to 'Inner Circle' countries (such as Britain, Australia and the United States), new varieties of English have evolved:

> which possess the common core characteristics of the Inner Circle varieties, but in addition can be distinguished from them by particular lexical, phonological, pragmatic and morphosyntactic innovations.
>
> (Brown 1995: 234)

This means, of course, that there is increasingly no one simple answer to the question of what is 'good' or standard English: the new Englishes, and their regional varieties within them, are standard within their contexts. A student coming to the United Kingdom from Pakistan, India or Nigeria for example, may find that what is standard English at home is not regarded as standard by native-speakers who seem to feel that they have some sort of monopoly over what is 'good' English on a worldwide scale. Differences in vocabulary, structure and pronunciation may even lead to students not being easily understood when as far as they are concerned, they are bilingual in English.

Another aspect of this problem is that of English-based creoles which have evolved, largely in former colonies, and often as a *lingua franca*. Students may speak them as mother-tongue or as a second language. Krio in Sierra Leone (Freetown), Bislama in Vanuatu in the South Pacific (Charpentier 1979) and the creoles of the Caribbean (see for example Craig 1971) amongst others, are languages in their own right, rather than varieties of English. Because most of the population speak the creole at home but are educated through the medium of a standard variety of English, the interaction between the two languages results in each individual's language performance being identifiable as lying on a point or covering a range of points somewhere on the scale between basilect (Creole) and acrolect (the standard language) (see for example Bickerton 1975: 189, for samples of Guyanese speakers). Craig (1971) points out that the learner is able, all the time, 'to recognise Standard English, far out of proportion to his ability to produce it' (Craig 1971: 377). He goes on to say:

The learning of Standard English can become arrested at a point where the quantity of unknown features...has become negligible, relative to social requirements, but at the same time the quantity of features known passively has remained relatively large and significant. The speaker in this situation would possess an adequate 'recognition' of Standard English and a consequent strong sense of knowing the language. These dispositions would reduce both his motivation to modify his language as well as his ability to perceive contrasts between what language he actually produces and what he aims to produce. Only the social effects of his Standard English efforts would be apparent to him.

(Craig 1971: 378)

Problems of this sort will of course be more marked in speech than in writing. In writing, one has the time to monitor one's work: patterns which are not habitual in speech can be produced when there is time to focus on form as well as content. Students' formal written English in cases like this may be far closer to a standard form than their spoken English.

When overseas students arrive in the United Kingdom with the variety of linguistic backgrounds described above, pre-sessional and ongoing courses in English and in study skills are provided by the host institutions of higher education. In addition to this, students' *informal* language skills should also develop very rapidly through daily contact with the native-speakers around them. It is unfortunate from the point of view of language development when students from the same country are housed together. It may be more homely and supportive and in some cases, necessary for religious or cultural reasons, but such students make slower progress in improving their English. Language *acquisition* in Krashen's (1982) sense requires massive intelligible input and constant use of the target language for real communicative purposes.

On the other hand, those students who integrate quickly into campus life often enjoy acquiring the colloquialisms and slang they hear around them. Learning discrimination in their use however is another matter. 'Please don't take me for a wimp' is racy and idiomatic English (and I was very impressed when I recently heard a Belgian student use it), but it may be socially inappropriate language in certain circumstances.

THE FOUR SKILLS

Successful study at an advanced level in a British university or college requires of the student communicative competence in English in all four language skills: listening, speaking, reading and writing.

The listening skill

In the past, listening was often mistakenly classified, along with reading, as a 'passive' skill. Today it would usually be termed a 'receptive' skill in recognition of the fact that a listener must be active in receiving, decoding, understanding and reacting to the message heard. Within the learning environment, the overseas student will need to be competent in listening in three main areas:

- understanding the content of lectures;
- following the more rapid and informal registers used in discussion;
- grasping instructions in more practical and/or face-to-face situations.

Understanding lectures

The responsibility for understanding a lecture does not, as some lecturers imagine, lie entirely with the student. The lecturer can do a great deal to make the task easier for students who are not native-speakers of English. For example, some support can be provided beforehand in the form of lists of the technical vocabulary to be used, a short and simply written introduction to the topic, or a simplified outline of the lecture, including key words and phrases. The students can then prepare and make sure that they are in a position where they know what to expect; it is much easier to understand when what is said is what is expected. (Coping with the unpredictable is a much higher-level listening skill.) The picking up of key words and phrases allied to a general idea of what the speaker is supposed to be saying can boost the level of listening comprehension a great deal in the early stages when newly arrived students may lack confidence.

During the lecture itself, the main problem for the overseas student is that of the strain of continuous listening for a long period. Short pauses, changes of activity and the visual build-up of the lecture outline on the blackboard or overhead projector can all give some respite and be supportive. This help is important because once the student has lost track of what is being said, what Krashen calls the 'affective filter' comes down, almost protectively, and reception stops (Krashen 1982: 32).

In order to increase the comprehensibility of what is being said, the following points are worth bearing in mind:

- It is easier to understand when one can see the face of the speaker (lip movements, paralinguistic features such as gesture and facial expression).
- Visual support in the form of pictures, realia and diagrams can make the comprehension of the spoken word less crucial.

- There is a great difference between spoken and written language. When we speak we use shorter sentences and fewer subordinate clauses. Speech also makes greater use of redundancy; there is more repetition and therefore more chance of catching an idea when it is repeated in a slightly different way. This being so, the lecturers who write out their lectures in flowing periods and then read them aloud are making themselves difficult to understand. What they say would be more comprehensible if they talked on the basis of skeleton notes. If they really have to write everything down, perhaps they should write their lectures in the style of the spoken word.
- EFL teachers who are used to communicating in English with pupils who as yet know little of the language, make sure that what they say is intelligible by restricting their vocabulary to what the pupils know or can guess and by controlling the structures that they use: little of what they say is expressed in unfamiliar terms. Whatever their actual message, they are very conscious of exactly what words and structures they are using to convey it. Sentences are repeated in different ways, using different words; new words are explained and jotted up on the blackboard.

If we can bring into lecturing this subtle awareness of the level of difficulty of the language we use and see the necessity for re-wording what we say to ensure comprehension, and if we can remember that our metaphors and references may be culture-specific and need elucidation, then our overseas students may find our lectures easier to understand.

Understanding in group discussions

When speaking, it is the learner himself who selects the language that is used. To some extent, therefore, he can compensate for deficiencies in his repertoire, through communicative strategies such as using paraphrase or simplifying his message. When listening, however, he cannot normally exercise any control over the language that is used: he must be prepared to extract meanings, as best he can, from whatever language is directed at him. It is therefore not enough that he should merely be able to understand the same range of language that he can speak: his receptive repertoire must be matched not against his own productive repertoire, but against the productive repertoire of the native speakers he will need to understand. In addition he must be prepared to cope with a wide range of situational and performance factors which are outside his control.

(Littlewood 1981: 65)

For an overseas student, the general impression in group discussions where the other group members are native-speakers, is probably that everyone is talking at once, and it is true that in lively discussion there is an overlap as new speakers break in at the end of what someone is saying. There are many things with which to learn to cope. Unlike in a lecture when there is one voice, usually speaking fairly standard English, which is being projected clearly in quietness, in discussion the voices are coming from all sides and perhaps in a variety of regional accents. Moreover, if several groups are working in the same room, there may be a high level of background noise. To make comprehension even more difficult, unless the discussion is highly structured, there is an element of unpredictability: what is said may be quite unexpected. Finally because a group is small and more sociable, the register of language tends to be less formal: speech is more colloquial and elliptical.

All these elements can make the group situation a testing one for overseas students who have not yet developed fairly advanced listening skills. Materials on which to base the discussion, firm structuring of the argument and care taken over location, group composition and choice of group leaders can all be helpful in making comprehension easier.

Understanding instructions

In contrast, in looking at the understanding of instructions, let us consider the one-to-one situation of a dissertation supervision.

Recently, a Nigerian student was asked at his viva why he had not included a copy of his fieldwork questionnaire in his dissertation. He replied that his supervisor had told him he did not need to do so. The supervisor had in fact said the very opposite. Here again, the responsibility of the tutor is clear: overseas students on the receiving end of personal supervisions are not only probably experiencing comprehension problems because of having to concentrate for a long period, but they are under stress because they are alone and the tutor's attention is focused on them. The good tutor makes sure that decisions, comments and instructions are listed during the supervision so that the student takes away a written record which can be referred to later. The final few minutes of the supervision will be devoted to checking over each item to make sure it is understood.

The speaking skill

Communicative competence goes beyond mere linguistic competence which requires only the ability to form grammatically correct sentences. For example if a tutor asks, 'Have you finished your essay?' and the student replies, 'Yesterday I bought some tomatoes', then the answer is linguistically competent, but it is not situationally appropriate. If the reply is 'Last night it was very cold', again we have an answer which is linguistically competent and apparently not situationally appropriate. A closer look however might suggest that what the student actually means is that he has not finished the essay because it was so cold the night before that he could not work. A sympathetic native-speaker therefore might pick up the clue and suggest: 'Ah! it was so cold you couldn't work?' The student replies 'Yes'. At this point communication has been achieved but what is still lacking is the important factor of social appropriateness: 'I am sorry I have not finished my essay but...' Linguistic competence and situationally and socially appropriate language are all required for communicative competence.

In traditional courses consisting largely of lectures, it is possible for an overseas student with poor speaking skills to work away quietly and avoid having to say anything to anybody. Courses which are more interactive, involving pair work, group work, discussions and student presentations obviously make more demands.

> When we use language, we are constantly having to create new higher-level plans at the level of ideas, meanings and conversational strategies. The effective execution of these plans depends on a high degree of automaticity at the lower levels. For example, in the course of a discussion conducted at normal speed, it would be completely impossible to devote conscious attention and effort to the construction of every sentence: this must occur automatically in response to the ideas we want to express at specific moments. Equally we must be able to adapt our plans as interaction proceeds.
>
> (Littlewood 1992: 42)

Because speaking is a productive skill, the demands it makes on the individual are more obvious than those made by the listening skill. Personality and culture factors also play a more important role (see for example Richards and Sukwiwat 1985; Cortazzi and Jin, this volume).

Tutors need to use a variety of techniques, such as pair work, to encourage non-native-speakers to contribute orally depending on whether the students are silent because of reticence or because they feel linguistically inadequate. Careful structuring of the oral interaction so that only short, safe answers are required can, for example, help to make a start. Pair work can be used in a supportive way to encourage oral participation, and incidentally helps to break down the monolithic structure of a lecture.

Pair work

1 Students are asked to work with a partner and to draw up a list of points with reference to the topic being taught, for example: *advantages and disadvantages* or *factors for and against* or *causes and effects.*
2 The stress of having to speak out aloud in front of the whole group is immediately removed. Within the pair, hesitancy, incomplete sentences and grammatical mistakes do not matter as long as communication is being achieved.
3 The students share ideas and jot down their points: the list will form a secure basis for oral production later.
4 The tutor can circulate, encouraging students and dealing with individual problems.
5 When most of the group has noted a reasonable number of points, each pair can be asked to contribute its ideas. With the confidence which comes from having something which is written down and needs only to be read out and which is, moreover, short, students tend to be more ready to contribute than they usually are.

Although pair-work techniques of this sort are being recommended here to encourage non-native English speaking students, they are also extremely useful for making reticent native-speakers more interactive.

The reading and writing skills

Reading in a foreign or second language can be a slow and clumsy process when the level of difficulty is beyond one's competence. It is helpful for overseas students if reading lists give some indication of which texts are most accessible and which should be left until later. Shorter, easier sources which are nevertheless useful can boost their confidence. Earnest and hard-working students sometimes plod dog-gedly through complete books, carefully looking up every unknown word in a dictionary. They need of course to be shown how to skim and scan and should be directed to study skills courses where these are available. In subject areas where students are expected to read a variety of sources and produce extended essays, proper training in the taking of notes whilst reading can be part of the effort to help students avoid plagiarism.

Plagiarism, where it occurs in the work of overseas students, can often be attributed to two very understandable causes. First, in some cultural traditions plagiarism is not recognised as a sin: it is normal academic practice to gather together what others have said into a sort of pastiche. Second, and more importantly, it is the fear of making mistakes in English which leads many students to stick too closely to their sources and prevents them from expressing their own ideas. Occasionally the plagiarism is brilliant: one essay I marked some years ago was composed entirely of individual sentences and phrases lifted from a great variety of sources but stitched together seamlessly. It was amazing that a student with the linguistic skills to perform such a feat should feel she could not attempt to use her own words. The combination of humility about one's own language competence and the traditional respect for what authors have written can result in a sort of plagiarism which lacks the deviousness and intention to deceive of the real thing. Handling this can be a delicate matter.

Where writing skills are concerned, particularly in essay work, it is not usually choice of lexis which is the main problem although students for whom English is a foreign language may sometimes use near-synonyms which render meaning rather nebulous. Minor grammatical mistakes are not serious either. The German student who starts sentences with the construction: 'Important it is that...' or 'Interesting it is that...' will quickly learn not to do it and in any case the meaning is clear. Errors associated with the use of the definite article in English do not disappear so quickly: essays are often dotted with definite articles which are not required or, more frequently, have most of the necessary ones missing. The correct use in English of the definite article, especially for students whose mother tongues do not feature this part of speech, is a late-acquired skill. Again, however, its misuse does not normally actually impede meaning.

It is lack of control over sentence structure which really distorts or disguises meaning and impedes communication. The likelihood of mistakes in sentence construction seems to increase in proportion to sentence length: the longer the sentence, the more likely it is that something will go awry in the deep structure. Encouraging students to write shorter, simpler sentences can often improve matters considerably.

Meaning can also be obscured or distorted by inapposite use of link words such as *however, nevertheless,* and *although.* Specialist help from the language support services is required here; they will have materials especially designed to sort out this sort of problem. Subject lecturers are not expected to be expert in the diagnosis and remedial treatment of students' language problems but they do have a duty to collaborate with language support services in helping the overseas student.

CONCLUSION

The language problems of students who are not native-speakers of English are bound to affect their academic work and make extra demands on those who teach them. Making the effort to ensure one is comprehensible in lectures, devising techniques to encourage students to participate in discussion and trying to make sense of what they have written can be both arduous and time-consuming. One is filled with admiration however for the courage and hard work of these students who tackle higher education courses in a language which is not their mother tongue, seeing only 'through a glass darkly' at first perhaps, but overcoming the linguistic problems successfully in the end and offering to their teachers and fellow students the opportunity to benefit from inter-cultural academic contact and friendship.

Chapter 10

Counselling for excellence
Adjustment development of South-East Asian students

Othman Mohamed

South-East Asia is a region with a mix of cultural entities but significant similarities in respect of ethnic and religious distribution. These are points which the first section of this chapter illustrates by means of pen-pictures of the countries in the region. These countries span westward to the Indian Ocean and eastward to the Pacific; they thrive on international trade in primary products such as timber, rubber, palm oil, cocoa, tin and petroleum; they have long been a focal point for traders of East and West; and they have a history of conquest, having been colonised by nations such as Portugal, The Netherlands, Britain, France, Spain and Japan.

South-East Asia has emerged recently as an important player in world economics. Malaysia, Singapore, Thailand and Indonesia have sustained an annual economic growth rate of 6–8.5 per cent between 1990 and 1995 within, for the most part, a relatively stable political environment. This combination of political stability and economic growth has led to a strong demand for skilled manpower in all sectors of the economy, and inevitably education has played a part in manpower development.

High economic growth was achieved through heavy investment in social infrastructure. In Malaysia, growth has created further impetus for social and economic restructuring, and economic planners are currently anticipating a further economic surge by the end of the century and, in the '2020 Vision' policy, preparing for full industrialised nation status by that date. Similar scenarios exist in Malaysia's neighbours: Singapore, Brunei, Thailand and Indonesia.

Malaysia's multi-racial population of 19.5 million comprises 48 per cent Malays, 31 per cent Chinese, and 8 per cent Indians; Iban, Bidayuh, Melanaus, Kadazan and Bajaus minorities represent 10 per cent, mainly in the Borneo states of Sabah and Sarawak, with the remaining 3 per cent composed mainly of aboriginal subgroups in the Malay Peninsula. Malay is the official language and the main medium of educational instruction, though Mandarin and Tamil are widely used by the Chinese and Indian communities respectively. English is a compulsory second language in schools, and widely used in trade and industry.

Ethnicity determines differences in the socio-cultural and religious make-up of the population. Islam is the religion of the Malays, whose way of life is in general the product of its responses to the challenges of its environment (Husin Ali 1970). Most Chinese, who are concentrated in the urban areas, are Buddhist or Taoist, though the several communities such as the Hokkien, Teochiu, Cantonese, Hakka and Hainanese share exclusive association and are bound by clan values and cooperation. The Indian community too is not homogeneous, though the majority are Hindus, with a minority professing Christianity or Islam (Ryan 1971). Similar cultural and religious diversity exists among the minority groups. Ibans, for example, may be Muslim, Christian, Buddhist or animist. Observations on the Malaysian socio-cultural perspective must therefore be made with caution.

The availability of tax benefits for international and multinational companies has led to a transformation in the industrial and commercial sectors and to increased employment opportunities, particularly in the larger cities. Expectation of employment has led many rural youths to migrate to the cities, a pattern which brought in its wake a predictable and, to western eyes, familiar range of social and economic problems. Hence industrialisation, globalisation of the communications network and increasing independence from the extended family system have all contributed to the changing values of youths in Malaysia.

The country's age profile is young, with some 39 per cent of the population aged 14 years or below, and government has identified education as a key aspect of the effort to enhance the techno-industrial performance of the economy. While education forms a large portion of the government's budget allocation, demand for technical higher education has continued to outstrip the availability of places in Malaysia's higher education institutions.

Changing employment structures have combined with a recent emphasis on vocational technically oriented career opportunities to create a tremendous need for vocational education. Fields such as electronics, engineering, food science, construction, agriculture and business are in great demand and, in a significant change of social attitude, vocational education now enjoys parity of esteem with more traditional academic specialities. Meanwhile, adherence to Islamic tenets which base the individual's existence on perceptions pertaining to the fundamental principles of Qadha and Qadar (good or bad) has increasingly given way to a less literal interpretation of these principles and, with it, an attitude which takes personal initiative, resilience and hard work as the bases of success. So while the basic tenets of Qadha and Qadar remain unchanged, individual initiative is increasingly believed to have religious significance, with Allah helping those who help themselves.

Such changing attitudes have an impact upon the behavioural mind-set of the Malay population towards education, the quest for knowledge and the desire for improved quality of life. Family expectations too are generated by the quickly changing economic structure and anticipated opportunities for career development available to the children. Among the Malay ethnic group high familial expectations still strongly influence the adolescent, and familial reputation may be staked upon the children's academic achievement and success in higher education.

In spite of rapid urbanisation many Malays, particularly from the lower income groups, still live in rural villages, and efforts towards democratising opportunities in education have led the government to build a number of high-quality residential schools for bright rural students, many of whom are sponsored to pursue their studies in technology-related fields in universities outside Malaysia, including Great Britain.

As elsewhere in the world, the countries of the South-East Asian region have come more closely together, predominantly for economic reasons but also for political purposes. In particular the formation of the Association of South-East Asian Nations (ASEAN) has led to a formalisation of trading links between Malaysia, Thailand, Indonesia, Singapore, Negara Brunei Darussalam, the Philippines and Vietnam. In this section we say a little about the other members of ASEAN.

Singapore's success in social re-engineering is seen as an example by many developing countries. Developing from a regional entrepôt to her present status as one of the most significant financial centres in world trade has been a remarkable feat. But an annual growth rate of 8–8.5 per cent is not achieved and maintained without hard work and a sense of mission, and strong social value is attached to these characteristics, with success being richly rewarded in both money and esteem.

Education has been a priority area for national development since independence in 1963. Singapore's education system is an adaptation of the British model. Being a multi-racial society (the main groupings being Chinese, 76.4 per cent, Malay, 14.9 per cent, and Indian, 6.4 per cent) the mores of the various ethnic groups are still adhered to in the traditions of family and community, and strongly advocated by the government which, for example, emphasises the need to support Confucian ethics as exemplary for the Singapore Chinese.

Thailand, the only South-East Asian country not to have experienced colonial occupation by a western country, is predominantly Buddhist. Of its population of 54.5 million, 29 per cent are under the age of 14 and 63.5 per cent are of working age (15–59 years), of whom (in spite of rapid industrialisation) 73.5 per cent continue to work in agriculture. The education system is Thai in orientation, with the Thai language the main medium of instruction throughout the school and university system.

There is a high literacy rate of 94.8 per cent (male) and 91.3 per cent (female).

Thai people adhere to the tenets of the Buddhist traditional wisdom of Annata that all entities are insubstantial, without permanent or enduring self-identity; and that nothing in the person is fixed, the self being ever changing, so enabling the person who does not like what he or she is to become otherwise. Indeed the self is construed as illusory and the main cause of all conflicting states of mind (Roccasalvo 1981).

Negara Brunei Darussalam is a Muslim Sultanate. With large petroleum assets and reserves Brunei is among the richest countries in the region, albeit one of the smallest in terms of land area, with only 5,770 square kilometres. Of its population of 294,000, 64 per cent are Malays, and 20 per cent ethnic Chinese, most of whom are Buddhist, and the official language is Malay. Education is free to university level for those who qualify. The population structure is young, with 34 per cent of the population below 14 years.

Indonesia, a predominantly Muslim country, is a chain of 13,500 islands on the Malay Archipelago, straddling the Indian Ocean and the South China Sea. With an ethnically diverse population of 203.5 million (though a Javanese majority), Indonesia is the largest and most populous country in the region. Malay is the official language and the main medium of instruction in the education system, though Dutch and English are used widely in government and trade. As with other South-East Asian countries, though still basically agricultural, Indonesia's economy is beginning to shift towards manufacturing industry.

The Philippines are an island archipelago between the Philippine Sea and the South China Sea. The 73.2 million population is 95.5 per cent Malay, of whom 91.5 per cent profess Christianity, with only 4 per cent Muslim. Tagalog is the official language, with English widely used in government, education and trade.

The sub-region of Indochina consists of Cambodia, Laos and Vietnam, countries which experienced war and strife from the end of World War Two to the very recent past, with desperate social and economic consequences. Recent increases in political stability and economic resurgence have led to increased international trade, though at present only Vietnam qualifies for membership of ASEAN. As a result of colonisation French is spoken widely, although the official language remains the indigenous one of each country (Khmer, Lao and Vietnamese), with English widely used in trade and official communications.

The majority of the population are Buddhist; life expectancy is low (49.5 years in Cambodia, 52.2 years in Laos and 65.7 years for Vietnam). Cambodia, with a literacy rate of 35 per cent, and Laos with 50 per cent have the lowest literacy rates in the South-East Asian region.

EDUCATION AND LEARNING STYLES

The various secondary education system in South-East Asia aims to produce versatile graduates with both an overall general education and the skills suited to meet the challenges of a rapidly developing country. This entails providing individuals with adequate knowledge of various learning styles and strategies. Green and Parker (1989) demonstrate the existence of a relationship between learning styles and student decisions on academic-major and job interest, science interest and numerical aptitude. The challenge facing educationalists is to enhance students' understanding of how to learn, while also helping them monitor and manage their learning styles. It follows that learning style is an important element in the teaching–learning process.

It is the responsibility of educational institutions to create a conducive learning environment, assisting students to master as many ways as possible of acquiring knowledge in a spirit of reciprocity with academic staff. In this regard institutions can assist individual students with their experiential learning development. Kolb (1984) identifies the three developmental stages of experiential learning as acquisition, specialisation and integration. Increasingly within higher education specialisation rather than integrative scholarship has characterised the curriculum as, in the rapidly developing economic climate of much of South-East Asia, workplace demands have increasingly influenced the mind-sets of the curriculum developers: competition is acute, as is the need to supply ready-to-work graduates.

Specialisation has inevitably led to a linear developmental growth at the expense of more dynamic multi-faceted creative academic pathways that, arguably, should be opened for students. It is not surprising that course transfers are becoming more prevalent, for mismatches between learning styles and the learning demands of the different disciplines accentuate the difficulties faced by students in coping with the differing academic demands of any specific specialism.

Over time the impact of specialisation may contribute to the formation of a correspondingly specific learning orientation. Individuals whose learning styles are not congruent with the specialised disciplines they are studying may manifest increasingly problematic performance and experience growing discomfort. All such students potentially need assistance, but for South-East Asian students studying overseas the scenario is complicated by several factors to do with adjustment, motivation and achievement.

RESEARCH FINDINGS ON STUDENT LEARNING AND ACHIEVEMENT

Several studies have been conducted on Malaysian student learning and achievement. In a study in the United States, Yusoff Ismail (1982) indicated significant relationships between achievement motivation and learning styles among Malaysian students, with students with high scores in achievement motivation being more likely to be abstract conceptualisers and those with low scores on achievement motivation being associated with the concrete experience domain. Another study of 216 Diploma of Education students in Malaysia produced a negative significant relationship between achievement motivation with concrete experience and reflective observation learning domains, and a positive significant relationship between achievement motivation with abstract conceptualisation and active experimentation domains (Yusoff Ismail 1986). However among male students ($n = 79$) there was a positive relationship between achievement motivation with active experimentation, and a negative relationship between achievement motivation with concrete experience and reflective observation domains; among female students, there was a significant relationship between achievement motivation with active experimentation domain ($n = 137$). The study also reported a significant difference between all the learning styles of the students, divergers, assimilators, convergers and accommodators with achievement motivation ($F(3, 212) = 8.839, p < .05$).

Abdul Halim Othman (1985) reported that variations in life-change stress may explain differences in perception of adjustment problems among Malay students overseas. Studies have indicated various causes of adjustment problems. Selye (1977) indicated that cross-cultural stress might emanate from a lack of friendly social contact and an obligation to follow customs and practices. A study conducted on seventy-two Malaysian students in Canada reported that male and older students from urban areas with an ability to speak more than two languages experienced low acculturative stress (Berry and Kostovcik 1983). Abdul Halim Othman (1986), in a relationship study on life-change stress with selected educational and demographic factors on a sample of Malaysian Malay students in the United States, found life-change stress to be higher among female than male students ($t (291) = -2.21, p < .028$). A higher life-change stress was also reported among single as opposed to married students ($t(291) = -2.00, p < .047$); in an ANOVA analysis the younger age groups (< 25 years) reported higher mean life changes scores than the older age groups (> 26 years) ($F(3,289) = 4.21, p < .006$). No significant difference was found in family background between subjects from urban and rural areas, and significant relationships were found between life-change stress and academic, personal and social problems.

Relationship studies on learning, stress and achievement have heightened our understanding of problems which influence student achievement; for example a study of a group of 188 low-achieving university students in Malaysia indicated that achievement motivation training can increase levels of achievement by means of a planned and structured training approach ($F(2,124) = 4.31, p < .05$) (Habibah and Wan Rafei 1994).

Wan Rafei (1980) found higher achievement motivation among Chinese than Malay or Indian students; Habibah and Wan Rafei (1994) showed that Chinese students benefited more from achievement motivation training than other ethnic groups, though a further study found that Malay students had the highest level of achievement motivation and a more positive attitude towards learning than Chinese or Indian students. Male students had greater control of self than female students (female Malaysian students being more fatalistic) and engineering students had the most positive study habits, a finding possibly indicative of the need for students in a more challenging discipline to be more systematic in planning an effective learning strategy (Habibah and Wan Rafei 1995).

Adjustment and academic performance may be influenced by learning styles. Kolb and Goldman (1973) showed that mismatches of majors or specialisation affect academic performance for economics and mechanical engineering undergraduates. Kolb described learning as a social process consisting of two dimensions: grasping and transforming information (Kolb 1984): information is grasped through concrete experience or abstract conceptualisation, the one involving feelings, the other emphasising thinking as the main domain; and transformed through reflective observation or active experimentation. The former involves internalisation, the latter emphasises an active external effort toward participatory experience. From these domains Kolb developed a four-stage sequence in the learning cycle process – concrete experience, reflective observation, abstract conceptualisation and active experimentation. The resulting learning styles are those of divergers, assimilators, convergers, and accommodators.

Othman Mohamed (1994) conducted studies on learning styles and plotted the overall profile of the Malaysian secondary school students from the mean identified by the various learning styles domain of the LSI. A kitelike learning styles profile of the students is shown as in Figure 10.1.

The intersections plotted from the resulting AC–CE and the AE–RO scales computed for the mean differences of the LSI determined the placement of the four learning styles on the quadrants: divergers, assimilators, convergers and accommodators (see Figure 10.2).

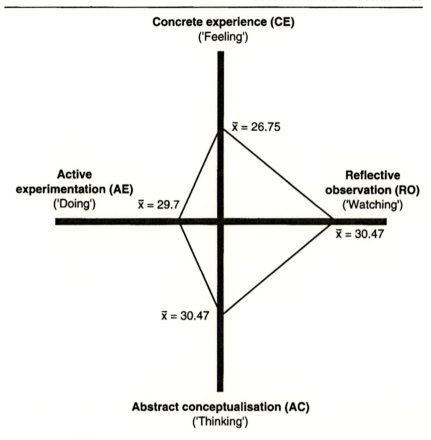

Figure 10.1 Learning style domain of Malaysian secondary school students

No significance was found in the mean differences of the LSI scales CE $(F(2,268) = 1.132, p > .05)$; RO $(F(2,268) = 0.25, p > .05$; AC $(F(2,268) = 1.05, p > .05)$; AE $(F(2,268) = 0.79, p > .05)$ with the dependent variable academic specialisation (Othman Mohamed 1994). A significant difference was, however, found for the concrete experience scale with gender $(F(1,273) = 5.86, p < .05)$. The mean for males was 27.66, SD of 5.41; for females it was 26.03, SD of 5.65. Significant difference was also detected for the reflective observation scale $(F(1,273) = 7.69, p < .05)$. The mean for males was 32.13, SD of 5.17; for females it was 33.95, SD of 5.57.

No significant difference was detected on the mean differences between the LSI scales with either urban or rural origin of the students. Significant differences were found in the active experimentation scale between Malay and non-Malay students $(F(1,273) = 7.89, p < .05)$. The mean for the Malay students was 30.25 with SD 4.87; for non-Malay students it was 28.47, SD 4.82 (Othman Mohamed, 1994).

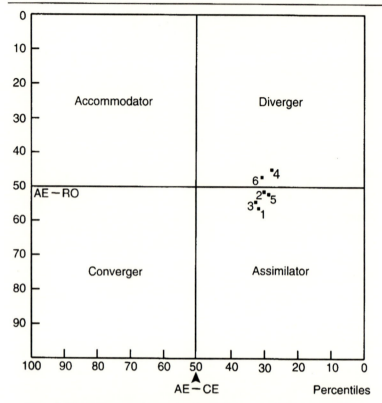

Key: 1. Overall secondary school students; 2. science students;
3. vocational students; 4. arts students; 5. female secondary school students;
6. male secondary school students

Figure 10.2 Learning style type grid of Malaysian secondary school students

Learning styles labels were detected only for two quadrants, divergers and assimilators on the LSI quadrants. The *t*-test analysis on the ethnicity variables indicated significance on the assimilators quadrant ($t(272) = 2.39, p < .05$). The mean value for Bumiputera subjects was –2.59 with SD 8.65; for non-Bumiputeras it was –5.34 with SD 8.86.

Overall these results suggest a pattern of learning style for Malaysian secondary school students with a bias on the reflective observation domain, average emphasis on the concrete experience and abstract conceptualisation domains, but minimal activity on the active experimentation dimension (Figure 10.1). Figure 10.2 suggests the preferred learning style of Malaysian secondary school students is assimilators.

Specific learning style patterns also emerge from the profiling. Predominant characteristics of students in the diverger quadrant are male, rural, arts, and Bumiputera Malay; while students in the assimilator quadrant are more likely to be female, urban, science/ vocational, and ethnic Chinese or Indian. Male students were oriented towards the concrete experience domain and female students towards the reflective observation domain; socialisation influenced male students towards impersonal and logical learning approaches; female students were inclined towards internalisation and the emphasis of feelings in their learning. These differences require attention if the needs of South-East Asian students in the West are to be met.

THE HELPING PROCESS

These elements of South-East Asian student profiles help elucidate the learning frameworks they are likely to employ. Factors such as motivation, life-change stress, learning styles and habits are relevant to performance, while demographic variables offer indicators of students' psychological readiness to grasp learning opportunities in an overseas environment. Helping students learn requires various approaches, and many possibilities exist, though the common element of any strategy is the student's own readiness to seek help, exposing him or herself to a significant other in a meaningful relationship.

Respect for an elder is embedded in the cultural milieu of South-East Asian students. Familial cohesion and piety plus the traditions of the Chinese clan, which include both cooperation and competitiveness, influence the motivation of Chinese students, while the traditions of respect for parents and teachers, group cohesion, faith and obedience to Islamic traditions within a cooperative community environment mould Malay students. Phenomena such as globalisation, information technology and Malaysia's determination to be a fully industrialised nation by the year 2020 have not fundamentally changed cultural characteristics of this kind. Hence students from South-East Asia have a sense of purpose, a commitment to fulfil any contract with a sponsor as well as to fulfil the personal ambition of achieving academic and professional competence in their field of studies.

COUNSELLING APPROACHES IN LEARNING

As we have seen, research on achievement motivation, life-change stress and learning styles provides indicators of appropriate counselling techniques and approaches to South-East Asians studying overseas. Nevertheless students' own social support systems have also to be taken into consideration. South-East Asian students are familiar with well defined and structured role preferences, and there is a normal expectation of self-restraint and formality in social interactions (Fernandez 1988). These learned behaviours may hinder social interactions in the

West, those who shy away from social interactions possibly being inundated with feelings of loneliness and helplessness, leading to an emotional disturbance which may exacerbate any academic problems.

It follows that a strong support system is necessary. Maznah (1993) studied social support preferences in addressing academic problems among upper secondary school students in Malaysia. The study, using Pearson's (1986) typology of twelve socially supportive behaviours, found three significant behaviour preferences: *guidance, knowledge* and *acceptance* (in order of perceived importance). Guidance reflects a need for advice, direction and spiritual guidance; knowledge emphasises information, expertise or instruction; acceptance is the sense of being respected and understood.

Guidance and knowledge suggest a need for cognitive related assistance consistent with academic problems; acceptance addresses needs of a more personal kind. Nevertheless, all categories, including love, encouragement, example, companionship, acceptance, guidance, comfort, giving/loaning, knowledge, honesty, and advocacy, ranged from important to very important, suggesting a need for multi-faceted help in the face of academic problems.

While clearly the nature of assistance required may shift between the onset of a problem and its resolution (Pearlin 1985), the multi-faceted support needs of students indicate that academic difficulties may be intertwined with other problems. Developing a social support system which helps sustain mental health by gratifying basic affiliation needs, maintaining self-identity and enhancing self-esteem, may therefore be a helpful strategy for overseas South-East Asian students (Cohen and Wills 1985; Pearson 1990; Shumaker and Brownell 1984). Moreover, such support may alleviate stressful incidents and increase students' confidence and capacity for personal control.

STAGES OF ADJUSTMENT OF OVERSEAS STUDENTS

Early in their stay South-East Asian students overseas undergo a process of acculturation. Atkinson, Morten, and Sue's (1979) study of the acculturation of minority groups, utilised by Fernandez (1988) in describing the acculturation of the South-East Asian students in the United States, proposes a Minority Identity Development model consisting of:

- conformity;
- dissonance;
- resistance and immersion;
- introspection and synergetic articulation;
- awareness.

Academic success is imperative for most South-East Asian students. For government-sponsored students enormous pressure results from contractual obligations as well as the need to save face, while differences in teaching and learning strategies further aggravate early adjustment anxieties. An awareness among counsellors and educators of the paradigm stages of adjustment of South-East Asian students will help reduce misperception while offering a framework within which to understand students' background and culture.

I propose the Role Identity and Integrative Maturity model as the optimal means of describing the learning adjustment of South-East Asians studying overseas. In this model South-East Asian students undergo a four-stage development process in their stay overseas:

- orientation and autonomy;
- transitions of self-worth;
- consolidation of role identity;
- competence and integrative maturity.

The orientation and autonomy stage: the moment of truth for South-East Asian students arriving in the host country is their ability to adjust well at the start to an experience which will be full of novelty, challenges and threats. They have to learn many skills in adjusting to new food, clothing, legal systems, housing, weather, commercial and financial transactions, social interactions and education – in short the whole plethora of a new culture. In the face of such demands their characteristic single-minded determination to succeed educationally is a considerable asset (Wehrly 1988).

This stage may last for two to three months, and entail stressful situations resulting from a lack of knowledge about systems prevailing in the host country. The excitement which stems from the novelty of being in a new environment only lasts so long as day-to-day needs can be met with ease, and this can only happen to the extent that students adjust to, for example, new social interactions, differing cues of language verbalisations and listening, food, and the teaching and learning environment. When the novelty is over, the stage can be characterised by homesickness and loneliness. Wehrly (1988) indicates that emotions may become especially intense for students unable to harness an immediate support system where they are studying.

The stage may also be landmarked by an opportunity to strive towards an independent, autonomous life style. For many students this will be their first attempt to live alone. Given all these uncertainties it is not surprising that, after their arrival at the host country, there often exist feelings of profound ambivalence.

The transitions of self-worth stage: lasting between three and six months, this stage normally entails students meeting the daily challenges of functioning in an alien culture with different values and expectations. This period can be the most stressful, and one characterised by ambivalence between resisting and complying with a new, different and questionably appropriate set of demands. The size of the financial commitment and the pressures on personal expenditure become increasingly clear, and worries about this and the need to create an expenditure routine can be overwhelming. It is not always understood that by no means all ˙overseas South-East Asian students are from wealthy families.

The normal expectations of western academic life too may be different when viewed from the South-East Asian perspective. Time-frame dimensions and punctuality requirements are different, and a student must adjust to the fast-paced time frame of the west. There is inevitable uncertainty as to whether they are meeting the expectations of the taskmaster: academic performance is still an unknown quantity at this stage in spite of the fact that sponsored students have demonstrated high levels of academic ability and undergone rigorous screening procedures.

Adjustment to the cultural milieu of the larger environment poses what in the West would be termed existential questions about one's self and the nature of one's own culture, customs and mores. Religious and cultural differences become important in day-to-day decision making; the extent to which one knows, values and holds on to one's sense of self-worth is an important dimension in the transitional 'mix and choice' between what has been learned in the home country and the complexities and constraints of the new environment.

The consolidation of role identity stage: during this stage awareness of the various systems becomes more pronounced. Learning needs may have been identified, though without the guided assertiveness of implementation; social interactions are slowly gathered and emphasis is placed on a collaborative effort, usually among the same national group (Wehrly 1988). There is increased understanding of and adaptation to the manner of financial transactions, such as utilising cheque book facilities. For many students the cheque book constitutes an important aspect of identity, for such a facility is rarely available to students in South-East Asia.

Many aspects of day-to-day experience, from weather to food, become part of the consolidation process, and if all goes well evidence of successful experimentation and a new awareness of self emerge. Nevertheless, for South-East Asian students the consolidation of self within the host environment coexists with the role identity which constantly demands educational success, reminding them that this is the primary purpose of their presence in the host country.

The competence and integrative maturity stage: this stage is characterised by the development of hope and confidence. It allows many the freedom to assume higher status and share their successes and failures with newer cohorts.

Most students are acutely aware of their family obligations. For those who are privately sponsored there is a sense of urgency to complete the course, while government-sponsored students become increasingly conscious of their contractual obligations. Some students will seek assistance and information about career pathing and opportunities. For most, returning home and contributing to meeting their nation's human development requirements remains an inspirational motivator to successful course completion, and this fact should not be undermined by a more characteristic western cynicism.

APPROPRIATENESS OF COUNSELLING PROCEDURES AND TECHNIQUES

Many counselling theories are premised upon personal growth through self-exploration (Fernandez 1988). The fact that South-East Asian students are characteristically reserved in regard to their personal problems does not mean they are necessarily unable or unwilling to disclose modestly to a counsellor matters pertaining to their immediate problems. At the beginning phase of the helping encounter the use of appropriate counselling skills and attending procedures is necessary to develop and maintain a trusting relationship, and this author believes that counsellor and educator characteristics of openness, genuineness and honesty deemed appropriate and effective in western counselling theory (see for example Truax and Carkhuff 1967) are equally appropriate in counselling South-East Asian students. The universal elements of a trans-cultural relationship pertaining to the credibility of the helper and the ability of the student to benefit from the helping encounter take precedence in the early stages of the relationship (Sue and Zane 1987).

Initially an overall empathic understanding is necessary for attending to these students. Students who study overseas have undergone a basic education of at least eleven years at primary and secondary levels. Over the past ten years many schools in Singapore, Indonesia, Negara Brunei Darussalam and the Philippines as well as Malaysia have introduced guidance and counselling services, so such services and expectations of the counselling relationship may not be alien.

While a pure form of person-centred therapy may not be appropriate, given South-East Asian students' likely expectation of a more directive approach (Maznah 1993), skills such as paraphrasing, reflecting and interpreting may valuably assist them in their task of the realisation of self. My counselling experience indicates, however, that such skills must not be used in isolation from the 'forward control' nature of the helper in the relationship. Subtle suggestions and alternatives as forms of encouragement can go a long way towards gaining a student's confidence, and hence facilitating the disclosure of personal distress.

Students experience various kinds of problems that need support. Church (1982) lists the most important as language difficulties, financial problems, adjusting to the new education system, homesickness, adjusting to social customs and norms, and, for some students, racial discrimination. Such problems could well be anticipated and encountered during the orientation and autonomy stage of the students' educational sojourn.

The helping relationship during the orientation stage is also a transition period marked by growing awareness on the part of the student. But while the identification of goal development is useful for students in need of assistance, and students who encounter assistance during this stage may well benefit from awareness of specific goals that could be worked together with the educator and counsellor, there is no clear-cut demarcation between different stages; nor are subsequent ramifications of procedures and counselling techniques rigid for each stage in the students' development.

During the transition of self-worth stage, distress may be at its peak. Basic counselling and attending skills are still necessary irrespective of a student's background. With South-East Asian students in particular it is necessary at this juncture to augment suggestive encouragement techniques with specific cognitive awareness techniques in order to introduce a reasoned purpose for a sense of hope to be instilled in the student.

Clear emphatic understanding will help enhance the overall awareness of the student in translating vague uncertainties and apprehensions into a specific effort towards goal development. South-East Asians studying overseas are generally high achievers, hard working, internally focused and with a highly developed sense of cognitive awareness. These considerable strengths should be utilised by helpers.

Resistance to change is common in any adjustment development process. The author's counselling practice has affirmed that reflective awareness procedures in tandem with cognitive restructuring techniques assist in reducing resistance and overcoming introversion. Helpers of South-East Asian students need a directive approach to the planned restructuring of false and ambiguous goals. Such an approach is consistent with the students' learning domain, especially that of Malay students, whose bias in the reflective-concrete domain is prominent (Othman Mohamed 1994).

During the helping process, reflective suggestions of alternative pathways to goal development may be given for consideration. Immediate goals should be encouraged, promoting a sense of hope and confidence and converting small steps into larger pathways. Students need to address problems encountered during this intermediate stage assertively: the self has to be adjusted towards the system in the host country. There is a Malay proverb describing this phenomenon: 'When a person enters the cattle pen he moos; when he enters the goat pen he bleats'. In the process, the adjusted self is disciplined without losing self-worth.

For many students, their period abroad is one of identification of self and of independence (Chickering 1972). At the stage of consolidation of role identity helpers should impart clear options in a purposive manner for consideration. Techniques such as imagery are often useful as a way of combining cognitive thoughts and reflective suggestions, and this combination can be a powerful helping tool not only for goal direction but also for the reinforcement of specific learning activities.

Helpers must know their own culture well and ideally the students' culture too. Helpers cannot be culture-encapsulated (Pederson 1976) and must be aware that for South-East Asian students respect for the authority of significant others is present as a legacy of the home upbringing. Hence a person with authority is usually held in high regard. However, students' acceptance of educators and helpers to assist them with their academic problems need not be related to preferences for control and authority (Rusnani Abdul Kadir 1993).

At this point students are aware of their sense of purpose, and learning can occur through observation, participation and explicit communication (Schild 1962). Over time, culture shock, identified by such symptoms as anxiety, irritability, feelings of helplessness, and longing for a predictable environment (Oberg 1960) is likely to lessen in view of students' increasing conformity to many day-to-day practices and experiences. The competence and integrative maturity stage is hence likely to be characterised by efforts to conform and adapt to what are perceived as the positive attitudes and practices of the host country.

Helpers must understand and acknowledge students' growing confidence and sense of achievement. For many it is a relief to have come towards the end of their stay, and reflections over what they have experienced and achieved are common. Accompanying any sense of accomplishment are likely to be different kinds of anxiety and uncertainties. Feelings of restlessness over the prospect of a meaningful career in the home country may become preoccupations. For students who accepted sponsorship immediately after secondary school for the opportunity of pursuing a higher education, and who may have reached some form of career maturity during their sojourn in the host country, ambivalence regarding a choice of career is probable. Although the main priority will continue to be academic success, feelings of homesickness and ambivalence may even lead to a surprising complacency in the immediate task of studying for good grades.

The demands of preparing for the transition from student life to the world of work must be instilled in a student's mind. For students who have been staying for several years in the host country, preparing for readjustment to life at home may be important, for such is the speed of social change in South-East Asia that students' home countries may differ markedly from that which they left some years earlier, and a transient culture shock in reverse may occur. In this regard, current information is easily accessible through relevant Homepages via the Internet. It is anyway wise for helpers to browse through the Internet to familiarise themselves with up-to-date economic, political and cultural information about the student's home country.

For helpers and educators, to find the best counselling approaches for South-East Asian students is a great and continuing challenge. The communication revolution and the globalisation of knowledge have taken a quantum leap in recent years, rendering temporary transmigration increasingly common among students all over the world, but in no way diminishing the need for nations to acknowledge the need for, and to provide, support systems for these wandering scholars of the late twentieth- and early twenty-first centuries.

Chapter 11

Supervising overseas students
Problem or opportunity?

Elizabeth S. Todd

INTRODUCTION

This chapter considers the learning support needs of students from overseas. Little detailed research exists into overseas students' experiences of studying and lecturers' experiences of supervising and teaching them (though for notable exceptions see Kinnell 1990; Ballard and Clanchy 1991; Harris 1995). Given the importance of overseas students to the income and culture of UK universities (Sherlock 1995; Woods and Woods 1995) and the widespread perception of them as problematic this is a surprising omission. Though there seems to be good practice in many universities little is documented about it.

In addition to research on students at UK universities (in particular those studying for an MEd at Newcastle University) I have drawn on research on overseas students, undergraduate and postgraduate, from other anglophone universities, principally in Australia, USA, and the University of the South Pacific (USP) in Fiji. I recognise that there will be differences in the cultures of these universities and students which may limit the extent to which such research can be applied to the UK context. My analysis relates primarily to postgraduate research and taught students, but much is also relevant to the teaching of undergraduate students.

How students generally learn and the effects of different teaching approaches have received much attention (Entwistle and Hounsell 1975; Brown and Atkins 1988; Entwistle 1992), but little of this work relates specifically to overseas students. Marton and his colleagues have drawn on students' own experiences to identify two different approaches to learning: deep and surface approaches (Marton and Saljo 1976a, 1976b, 1984). A broadly defined information-processing model can be applied to this finding, conceptualising different approaches to learning as leading to different levels of processing. Approaches to learning affect learning outcome (Svensson 1977; Saljo 1982), and distinctive differences exist in the development of people's conceptions of learning (Saljo 1979, 1982).

Social and emotional factors have been shown to influence learning (Rogers 1969, 1978) and students' metacognitive skills (awareness of the way they learn) affect learning outcomes (Ausubel 1978; Entwistle 1992). There is also an extensive literature on socio-linguistic factors relating to student learning, some of which will be drawn upon in this paper.

Overall there is far greater awareness today that learning outcomes reflect not just individual student characteristics or particular teaching methods, but the socio-cultural context in which learning takes place (Rogoff and Lave 1984; Entwistle 1992). This perspective is reflected in the present chapter, which argues that students' problems can be conceptualised as manifestations of cultural differences in beliefs about the construction of knowledge.

In this chapter I first investigate to what extent study problems of overseas students can be understood as problems in English language. I argue that quite often the problem lies not so much in language difficulties but in students employing study strategies that have worked in their previous academic lives and finding that this is not what is expected in the UK. I explore how differences in expectation can lead both students and staff to frame the other as problematic, or as 'failing', and how cultural differences in the construction of knowledge underlie these expectations. Moreover, such differences are not characteristic of overseas students alone, but can also be applied to local students. I look at ways we can structure student supervision to reduce problems and reframe previous experience in a positive light.

Are overseas students to be seen as problematic principally because they demand so much of our time? Or are they to be seen in terms of opportunity? They provide us with an opportunity to understand more about teaching and learning processes as we find ways to meet their needs. Perhaps more importantly, improving postgraduate education for overseas students would help us develop 'an appropriate...culture which would help equip us for operating in the emerging bi-polar world of the twenty-first century' (Woods and Woods 1995: 212).

HOW MUCH OF A PROBLEM ARE ENGLISH LANGUAGE DIFFICULTIES?

Many overseas students have difficulties with English language. One survey suggests that only 12 per cent of overseas students are first-language English speakers (United Kingdom Council for Overseas Student Affairs 1989). Another, of 1,800 students, found that 34 per cent experienced problems with English and that for 13 per cent this was their most serious problem (Williams, Woodhall and O'Brien 1986). Students differ in language skills, though Commonwealth students are less likely than others to have difficulties, having been more likely to have experienced English as a means of instruction at school (UKCOSA 1989; Nixon 1993). However, there are wide variations in English language proficiency in every country.

For example in Burns' (1993) study of the psychosocial problems of undergraduate students at Curtin University, Australia (133 from overseas and 76 resident in Australia) half the overseas students rated themselves as being less than competent to use language effectively. Writing caused the most problems, reading the least but hardly any local students perceived themselves as inadequate in these areas, though some rated themselves as poor. Malaysian students rated themselves lower than did students from Hong Kong or Singapore. Samuelowicz (1987) obtained questionnaire responses from 145 members of staff and 136 overseas students at the University of Queensland. Over half ranked language difficulties as 'very important' or 'important' and 60 per cent expected language to be a problem. Burke (1986) found that under-graduate overseas students reported their major study difficulty as being in understanding lectures, asking questions, participating in class discussions, formal essay writing and selecting appropriate English to express ideas.

Much attention has therefore been given to language issues in teaching overseas students. However, to see their problems as solely arising from linguistic limitations is an oversimplification. If language problems were central we might expect students' difficulties to be solved by upgrading language skills, and that more stringent use of English language tests at the point of selection would lead to a reduction in study difficulties. I will look at the way problems in either course of action lead to an alternative framing of student difficulties.

Ballard (1991) argues that improving vocabulary or grammar, or editing essays or thesis chapters does not necessarily lead to higher grades. Language problems are sequential: once one is solved another surfaces. For example, as difficulties in listening and speaking decrease students may become more aware of their difficulties in assimilating the quantity of required reading and in negotiating academic writing. On the other hand language help can make a student's writing easier to read, and therefore examiners are more likely to identify problems of content. Ballard argues that it is more effective to help students think about and express their ideas in order to increase their capacity to write what they mean.

Some writers argue for a stricter use of language-proficiency tests at selection. However, studies on the ability of English language proficiency to predict academic success are inconclusive (May and Bartlett 1995). Experience at Newcastle would support this: students may have good language skills but be unable to negotiate analytic writing in conventional western terms. The opposite is also true: students with poor language scores can do high-quality work. Test scores can fail to reflect students' proficiency through deficiencies in administration (language tests can be used in a discriminatory way by not being applied with uniform consistency) or validity. Tests may also be insensitive to particular group characteristics – for example students from Papua New Guinea often have difficulties with register, using colloquial language in an academic context; those from an African country often use language very formally and legalistically, which is just as inappropriate in modern academic communication (May and Bartlett 1995).

It can be easy for lecturers and students to see language skills as the source of problems partly because students and staff expect them to be so. However, it can still come as a shock to students if, as Ballard (1991) reminds us, they were previously seen as having very good English. Whilst language skills are very important, the major problem for students has less to do with difficulties in language skills than with ways of studying. Students may simply not understand what is involved in writing, thinking and talking in the UK, particularly at postgraduate level. Cultural differences in studying can lead to differences in student and staff expectations about what is required (Ballard 1995). Such issues are now widely accepted by many university departments involved in supporting students' study and language skills (Ballard and Clanchy 1991; Ballard 1991; Connell and Hodson 1995; May and Bartlett 1995) and by educational linguists who argue that 'genre provides a better starting point than grammar for relating education and language' (May and Bartlett 1995: 6; for a general overview see Hammond 1987).

ARE THERE CULTURAL DIFFERENCES IN STUDYING?

We should be able the better to understand the issues involved in teaching overseas students by examining the views of lecturers and overseas students themselves. Some lecturers characterise the learning strategies of overseas students as relying on rote learning and memorisation, and being unable to participate in class discussions or to think critically and analytically (Benn 1961; Phillips et al. 1985; Bradley and Bradley 1984; Samuelowicz 1987; Ballard and Clanchy 1991; Ballard 1991, 1995; Nixon 1993; Stapleton 1995). However, this is not surprising if we consider how students' educational backgrounds have shaped their expectations. Whereas in the UK postgraduate students are required to demonstrate that they appreciate that other findings are not to be simply accepted and reproduced, and to show that they understand how knowledge in a certain discipline is constructed (Bloor and Bloor 1991), many overseas students achieved success by reproducing what their teacher gave them. Many students believe there are correct answers, and such answers should be supplied by the lecturer. They quote the lecturer and expect to be rewarded, but to many lecturers this is inappropriate.

Long experience of memorising and respecting the written word may lead students to try to read everything on a reading list in impossible detail (Bradley and Bradley 1984). When students are required to reproduce the teacher's ideas there is no need for self-directed research, discussion or critical thinking. Not only this, but students often come from an environment where they are not allowed to criticise teachers, raise questions that could embarrass them or correct them if they make a mistake. It is therefore not surprising if they find it hard to put forward their own ideas.

Such differences in expectations can lead both lecturers and students to characterise the behaviour of the other as deficient and failing. For example an MEd student from Hong Kong at Newcastle University told me that in his first few weeks he believed the lecturers to be lazy, since they did not prepare detailed notes for him to memorise, but gave him reading lists and an open question to research in the library. Similarly some lecturers complain that students expect to be spoon-fed and feel this indicates a lack of ability.

Many overseas students have little experience of some of our teaching methods. For example, Samuelowicz (1987) found that only 28 per cent of overseas students at the University of Queensland were familiar with tutorials, and 18 per cent with any form of group discussions. However, students may realise there are different expectations of them in their new learning environment (Samuelowicz 1987; Ballard 1991; Burns 1994; Landbeck and Mugler 1994) and have reasonable awareness of their own study difficulties (Bloor and Bloor 1991). Burns (1994) found that overseas students rated themselves significantly ($p < 0.05$) less competent than did local students at almost all academic skills (expressing ideas clearly, using logical argument, taking notes in lectures). Students may have difficulty leaving behind old behaviours and be unsure of what the new expectations are. They may therefore need more reassurance that their work is appropriate; this may help account for lecturers, who may not recognise and give credit for the major changes students are already making, characterising them as very demanding. For example, Brunei students report talking more in the class than ever before in their entire education (Bradley and Bradley 1984).

Overseas students may have very different expectations of the teacher–pupil relationship, the roles of student and lecturer and the locus of responsibility for learning. One would expect students who are used to seeing teachers as the source of knowledge to view them as mostly responsible for the level of students' achievement. This view was confirmed by students on the MEd course at Newcastle, while lecturers on the same course believed students had responsibility for what happened – albeit that when students were in danger of failing most lecturers behaved as if the failure was their own. Students from some cultures may expect teachers to adopt an almost parental role towards them. For example Vietnamese students are quoted as expecting lecturers to help with any problems and guide them to the right path in life (Bradley and Bradley 1984). Feedback following course evaluations indicated that the MEd students at Newcastle valued being able to talk to their dissertation supervisor about personal problems which could impede study, though some students might, through concerns about loss of face, find it hard to approach tutors with such problems (Burns 1994).

If overseas students experience formalised relationships with their teachers at home they may find it hard to adjust to the relative informality of academic relationships in the UK. The Newcastle MEd students, while acknowledging that such differences in teacher–student relationships existed, appreciated this informality and the scope it gave for discussing a wide range of problems. This is not a universal experience: Burns (1994) found that most students at an Australian university, overseas and local, felt staff were hardly aware of their problems, whether academic, social, emotional or health-related, and lacked interest in helping them; only a third of overseas students even felt staff were interested in helping with academic problems.

ARE THERE DIFFERENT APPROACHES TO KNOWLEDGE?

Differences in expectations between students and lecturers can be variously understood, but all seem to relate to the way authority is viewed and knowledge constructed. Ballard (1991) suggests this issue should be considered in terms of a continuum of attitudes to knowledge. At one extreme is a *conserving* attitude in which students reproduce what is given to them, at the other an *extending* attitude which advocates questioning and extending what the student is given. At the far end of the extending attitude is a *speculative approach* particularly characteristic of postgraduates.

It is likely that many overseas students will be used to a more conserving education system than exists in the UK, though claims that particular cultural attitudes to knowledge produce approaches to learning which in turn result in related teaching and learning strategies (Ballard and Clanchy 1991) ignore the complex relationships between culture and learning. They also fail to recognise the validity and complexity of different cultures' approaches to knowledge (for evidence of the efficacy of the repetitive learning approaches characteristic of Confucian-heritage students see Chan and Drover's chapter in this book), and the influences of western education on other countries. Characterising overseas students as coming from more conserving societies is likely to stereotype such students as problematic in a way which leads to an underestimation of their skills and abilities. Differences in the learning approaches of overseas students should therefore be understood as resulting from valid formative experiences, not be seen as deficiencies or the consequences of 'poor English' (Ballard 1995).

A COMPLEX ANALYSIS OF ABILITY AND NEED

Generalisations about the learning strategies of overseas students may be incorrect in a way that hinders our ability to teach them. For example students from Pacific island countries are often described as learning by rote and being reluctant to adopt a more extending approach. However, Landbeck and Mugler (1994) found that this was an oversimplification, their research at the University of the South Pacific showing that students had two different meanings for learning. One was the process of acquiring knowledge or broadening existing knowledge and could be related to, amongst other things, the process of memorisation. The other was a deeper meaning denoting coming to an understanding of the knowledge. In spite of years of a conserving education system most students had adapted to the need for independent learning at university and demonstrated this latter approach.

Landbeck and Mugler also suggest that when students try to change, their efforts may be frustrated by systems we have put into place. When explaining their continued use of memorisation, most students referred not to their primary or secondary education but to their current higher education. Students were aware that in their university study they often relied on memorisation, but regretted this and said it came from the stressful demands of the examination system used by the university. This suggests that in the right setting even overseas students from a conserving society are capable of analytic thinking (Ballard 1991; Landbeck and Mugler 1994) and change (Hyland 1994, of Japanese students).

None of the overseas MEd students at Newcastle lives completely up to stereotypes, and as in all groups there are wide differences between students in terms of capabilities and willingness to embrace new situations. For example, contrary to cultural expectations a student from South-East Asia had experienced many opportunities for discussing her own ideas in her home university education, and in conventional western terms her standard of analytic writing was very high.

The literature often assumes that the needs of overseas students differ from those of home students. This is to ignore the cultural complexities of the UK and the fact that we can find evidence of the whole range of attitude-to-knowledge continuum in our own country, within institutions and between institutions and disciplines. The culture of the institution and the rules of academic writing are therefore often difficult for many UK students, including those who have English as their first language.

School leavers may require considerable help in making the transition to tertiary learning (Ballard 1991). May, Bartlett and Holzknecht (1994) found that some home students in Australia needed as much help as overseas students in coming to grips with issues such as being critical and analytical, how to write a research proposal and how to present work in writing and in seminars. They found that all students had difficulty in understanding exactly what was needed of them in postgraduate study. Similarly at Newcastle the dissertations of home postgraduate students are variable and sometimes poorly structured, possibly reflecting less supervision in the expectation that home students know how to write. However, those of overseas postgraduate students are often well structured but in a uniform way that probably reflects close supervision. It is therefore likely that some home postgraduate students have unmet supervision needs.

Academic problems are often very difficult to unravel, another factor which may lead lecturers to attribute difficulties too quickly to language or ability problems. Students are having to make several complex transitions, from graduate to postgraduate, from one academic culture to another, from being a teacher/education officer/researcher to being a student, from being someone who knows the rules to being someone who has to find out what they are (May and Bartlett 1995; Wheeler and Birtle 1993). Experience supervising a student from southern Africa illustrates how difficult it can be to' unravel the study problems of overseas students. By the end of the first term the student manifested both academic and health problems, was unable to sleep and was missing his young family. He returned home in the middle of the year to carry out field research and, though this was not without problems, when he returned he seemed a different person, able to focus on his research question and fully in command of how he wanted to write his thesis; his health was under control and sleep had returned. This experience taught me to be less hasty about making quick judgements about a student's capabilities.

However, it does not make solutions to students' problems any easier to find: a trip home will not be possible or even desirable for every student. Schneider and Fujishima (1995) discuss Zhang, a thirty year old native Chinese speaker from Taiwan. He experienced only limited academic success at a postgraduate course in the USA despite high ability, motivation and discipline. They suggest that familiarity with the larger university culture and disciplinary subcultures, including accepted patterns of interaction, are crucial in allowing students to adjust to the expectations of life in their new setting. Burns (1994) suggests from his literature survey that coping students have social contact with local students, are older, male, from an urban country, and have been in the host country for longer.

Viewing overseas students as problematic can create problems and reduce the benefits of cross-cultural dialogue. A colleague at Newcastle expressed concern that our overseas students might be deskilled by their time there. Most of our students are educational professionals in their own country, and although we try to encourage them to use and reflect on their experience they quickly fall into the role of students needing detailed guidance from the tutor. Nevertheless overseas students have by definition chosen to join the international community and we have to help them understand what is needed to participate in that community (Bloor and Bloor 1991). Indeed, some students choose our courses precisely because of the different study approach: for example a student from Hong Kong chose to study for his MEd in the UK rather than Hong Kong because it would force him to carry out more independent literature and field research.

It is easy to characterise students as lacking the ability to be critical and analytical. However, academic writing from other cultures suggests that criticism is not absent but expressed in different ways. Bloor and Bloor (1991) suggest that German and Polish writing is much more direct than British, while Japanese writing is far less direct. A Japanese MEd student confirmed this, explaining that in a Japanese academic article the reader would have to infer the writer's views from subtle signals, since there would never be direct criticism. In Polish there are no repetitions, and none of the paraphrasing or in-text summaries essential in English.

Bloch and Chi (1995) found far fewer critical citations in Chinese than in American social science articles (an average of 1 against 4), indicating that while taking a critical position may be acceptable and important in Chinese academic writing, criticism is differently expressed. The expression 'it is worthwhile to reconsider and discuss' was frequently used by Chinese writers to make an indirect criticism, as was the phrase 'some people have said', used without naming the people. In American academic writing, a different balance was found among various types of citations (background, supporting an argument, denoting criticism) in social science and science, indicating that writing happens in a particular way in different disciplines in American academic writing. It is not that some cultures are critical and others not, but that cultures express criticism in different ways. We may not recognise, in students' writing, their use of their own genres, or their attempts to adopt ours, simply perceiving a 'lack of critical dimension'. It follows that it may not be enough to ask students to write in a critical way; they may need more detailed help about exactly how to discuss and how to be critical (Bloor and Bloor 1991).

Similar issues arise with plagiarism, which is clearly understood as dishonesty in the West, but may reflect cultural differences in how we look at and use what has been written before, and more generally, in what constitutes private property. Bloch and Chi's (1995) investigation of the characteristics of citations in Chinese writing suggests that there plagiarism can be considered an expert strategy reflecting how composition has traditionally been taught. An MEd student from a northern African country thought it was legitimate to copy from books since he agreed with the ideas and found similar ones in many books. Bloor and Bloor (1991) suggest plagiarism may be a compensatory strategy for difficulties in language or lack of time and that, even for experienced writers, there is a fine line between acceptable and unacceptable use of sources. They talk of 'free and non-free' goods and point out that some ideas and terms have become so accepted that they can be used without reference. However, there is also the possibility that different cultures may not place the same taboo on plagiarism as does the West.

It is possible that we may be able to move to a position where we can allow overseas students to write in ways more consistent with their cultures without losing sight of our own ways of writing and thinking. Further research is needed to enable us to have a greater understanding of what students are doing, and how this relates to our disciplines. Such an understanding might enable us to regard overseas students as achieving a similar standard of analytic thinking and writing but expressing it in different ways. Debate is needed between us and our students about this, to discuss different genres and their relationships with different ways of conceptualising knowledge. As an intermediate position, students' prior cultural and learning experiences need to be recognised and valued by the university community (Keech 1994).

IMPLICATIONS FOR THE SUPERVISION OF OVERSEAS STUDENTS

Once lecturers look beyond language, student problems can seem so complicated that they feel powerless to address them, particularly if their solution depends upon a critical look at teaching and supervision methods. Kinnell (1990) claims that these problems typically arise from a mismatch between the needs of the students and the responses of the universities. But what kind of response is appropriate, who should be responsible for it, how should it happen, and what, exactly, should be communicated? Should help be given in stand-alone pre-sessional courses or in the process of, and integrated with, a student's course, or is there some other model?

Specialist language and study-support staff may have greater awareness of language and study-skill issues, but the help they can give is restricted by lack of discipline knowledge (Shaw 1996). There are also likely to be differences in focus between language and discipline specialists, the former focusing on presentation and the latter on content

(Bush 1994); as well as between individuals in all professional groups. There is evidence of inconsistency among lecturers both in determining criteria for grading written work and in identifying agreed criteria in specific essays (Leki 1995). Language and discipline specialists have complementary skills and should work together to allow early and accurate identification of problems, and to focus on the specific demands of the discipline (Keech 1994; May and Bartlett 1995). It is likely that certain centres and institutions are better equipped than others to cater for international students due both to the collection of experience of a cross-cultural context and to the nature of support they can provide.

There is disagreement in the literature as to the most appropriate model of support: should there be stand-alone courses? If so should they take place before postgraduate study commences or during the course? Or is an integrated model preferable? Preparatory programmes can help orientate students gradually into the desired study approaches, serving as an advance organiser of metacognitive skills. One example of this is the sixteen-week bridging programme provided by the Asian Institute for Technology in Thailand for postgraduate students from other Asia-Pacific countries. This course uses a learner centred approach and open-ended research tasks to strengthen students' ability to undertake self-directed learning in English. May and Bartlett (1995) describe preparatory courses provided for all students by the Australian National University on library and research skills, computing, writing, seminar presentation skills, cross-cultural communication and a range of personal adjustment areas, and report that students with problems are disproportionately likely to be those who have missed the courses.

Preparatory courses can help orientate students into desired study approaches, but it is only in actually taking a course that study demands become clear. Students gradually learn the different facets of postgraduate study by listening to lectures, taking part in seminars, preparing writing and receiving feedback. May et al. (1994) argue that the key to carrying out independent and innovative research is the quality of teaching and supervision during the course itself, as this helps establish a confidence and skill base. Such thinking has led some institutions to abandon preparatory courses (Ballard 1991), and several writers underline the importance of a discipline-based approach, since each discipline has slightly different genres, and requirements for writing, speaking and constructing knowledge (May et al. 1994). May and Bartlett (1995) aim their programmes equally at both overseas and home students, and argue against describing them as 'support', since this implies they are not central to the process of studying a course, but are for students who are somehow deficient.

The content and methods of communicating study expectations to students are widely debated by socio-linguists, learning theorists, tutors of English for academic purposes and discipline specialists (McKenna 1987; Ackers 1987; Swales 1990; Shaw 1991), and I can only consider the issues briefly in this chapter. Shaw (1995) asserts that what is crucial is not so much telling students how to structure a thesis as helping them become, or at least sound like, insiders in their discipline. This entails different ways of signalling knowledge, and Shaw provides examples. But students are not socialised into disciplinary communities in uniform and predictable ways as a result of immediate, local and interactive factors that impinge on individuals as they write (Casanave 1995); and Shaw therefore argues that students are best helped by upgrading their use of the self-help skills they already have.

Discipline specialists who are skilled thinkers, researchers and writers in their subject may not necessarily be skilled in communicating what they do. It is difficult to see how lecturers can help students become 'insiders' other than through osmosis if the lecturers themselves do not have this awareness. Our learning culture is biased towards osmosis: today's academics presumably received few clear guidelines when they were students (May and Bartlett 1995), and for a student to press for explicit instructions is viewed as bordering on cheating. However, the need for discipline specialists to be trained in teaching approaches has more recently been accepted, and is compulsory for new lecturers in many universities. The existence of wide variations in the criteria for written postgraduate work may be framed as poor educational practice, and is certainly problematic for students new to our systems. However, there will always be different views about what is an acceptable approach; indeed, particularly at postgraduate level learning has to be self-directed since it is part of the process of acculturation to the specific norms of the academic community (Shaw 1991), and an expectation of most disciplines. Nevertheless broad areas of within-discipline consensus as to criteria for postgraduate work exist, and students need to have these areas explained, while also understanding that no one style is universally favoured and that they will accordingly have to adjust to different expectations (Bush 1994).

Action can be taken to improve the supervision of overseas students at both departmental and supervisory levels. Departmentally, issues for discussion include setting and communicating criteria for academic research and writing, including ranking criteria and negotiating acceptable levels of variations; determining which methods (written guidelines, stand-alone sessions, supervisions) are most appropriate for communicating these criteria; priority topics to be communicated in supervision; points which have proved particularly useful; supervisory difficulties and possible solutions. Such discussions could lead to a departmental policy on supporting postgraduate students from overseas.

At the level of the supervisory relationship students need clear explanations of how the relationship will work, what is expected of them, and what the supervisor will do. Some students may need encouragement to adjust to a more independent and self-directed role whilst others may be reluctant to take advice and may need to be encouraged to adapt to a more cooperative approach (Craswell 1994). There are several strategies that can be employed by the supervisor to facilitate the supervision process, as follows:

Avoid editing and concentrate upon early and constructive feedback on and discussion about written work. Editing seems to be a popular supervision task, particularly when deadlines are looming, but it may not be the best way to help (May et al. 1994; Shaw 1996) since students are likely to accept corrections without spending time understanding the reason for them. It is far better to ask students for written work early on in their course so discussions can take place. Rewriting work should always be avoided. Instead, find out the students' intentions and explain clearly but positively why there are problems. If editing of English has to happen it is better to concentrate on one or two particular mistakes, since correcting everything may infuriate the supervisor and demoralise the student. Repeated errors are likely to happen for a reason, and discussion may be more likely than correction to lead to a lasting solution. For example, an overseas postgraduate student at Newcastle seemed to use commas and semicolons randomly. He explained that he used a comma whenever he stopped to think, and the supervisor was able to discuss a more appropriate use of punctuation. Supervisors could aim for a level of intervention which decreases over the time of the course.

Give students different opportunities to experience the kind and variety of analytic behaviour needed in the thinking and writing of a particular discipline. This can help students to carry out their own editing and it can happen in a variety of ways:

- direct students to models of good practice such as previous, successful dissertations, focusing on general features of style and structure. Shaw (1995) found students used previous dissertations for guidance about the form of the whole dissertation, the chapter structure and useful phrases;
- ask students to read and discuss different kinds of writing, to evaluate several past essays or give an example of an essay or thesis chapter with comments. Particular aspects of writing could be pointed out, such as the concept of an audience, and the notion that the writer needs to make points clear to the reader;
- model the kind of analytic behaviour required by the way information is presented in lectures and seminars, moving through possibilities, ranges of interpretations and showing why the lecturer regularly chooses one rather than another;

- help students compile glossaries of words and phrases, since this can help them assimilate the conventions and registers of their subject;
- devise exercises in paraphrase and synthesis, writing styles which figure significantly in anglophone academic writing (Shaw, 1991);
- do not talk about prohibitions on plagiarism without discussing how sources can be used, and helping students to use sources appropriately. Discuss phrases appropriate for reuse, since this can help distinguish these from plagiarism. Students may need help to look at sources from the standpoint of their own ideas rather than from those of other people, and to know their own ideas are valued if they are to have confidence in them. Moreover, they may need to know that writing makes the greatest sense once the structure is determined by their own thinking about their essay or research question.

We should also not lose sight of the broader aim of our courses, which is not just to produce a well structured thesis. For MEd students at Newcastle the process of learning is of prime importance: we want students to become engaged in, even excited about, their research, and be able at the end to return home confident of their ability to use research skills to pursue questions. Supervision should therefore encourage students to develop metacognitive awareness and recognise when they are competently using such skills.

CONCLUSION

In our supervision of overseas students we need to be clearer about our own expectations for writing in our discipline, and to discuss these with colleagues in order to clarify ideas and aid understanding of inter-disciplinary differences in genre. We should communicate expectations in ways that recognise students' own skills and experience, and that allow them to find ways to express themselves. Even modest attention to this is likely to have a significant positive effect on students' learning experiences. A deeper and more complex understanding of how cross-cultural problems can arise can help the course designer, teacher and student to make reasoned choices at the rhetorical and stylistic levels (Bloor and Bloor 1991). Academics in the UK need to continue to address the issues raised in this chapter, to come to a greater understanding of the relationship between culture and learning at a postgraduate level, and to find ways to ensure that educating overseas postgraduate students becomes a genuine process of exchange.

Chapter 12

Evaluating UK courses
The perspective of the overseas student

Jim Ackers

'If they don't like our courses they wouldn't come would they?'
'I haven't heard anyone complaining, have you?'
Attitudes such as these, though seldom voiced loudly or publicly, may be covertly present in many higher education institutions. Nevertheless, in spite of the fact that all too many institutions see overseas students solely or mainly in financial terms they are also an important educational resource, bringing fresh perspectives to our culture and are by no means simply a lucrative nuisance to be tolerated.

This chapter discusses key issues in evaluating UK courses from the perspective of the overseas student. This is no simple task, not least because although I have worked for many years overseas in Africa and the Middle East I have never actually been an 'overseas student'.

There is, first of all, a well established problem of defining what precisely we mean by 'overseas students' and, even if we have a good enough definition, of classifying them appropriately. The term evokes an image of homogeneity yet refers to a heterogeneous conglomeration of people from many countries, further differentiated by non-geographical factors, religion, ethnicity, culture and climate, as well as by individual variables such as educational level and familiarity with the UK before arrival, type and length of course studied (short or long, research or taught), and reasons for coming to the UK, which may at times be as important as the academic imperative.

Overseas students may be further categorised according to whether they are self-financing or sponsored, this being particularly significant when one considers that several prior evaluations of overseas students' experiences in the UK, including some discussed in this chapter, have also addressed the interests of the sponsor and host governments. In cases such as these our subject-matter must embrace not only the student's evaluation of courses but also that of other stakeholders.

The reader must also bear in mind that the writer's perspective reflects the fact that he has been working in an autonomous international centre within a university department of education. With substantial overseas student clusters it may be easier to receive evaluative feedback than is the case when overseas students are dispersed across departments. This chapter does, however, relate personal insights and experience to the wider literature. I take a broad and multi-faceted approach to evaluation, and here address the key questions of why, how and when evaluation should take place.

ATTRACTING OVERSEAS STUDENTS

So how should we continue to attract this invaluable resource? There are three main approaches:

- improve the affordability of the product
- improve awareness of the product
- improve the quality of the product.

While the first approach threatens to undermine the latter two in today's competitive climate it is nevertheless the latter two on which this paper focuses.

If as much energy went into analysing how overseas students evaluated their experience in our institutions as is spent on recruitment publicity, not only would there be a larger literature on which to draw for this chapter but recruitment would itself be more sustainable. Marketing literature stresses the importance of basing what we produce on an analysis of customer expectations and the necessity of ensuring that our products satisfy them. This is particularly the case today where the customer is more discerning and demanding and has a wider range of international options from which to choose – not only in Britain but in North America, Australasia and other European countries, as more institutions throughout Europe run courses through the medium of the English language.

White et al. (1991) rightly argue that those in the educational market place must cease to deride 'marketing' by confusing it with 'selling' and assuming that marketing is selling plus frills:

> good marketing is primarily a matter of attitudes, organisation and orientation. ... Its essence lies in a real belief running throughout the *whole* organisation in giving the customer value for money, offering dedicated *service* as well as good quality *services*. It is not just a combination of activities like advertising and public relations, but a total approach to the business and in that way should permeate everything.
>
> (White et al. 1991: 200)

While we must be wary of market forces alone driving higher education curricula we must be mindful of the need to satisfy our customers. A good source of income needs also to be a target for investment, yet in spite of the fact that overseas students are increasingly aware of their consumer power, many institutions make little separate provision for them, slotting them into large lecture-based programmes designed for home students, or even expecting them to attend evening courses with British professionals, providing at best only token support in respect of language and study skills.

Doubtless some institutions depend on famous names, worn like designer labels, to attract overseas students. Yet their future recruitment will be endangered if they do not properly evaluate student needs and the extent to which their courses satisfy them. It is only a slight exaggeration to observe that while a reputation can take decades and more to build, it can be destroyed by just one poor course.

Institutions cater for overseas students in a variety of ways. Some run special courses for groups of overseas students (probably the ideal formula); others, such as international centres, run courses with an overseas perspective, designed specifically for overseas students from various countries; others again accommodate overseas students on mainstream general courses. All these options are potentially appropriate if proper back-up support is provided, though it is difficult to provide adequate support for small numbers of overseas students with language and cultural problems on large intake courses designed for home students.

Overseas education centres such as the Centre for International Studies in Education (CISE) at Newcastle University can give the support necessary to ensure that their overseas students at least hold their own compared to their British peers in terms of academic success. Figures for MEd students for the years 1993–5 show a percentage pass and distinction rate for overseas students equivalent to that of their British peers. While it is proper to regard such figures with caution, it is the case that the overseas students are on full-time courses tailored to an international audience, with tutors (whose role is broader than is typically the case in the UK university system) with overseas experience, and a staff–student ratio of 1:10.

For the overseas student appropriateness is a central component of quality. It is important for institutions to develop their own performance criteria to reflect the work which they undertake, in order that they may be encouraged to give sufficient time and effort to their students and not be deflected from doing so by other priorities. Hence CISE has developed a list of core activities which reflect its purposes as a centre and which serve as the basis of individual appraisals.[1] In departments where overseas students are dispersed, specific tutors may be selected to care for overseas students. Again the work of such tutors should be recognised as valuable and distinct.

EVALUATION: ACCOUNTABILITY OR DEVELOPMENT?

The purposes of evaluation may be considered on two axes: development and accountability. Figure 12.1 suggests that it may be difficult to satisfy both these demands in one evaluation exercise. For example, top-down line management appraisals are effective in providing accountability and organisational knowledge but less effective than peer appraisals in providing ideas for personal development. We must therefore explore complementary methods of evaluation (see Figure 12.2 on p.194) if we are to foster effective development while also demonstrating accountability to students, sponsors, governments, our own institutions and the Higher Education constituency as a whole.

Due to a decline and reorientation of donor spending there has been a shift in recruitment focus from those countries with the need for training to those individuals who are able to pay; from less developed nations to the Asian tigers of the Pacific Rim; and perhaps a concomitant shift of focus from predominantly national to predominantly individual needs. The profile of the 'typical' international student at CISE has changed dramatically in recent years. Twenty years ago *he* had a predominantly

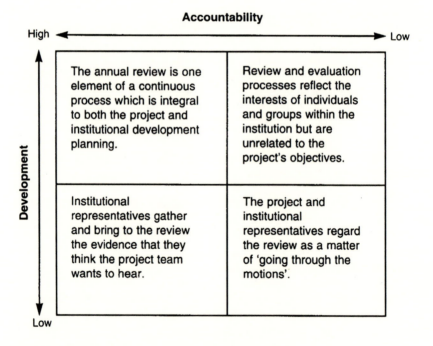

Figure 12.1 Evaluation for accountability or development?

male Afro-Caribbean complexion, now *she* has more of a female Asiatic complexion. In 1995-6 half our students were from South-East Asia and only a third from sub-Saharan Africa; three quarters were female. Though this is not to suggest that this shift in gender balance is reflected system-wide (see Wright's chapter in this book), such a shift in recruitment necessitates a re-evaluation of courses developed over the years, of materials used, of examples and case studies drawn on for teaching purposes, and of staff recruitment patterns.

However this has been a shift and not a total reorientation. In the case of CISE the number of students from developing countries is still relatively high, many still being sponsored by the Overseas Development Administration, other international aid agencies or national governments; whereas according to Maxey and Preston's interpretation of the Department for Education's 1991 figures 32.2 per cent of postgraduate students were from overseas but only 15.4 per cent of these were from developing countries (Maxey and Preston 1994).

At times where there is a contract between donors and providing institutions, responsibility to the former takes precedence over that to the student, for example in terms of choice and length of course. Given that in this situation the funding organisation, not the student, is the university's client it is very important for the university to convince overseas governments of the quality of resource they offer. The 1993 African Education Trust (AET) survey of Namibians returning from overseas training notes:

> concern within Namibia that [courses in the UK] have little credibility because the qualifications they provided were not recognised for labour market entry.
>
> (Preston and Kandando 1993: 24-5)

Encouragingly some developing countries such as Botswana now invest in sending their personnel for training overseas without external donor aid in order to build future capacity at home. In such cases evaluation is a simpler process between student, ministry and providing institution without a further donor party being involved – though more responsibility naturally falls on the receiving institution if the British Council is not involved in supporting the student during his or her period of study.

With the blacklisting of certain UK institutions in Hong Kong and lists of recommended institutions in Malaysia based on points systems (Rogers 1994), the credibility of qualifications at home is a crucial issue, and it is important for all institutions to strive to maintain the reputation of UK Higher Education, particularly when the actions of a number of overseas governments make it plain that the idea that there remains a 'gold standard' in terms of academic awards is regarded with extreme scepticism. In such a difficult context it is the more unfortunate that some overseas governments, as well as the British government, construct league tables on the basis of inappropriate or only partially appropriate criteria, for example research assessment ratings, rather than in relation to the quality of teaching and support for overseas students.

EVALUATION

The Open University (1982: 30) argues that effective evaluation should:

- be fair and perceived as such by all the parties involved
- be capable of suggesting appropriate remedies to problems as they arise
- yield an account that is intelligible to its intended audiences
- be methodologically sound
- be economical in the use of resources
- offer an acceptable blend of centralised and delegated control.

Aspinwall et al. (1992: 4) argue that effective evaluation involves making judgements, is at its best open and explicit, and contributes to decision-making. Nevertheless, at complex institutions like universities there is a problem of determining what elements of evaluation should take place at the institution's centre and what at the teaching-unit level, and how these different levels of evaluation are best linked. University statements of good practice are awakening to the need to evaluate practice with overseas students, and to disaggregate students according to particular needs. Such a statement from one university, for example, states that:

> General academic support is provided for all students and special attention is given to identifying any specific support needs arising from the particular demands of a programme or of particular students, for example, postgraduates, those from other countries, mature students and those with non-traditional qualifications.
>
> (University of Newcastle 1995: 5)

Many overseas students fall into all these categories if 'non-traditional qualifications' are interpreted broadly to include education within different systems and academic cultures (for an example of work on inter-cultural understanding between Chinese students and British tutors see Cortazzi and Jin 1995, and in this book). At Newcastle the need to cater for the needs of overseas students and the mechanisms by which these needs should be assessed (including regular module and programme evaluation by anonymous questionnaire) are recognised institutionally (University of Newcastle 1995: 7).

Overseas students benefit from the strong domestic pressure to make universities more accountable for quality, and more transparent and consumer-based in how they measure it. Aside from the course, however, there are many other factors to consider when evaluating the student's overall experience in the UK, and surveys which neglect wider issues are likely to produce inadequate data. No doubt students choose to study in the UK for a variety of reasons such as to learn about British culture or to make professional and social contacts which may be of help on their return home. An African refugee student at CISE made the following comment just after handing in his final dissertation.

> I feel that I have just come out of a tunnel where the dissertation was the light at the end. Now I have arrived there I look around and realise that there is so much that I have to do and should have done to help my project but I haven't have the time, so I feel happy but at the same time disappointed.

Evaluation is typically characterised as an impure form of research, but in reality it shares similar methodological concerns, constraints and limitations with other research approaches. So how do we conduct an evaluation of programmes and courses in a manner both methodologically sound and economic? And how do we ensure that our investigation has practical effect?

We have to be clear about the reasons for conducting evaluations and select our tools appropriately. Anonymous questionnaires may yield more objective results than signed ones but their developmental potential is diminished by the obvious impossibility of contacting respondents who signal serious problems. Perhaps unsurprisingly, one method is seldom sufficient and a triangulated response is required.

Informal means of evaluating students' experiences may produce some of the most valid information. Students should be provided with as many informal opportunities to meet staff as possible. International student evenings, organised outings and entertaining tutor groups at tutors' homes allow the development of trust and friendship between students and tutors as well as enabling tutors to spot behavioral danger signals. As such their importance cannot be overestimated. However such means are too haphazard to be sufficient in themselves, and formal methods of evaluation are also necessary.

Figure 12.2 demonstrates the existence of an elaborate collection of formal means of evaluation, traditional mechanisms for quality control being supplemented by new internal measures and initiatives from outside the universities. There is however little systematisation and linkage between these mechanisms, which can too easily be characterised by incoherence. There can be an untidy coexistence of mandatory and voluntary procedures, and monitoring and evaluation are frequently managed in a haphazard manner – for instance social welfare needs are ignored in many evaluation exercises. Nevertheless such a multifarious system is likely to be able to provide a more rounded qualitative picture than systems which lack either direct contact between students and tutors or an external perspective.

Often the questionnaire is the principal evaluative instrument, its chief benefits being the possibility of preserving anonymity, ease of delivery, ease of analysis and cost-effectiveness. The questionnaire's utility may, however, be more symbolic than real: not for nothing is it sometimes dubbed 'the happy sheet', eliciting generalised, superficial and sentimental data at the end of a course or year when it is too late to do anything to assist the respondents themselves. Thus used, the questionnaire may become a ritualistic device and not a serious evaluation tool.

It has been suggested that spring is the best time for surveys, students having had sufficient experience to make an informed comment but being free of immediate examination pressure (Rogers 1994: 7) and the institution having time to react to the findings before the end of the academic year. Of course more specific surveys may take place at different times: at some institutions, for example, questionnaires are administered at the end of induction week and on completion of all modules, with a main survey near the end of the year.

An excess of surveys can, however, promote an anti-survey culture, and voluntary surveys normally produce a low return rate. For example a 1992 Southampton survey described by Rogers cites a return rate of 23 per cent, (Rogers 1994: 8) the lowest return being from North American students who may well have been numbed by long, indeed seemingly

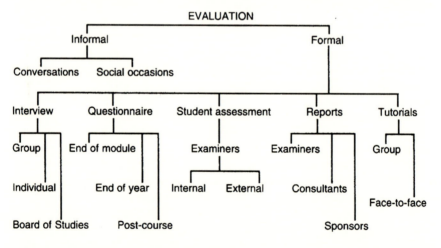

Figure 12.2 Summary of means used to obtain evaluative feedback on the academic and general welfare of students

endless, experience of customer-service surveys. The CISE return rate is normally 100 per cent because time is set aside for the evaluation event and all students are expected to attend. It is worth considering whether the completion of evaluation forms should be mandatory, since low returns may yield partial and distorted results. In departments where students are dispersed, administrative staff might ensure that students complete and return questionnaires, with systems such as the polling booth being used to ensure anonymity.

Questionnaire design is crucial. Ideally it should have several audiences in mind, including the students themselves, the providing institution, sponsors and other interested parties. There are ways of ensuring that students' concerns are addressed: they should be involved in the design and updating of the questionnaire, be informed of results, especially any key issues raised, in order that these may be discussed in greater depth. The opportunity for anonymity is crucial, though it is important to encourage students who wish their comments to be followed up to identify themselves if they wish. At CISE a group discussion with the entire student body follows questionnaire completion, and students who have expressed concerns and named themselves are subsequently contacted so that they may have the opportunity to discuss their problems.

Evaluation is necessary before, during and after the course. First, authors such as Dickinson and Houghton recommend *pre-arrival surveys* (in Rogers 1994: 7). It is important for an institution to be aware of the needs and expectations of students prior to their arrival, and it is good practice for potential tutors to correspond directly with applicants before and after they have been offered places. Not only is it helpful to ascertain, for example, that course content is appropriate to their needs and expectations but it is reassuring for students to arrive having established a rapport with their tutors through correspondence.

Further guidance needs to be made available during induction week, when students choose their options, some even changing their main areas of study. There is similar pre-arrival correspondence with donors. At times these may raise complex issues and precise demands involving, for instance, and depending on the management of the internal economy of the institution concerned, buying into courses in other departments or arranging secondments to schools or local education authorities. In particular, meeting sponsors' expectations is an essential aspect of responsible recruitment (UKCOSA 1986a).

Second, the importance of continual evaluation *during the programme of studies itself* need hardly be stressed. As we have seen, both the focus and the timing of course-related evaluation activities will vary according to their purposes, with the questionnaire often a key instrument. Here, however, I explore other means of evaluation:

- the evaluation of student needs as well as achievements should be central to the process. Both taught and research students should be encouraged to produce work which will alert supervisors to problems at an early stage. At this time offering detailed feedback, having and explaining explicit examining criteria and providing an opportunity for overseas students to have informal advice before they formally submit early assignments are important. Many overseas students experience problems adapting to the academic style required in western universities (see Cortazzi and Jin 1995, and in this book), and it is unfair to assess students before they have learnt the rules of the game;
- the views of external experts can be used to enable overseas students to comment on their course experience. At Newcastle external examiners hold individual and group vivas during which students are invited to comment candidly on the quality of both teaching and assessment. External examiners' reports, of course, provide very useful feedback to course tutors, but in addition the use of external consultants can provide fresh perspectives to any organisation. We have always found that visiting lecturers from overseas provide useful insights, and we therefore try to treat them as part of the team, not as 'one-off' lecturers with no functions outside their paid hours;
- representation on boards of studies (or their equivalents) ensures that students can voice any concerns directly to the Dean;
- reports to sponsoring bodies (such as the standard progress report for British Council sponsored students) help ensure the formative evaluation of sponsored students during the year; while internal annual reports provide an opportunity for students to appraise the quality of support the university and specifically their tutor, provides. Nevertheless such forms are normally completed cautiously, in the interests both of the future career of the student and of the tutor–student relationship, and sometimes for cultural reasons. Informal contacts with sponsors, normally by telephone, are therefore necessary to complement such formal channels;
- it is important for overseas students to experience one-to-one tutorials. International centres can provide the opportunity for frequent tutorial contact time to discuss personal problems as well as academic issues. It is also good practice for students to see specialist lecturers for tutorials related to assignments that they have set and be encouraged to seek out another member of staff if they have a problem they do not wish to discuss with their principal tutor.

Third, *post-course evaluation* is important in spite of the fact that, as Iredale claims, very few initiatives exist to enable universities to keep in touch with their overseas alumni and alumnae (Iredale 1992). In recent years there has been far more concern regarding the relevance of courses to the individuals and countries concerned, particularly in the case of developing countries. Accordingly, a number of tracer studies have been carried out, some focusing on individual students, others on larger groups of students. Here I mention briefly three surveys concerning the impact of UK courses on overseas students returning home.

First, Williams (1985) sought to evaluate the success of Technical Cooperation Training for British Council- and ODA-sponsored scholars attending UK courses in 1981. Though the findings were largely favourable, with only 17 per cent expressing overall dissatisfaction, 24 per cent of respondents complained that course content was not what was hoped for (a factor closely linked to lack of pre-course information), 22 per cent (particularly those engaged in more applied areas such as education or engineering) claimed that there was insufficient opportunity for practical training, and the view was also expressed that courses tended to be too short and rushed. Certainly experience at CISE suggests that students on two-year programmes show significant improvements in their second year, and one can only wonder about the value of courses of less than twelve months duration, particularly where there are problems of linguistic and cultural orientation to overcome.

The study is limited by the fact that Williams looks only at the perceptions of the study fellows themselves and not at those of their government sponsors or their institutional hosts. He also focuses exclusively on expectations rather than realisations of success, and 'development' and 'developmental impact' are very difficult concepts to define (see Rogers 1992; Ackers 1995) and Williams himself argues for long term career referenced tracer studies:

> Follow-up studies of returned Study Fellows' careers seem essential to total programme evaluation with its considerations of developmental impact of overseas training.
>
> (Williams 1985: 17)

The study addresses the key issue of the impact of training on practice, whether measured individually, organisationally or nationally – an issue of which overseas governments are becoming more aware when advising nationals on which courses to take in the UK, and when determining the equivalence of overseas qualifications to their own. Doubtless connected with this point it is becoming increasingly the norm for institutions to arrange visits to countries from which they enjoy substantial recruitment. CISE, for example, arranges annual meetings with former students in Hong Kong. This makes sense from both marketing and developmental perspectives, is increasingly expected by donor agencies and overseas governments, and will doubtless contribute to more focused and responsible recruitment drives on the part of many universities and their departments.

Secondly, the African Education Trust sponsored a survey to 'assess the relevance of education and training of Namibians abroad to labour market structures and needs on their return home' (Preston and Kandando 1993: 30). This study challenges the hesitancy of donors to assist refugees to study outside their countries on the grounds of lack of relevance of training. In the foreword to the study Brophy, the AET Director, attacks the emerging third-country training panacea – the argument that developing country students would benefit more by studying in a neighbouring developing country – stating that 'in most parts of Africa access to national institutions by foreigners is in fact rather difficult... universities in neighbouring African countries are simply so overcrowded' (in Preston and Kandando 1993: iii). The study also challenges the myth that studying in the UK is inappropriate to the needs of the African or other non-UK nationals on their return home. Taking a broader view of education and training in the context of a country reconstructing itself, the report of the National Institute of Namibia notes:

> not only were 95 per cent of those traced in employment in Namibia, but... the work requires skills closely related to those acquired on UK courses.
>
> (Preston and Kandando 1993: iv)

A third study asks why skill transfer is reputedly so problematic after study fellows return to their place of work. It singles out lack of communication skills as a key factor on the ground that neither employer nor employee has formal or informal expertise in skill transfer (Maxey and Preston 1994). In identifying communication strategies as lying at the heart of the problem the authors avoid discussing more deep-seated structural problems such as traditional status relations which may be challenged upon the study fellow's return. Such problems are compounded by inappropriate selection of study fellows – for example, where classroom teachers are sent overseas to learn teacher evaluation only to be shunned on their return by inspectors already in place, and responsible for such work.

Communication strategies may alleviate problems but will not solve them. More effective joint planning between the host government and the donor agency's project coordinators at selection stage would reduce the perennial problem of 'failed matrimony' (Leech 1993). Explicit planning for what will occur when study fellows return home would give a sharper focus to their overseas study. If I may be permitted a personal anecdote, as a British Council officer in Senegal I used to insist that teachers coming to train in the UK gave a presentation to their colleagues on their return: problems of reintegration are two-way, and for returning graduates to be able to give of their best in their own countries their future colleagues have to be able to exploit to the full what they have to offer.

The study's value is vitiated both by leading questions (it is not surprising, for example, that nearly all respondents replied positively to being asked: 'Would a short intensive course on teaching skills have been useful to you?') and by a very low return rate of 17.5 per cent, a problem which demonstrates why Williams argues that: 'for tracing purposes, the immediate post-course evaluation with its access to a still "captive" group of informants has great advantages' (Williams 1985: 17). Nevertheless the study is a brave attempt to identify and elaborate a key problem; it suggests solutions to the problem of reintegration, arguing that programmes should contain communication training and that such a provision would be popularly received. However it also recognises the difficulty of organising such courses from a financial and timetabling point of view, and it may be that the skills described could be developed within mainstream courses themselves if lecturers took a more student-centred approach by, for example, encouraging students to make presentations to each other in seminars.

The study argues that reorientation and dissemination are of central importance for achieving the multiplier effect which is a goal of most training programmes. In terms of reorientation training UKCOSA has produced a useful pack (Unterhalter and Hayton 1993) designed to minimise 'reverse culture shock' and to ensure that trainees are able to use their newly acquired skills on return to the workplace. Certainly we should not be too pessimistic about the impact of courses on the professional practice of the returning student. Many institutions attempt to orientate students prior to their departure by, for example, drawing up action plans to implement ideas developed in dissertations. Feedback on the success of such planning is at present largely ad hoc though still useful. In 1994–5, for example, a group of leading Zimbabwean educators came to Newcastle to study educational guidance and counselling, and before returning home drew up an action plan with their tutor. In November 1995 we received a letter containing the following:

> J and T are also here.... This morning we shall present the paper entitled *Quo Vadis Guidance and Counselling Zimbabwe?* ... to Deputy Regional Directors, Chief Education Officers and other education officials. Hopefully, a clear national policy on G and C will be enunciated as a result. I know L (my tutor) will be thrilled to know this.

L was indeed thrilled to know this and is planning a visit to Zimbabwe to meet her former students and Ministry officials to discuss the development of a joint training initiative. Many other centres dealing with overseas students will be able to cite similar instances of encouraging feedback.

A number of points seem clear:

- training in the UK brings a number of students together who learn much from each other as well as from their tutors;
- the UK still has much to offer in terms of models of practice;
- training in the UK need not be followed by disappointment on returning home if study fellows are appropriately selected in the first place and properly prepared – that is, if they have the power to put ideas into practice;
- UK institutions need to build longer-term links with their students for the optimal transmission of ideas as well as for marketing purposes;
- there is no better evaluative and developmental tool than getting to know your students socially and professionally.

CONCLUSION

Currently a number of rather ad hoc mechanisms exist through which overseas students may evaluate their experience of studying and living in the UK. UKCOSA publications may offer a road forward and provide coherence in a rapidly developing world. Research into the longer-term effects of studying overseas, in particular its relevance on return, has some way to go if it is to transcend the immediate task of satisfying sponsors and significantly influence programme design.

Overseas students are an amorphous group, but their needs must be met at individual, sponsor and country level if British academia is not to fall victim to the same fate as other British industries, which survived for too long on reputation alone. In many African countries people have turned from the time-honoured Landrover to Japanese four-wheel-drives because the Landrover has no support systems in terms of garages and spare parts. How many of our institutions provide effective after-sales care to their students? We need to develop new quality control structures if we are to sustain our status as major providers of education overseas. We must be able to identify and respond to overseas student needs before, during and after the course if our comparative advantage is to be maintained. Viewed positively, evaluation is as much about celebrating success as identifying problems. It provides the basis for a continuous development of good practice in a fast-changing world, enabling us to marry the best of our inheritance with the best of our creative potential.

NOTE

1   A copy of this document is available from the author on request.

Bibliography

Abdul Halim Othman (1985) 'Malay students in the United States: a study of adjustment problems and perception of problem solving resources', *Nusantara*, 12, 1–36.

——(1986) 'Life change stress of Malay students in the United States', *Jurnal Psikologi Malaysia*, 2, 129–39.

Acker, S. (1984) 'Women in higher education: what is the problem?', in S. Acker and D. Piper (eds) *Is Higher Education Fair to Women?* Guildford: Society for Research into Higher Education and NFER-Nelson.

Acker, S. and Piper, D. (eds) (1984) *Is Higher Education Fair to Women?* Guildford: Society for Research into Higher Education and NFER-Nelson.

Ackers, W.J. (1987) 'A rationale for the application of individualised learning to an in-sessional service English context', unpublished MA dissertation, University of Leicester.

——(1995) 'The impact of an ELT project on socio-economic development in a French-speaking West African country', in *Bristol Papers in Education*, Bristol: Centre for International Studies in Education.

Adler, P. (1975) 'The transition experience: an alternative view of culture shock', *Journal of Humanistic Psychology*, 15, 13–23.

Allen, A. and Higgins, M. (1994) *Higher Education: The International Student Experience*, Leeds: Heist, in association with UCAS.

Alptekin, C. and Alptekin, M. (1984) 'The question of culture: EFL teaching in non-English-speaking countries', *ELT Journal*, 38, 14–20.

Anonymous (1985) 'An overseas student's view of support services: we have to tell them everything and they tell us nothing', in Further Education Staff College, *Coombe Lodge Report: Developing a Policy for Recruiting Overseas Students: Part I*, Coombe Lodge, Bristol: Further Education Staff College.

Appadurai, A. (1990) 'Disjuncture and difference in the global cultural economy', in M. Featherstone (ed.) *Global Culture: Nationalism, Globalization, and Modernity*, London: Sage Publications.

Argyle, M. (1979) 'New developments in the analysis of social skills', in A. Woldgang (ed.) *Non-Verbal Behaviour*, London: Academic Press.

Aspinwall, K., Simkins, T., Wilkinson, J. and McAuley, M. (1992) *Managing Evaluation in Education: a Developmental Approach*, London: Routledge.

Atkinson, D., Morten, G. and Sue, D. (1979) *Counseling American Minorities: a Cross-Cultural Perspective*, Dubuque, Iowa: William C. Brown.

Atzet, A. (1995) 'Meeting the needs of students from Cambodia, Laos and Vietnam: the Asian Institute of Technology Bridging Programme', in P. Thomas (ed.) *Teaching for Development: an International Review of Australian Formal and*

Non-Formal Education for Asia and the Pacific, Canberra: National Centre for Development Studies, Australian National University.

Au, D. (1969) 'The influence of contact with host nationals on foreign students' attitudes', unpublished thesis, University of New South Wales.

Ausubel, D. (1978) 'In defense of advance organisers: a reply to the critics', *Review of Educational Research*, 48, 251–7.

Ausubel, D., Novak, J. and Hanesian, H. (1978) *Educational Psychology: a Cognitive View*, New York: Holt, Rinehart and Winston.

Ayuru, R. (1995) 'Politics of access to higher education: gender considerations', in R. Moodley (ed.) *Education for Transformation: Black Access to Higher Education*, Leeds: Thomas Danby Publications.

Baker, D. (1993) 'Compared to Japan, the US is a low achiever... really: new evidence and comment on Westbury', *Educational Researcher*, 22, 3, 18–20.

Ball-Rokeach, S. (1973) 'From pervasive ambiguity to a definition of the situation', *Sociometry*, 36, 133–45.

Ballard, B. (1991) *Helping Students from Non-English Speaking Backgrounds to Learn Effectively*, Melbourne: Educational Research and Development Unit, Royal Melbourne Institute of Technology.

——(1995) 'Creative tensions: teaching in programmes for international students', in P. Thomas (ed.) *Teaching for Development: an International Review of Australian Formal and Non-Formal Education for Asia and the Pacific*, Canberra: National Centre for Development Studies, Australian National University.

Ballard, B. and Clanchy, J. (1984) *Studying Abroad: a Manual for Asian Students*, Kuala Lumpur: Longman.

——(1991) *Teaching Students from Overseas*, Melbourne: Longman.

Barnett R. (1994) 'Power, enlightenment and quality evaluation', *European Journal of Education*, 29, 165–79.

Bauman, Z. (1990) 'Modernity and ambivalence', in M. Featherstone (ed.) *Global Culture: Nationalism, Globalization, and Modernity*, London: Sage Publications.

Becher, T. (1989) *Academic Tribes and Territories: Intellectual Enquiry and the Cultures of Disciplines*, Milton Keynes: Open University Press.

Belcher, D. and Braine, G. (eds) (1995) *Academic Writing in a Second Language: Essays on Research and Pedagogy*, New Jersey: Ablex.

Benn, R. (1961) 'The adjustment problems of a group of Asian students at an Australian university', unpublished MA thesis, University of Sydney.

Bernstein, B. (1975) *Class, Codes and Control*, London: Routledge & Kegan Paul.

Bickerton, D. (1975) *Dynamics of a Creole System*, Cambridge: Cambridge University Press.

Biggs, J. (1990) 'Asian students' approaches to learning: implications for teaching overseas students', in M. Kratzing (ed.) *Eighth Australasian Learning and Language Conference*, Queensland: Queensland University of Technology Counselling Services.

——(1991) 'Approaches to learning in secondary and tertiary students in Hong Kong: some comparative studies', *Educational Research Journal*, 6, 27–39.

——(1993) 'What do inventories of students' learning processes really measure: a theoretical review and clarification', *British Journal of Educational Psychology*, 63, 1–17.

——(1994) 'What are effective schools? Lessons from East and West', *Australian Educational Researcher*, 21, 19–39.

Blackmore, J. and Kenway, J. (eds) (1993) *Gender Matters in Educational Administration and Policy*, London: Falmer Press.

Blake, V. (1995) 'From access student to access course director: a personal perspective', in R. Moodley (ed.) *Education for Transformation: Black Access to Higher Education*, Leeds: Thomas Danby Publications.

Blaug, M. and Woodhall, M. (1981) 'A survey of overseas students in British higher education, 1980', in P. Williams (ed.) (1981) *The Overseas Student Question: Studies for a Policy*, London: Heinemann for the Overseas Students Trust.

Bligh, D., Jaques, D. and Piper, D. (1981) *Seven Decisions when Teaching Students*, Exeter: Exeter University.

Bloch, J. and Chi, L. (1995) 'A comparison of the use of citations in Chinese and English academic discourse', in D. Belcher and G. Braine (eds) *Academic Writing in a Second Language: Essays on Research and Pedagogy*, New Jersey: Ablex.

Bloor, M. and Bloor, T. (1991) 'Cultural expectation and socio-pragmatic failure in academic writing', *Review of ELT* (special issue on Socio-cultural Issues in English for Academic Purposes), 1, 2, 1–12.

Blumenfeld, P., Mergendoller, J. and Swarthout, D. (1987) 'Task as a heuristic for understanding student learning and motivation', *Journal of Curriculum Studies*, 19, 135–48.

Bochner, S. (ed.) (1982) *Cultures in Contact*, Oxford: Pergamon.

Bochner, S., Buker, E. and McLeod, B. (1976) 'Communicational patterns in an international student dormitory', *Journal of Applied Social Psychology*, 6, 275–90.

Bochner, S., McLeod, B. and Lin, A. (1977) 'Friendship patterns of overseas students: a functional model', *International Journal of Psychology*, 12, 277–99.

Bochner, S. and Orr, F. (1979) 'Race and academic status as determinants of friendships formation: a field study', *International Journal of Psychology*, 14, 37–46.

Bock, P. (ed.) (1970) *Culture Shock: a Reader in Modern Psychology*, New York: Knopf.

Bok, D. (1982) *Beyond the Ivory Tower: Social Responsibilities of the Modern University*, Cambridge, MA: Harvard University Press.

Boswell, T. (1994) 'Quality and Europe', in G. Bradley and B. Little (eds) *Quality and Europe: Papers Presented at a Conference*, London: Quality Support Centre and the Open University.

Bourdieu, P. (1977) 'Cultural reproduction and social reproduction', in J. Karabel and A.H. Halsey (eds) *Power and Ideology in Education*, New York: Oxford University Press.

Bowles, S. and Gintis, H. (1976) *Schooling in Capitalist America*, London: Routledge & Kegan Paul.

Bradbury, M. (1959) *Eating People is Wrong*, Harmondsworth: Penguin Books.

Bradley, D. and Bradley, M. (1984) *Problems of Asian Students in Australia: Language, Culture and Education*, Canberra: Australian Government Publishing Service.

Bradley, G. and Little, B. (eds) (1994) *Quality and Europe: Papers Presented at a Conference*, London: Quality Support Centre and the Open University.

Brann, C. (ed.) (1970) *French Curriculum Development in Anglophone Africa: a Symposium and Guide*, Occasional Paper no. 9, Ibadan: University of Ibadan Institute of Education.

Brennan, J. (1993) 'Higher education quality: a European dimension', in J. Brennan and F. van Vught, *Questions of Quality: in Europe and Beyond*, Quality Support Centre Higher Education Report no. 1, London: Quality Support Centre and the Open University.

Brennan, J. and van Vught, F. (1993) *Questions of Quality: in Europe and Beyond*,

Quality Support Centre Higher Education Report no. 1, London: Quality Support Centre and the Open University.

Brennan, J. Goedegeburre, L., Shah, T., Westerheijden, D. and Weusthof, P. (1993) *Towards a Methodology for Comparative Quality Assessment in European Higher Education*, London, Enschede and Hanover: Council for National Academic Awards, Centre for Higher Education Policy Studies and Hochschule Information System.

Brennan, J., Frazer, M., Middlehurst, R., Silver, H. and Williams, R. (eds) (1996) *Changing Conceptions of Standards*, Quality Support Centre Higher Education Report no. 4, London: Quality Support Centre and the Open University.

Brewin, C., Furnham, A. and Howe, M. (1989) 'Demographic and psychological determinants of homesickness and confiding among students', *British Journal of Psychology*, 80, 467–77.

Brislin, R. (1979) 'Orientation programmes for cross-cultural preparation', in A. Marsella, R. Thorp and T. Cibrowski (eds) *Perspectives on Cross-Cultural Psychology*, New York: Academic Press.

Brislin, R., Bochner, S. and Lonner, W. (eds) (1975) *Cross-Cultural Perspectives on Learning*, New York: Wiley.

British Broadcasting Corporation (1994) 'Is the future female?', *Panorama*, BBC1, 24 October.

British Council (1980) *Study Modes and Academic Development of Overseas Students*, London: British Council.

——(1995) *Studying and Living in Britain 1995: the British Council's Guide for Overseas Students and Visitors*, Plymouth: Northcote House in association with The British Council.

British Council Education Counselling Service (n.d.) *Code of Practice: Educational Institutions and Overseas Students*, Manchester: British Council.

Brock, C. and Ryba, R. (eds) (1980) *Volume of Essays for Elizabeth Halsall*, Aspects of Education no. 22, Hull: University of Hull.

Brown, G. and Atkins, M. (1988) *Effective Teaching in Higher Education*, London: Routledge.

Brown, K. (1995) 'World Englishes: to teach or not to teach?', *World Englishes*, 14, 233–45.

Brown, P. and Scase, R. (1994) *Higher Education and Corporate Realities*, London: UCL Press.

Bruthiaux, P., Boswood, T. and Du-Babcock, B. (eds) (1995) *Explorations in English for Professional Communication*, Hong Kong: City University.

Burke, B. (1986) *Experiences of Overseas Undergraduate Students*, Bulletin no. 18, Student Counselling and Research Unit, Sydney: University of New South Wales Press.

Burns, D. (ed.) (1965) *Travelling Scholars: an Enquiry into the Adjustment and Attitudes of Overseas Students Holding Commonwealth Bursaries in England and Wales*, Slough: National Foundation for Educational Research in England and Wales.

Burns, R. (1994) 'Study and stress among overseas students at an Australian University', unpublished paper presented at the 8th Australian and New Zealand Student Services Association International Conference, Adelaide, January.

Burstyn, J. (1984) 'Educators' response to scientific and medical studies of women in England, 1860–1900', in S. Acker and D. Piper (eds) (1984) *Is Higher Education Fair to Women?* Guildford: Society for Research into Higher Education and NFER-Nelson.

Bush, D. (1994) 'Academic writing: faculty expectations and overseas student performance', unpublished paper presented at the National Australian Council of TESOL Associations Conference, Western Australia.

Buttjes, D. and Byram, M. (1990) *Mediating Languages and Cultures*, Clevedon: Multilingual Matters.

Byram, M. and Fleming, M. (eds) (forthcoming) *Foreign Language Learning in Intercultural Perspective*, Cambridge: Cambridge University Press.

Byrnes, F. (1966) *Americans in Technical Assistance: a Study of Attitudes and Responses to their Role Abroad*, New York: Praeger.

Calleja, J. (1995) 'International education: a common direction for our future', in J. Calleja (ed.) *International Education and the University*, London: UNESCO and Jessica Kingsley.

Cammish, N. (1980) 'Bilimbis et Colilibris: a French curriculum development project in Seychelles', in C. Brock and R. Ryba (eds) (1980) *Volume of Essays for Elizabeth Halsall*, Aspects of Education no. 22, Hull: University of Hull.

Carey, A. (1956) *Colonial Students*, London: Secker and Warburg.

Casanave, C. (1995) 'Local interactions: constructing contexts for composing in a graduate sociology program', in D. Belcher and G. Braine (eds) *Academic Writing in a Second Language: Essays on Research and Pedagogy*, New Jersey: Ablex.

Channell, J. (1990) 'The student–tutor relationship', in M Kinnell (ed.) *The Learning Experiences of Overseas Students*, Buckingham: Society for Research into Higher Education and Open University Press.

Charpentier, J. (1979) *Le Pidgin Bislama et le Multilinguisme aux Nouvelles Hébrides*, Paris: Société d'Etudes Linguistiques et Anthropologiques de France.

Chen, J. (1990) *Confucius as a Teacher*, Beijing: Foreign Languages Press.

Chickering, A. (1972) *Education and Identity*, San Francisco: Jossey-Bass.

Chiu, L. (1993) 'An examination of the delivery of social services to the Chinese community in Britain', unpublished MA dissertation, University of Hull.

Choi, P-K. and Ho, L-S. (eds) (1993) *The Other Hong Kong Report*, Hong Kong: The Chinese University of Hong Kong.

Christopher, R. (1984) *The Japanese Mind*, London: Pan Books.

Church, A. (1982) 'Sojourner adjustment', *Psychological Bulletin*, 91, 540–72.

Cleveland, H., Margone, C. and Adams, J. (1963) *The Overseas Americans*, New York: McGraw-Hill.

Cobb, A. (1976) 'Social support as a moderator of life stress', *Psychosomatic Medicine*, 38, 300–314.

Cochrane, R. (1983) *The Social Creation of Mental Illness*, London: Longman.

Cockburn, C. (1995) 'Fundamentalisms', unpublished paper presented to the New Thinking on Women Conference, Birkbeck College, University of London, 11 November.

Cohen, S. and Syme, L. (eds) (1985) *Social Support and Health*, New York: Academic Press.

Cohen, S. and Wills, T. (1985) 'Stress, social support, and the buffering hypothesis', *Psychological Bulletin*, 98, 310–57.

Coleman, H. (ed.) (1996) *Society in the Language Classroom*, Cambridge: Cambridge University Press.

Collett, P. (1982) 'Meetings and misunderstandings', in S. Bochner (ed.) *Cultures in Contact*, Oxford: Pergamon.

Commission of the European Communities (1991) *Memorandum on Higher Education in the European Community*, COM(91) 349, Luxembourg: Office for Official Publications of the European Communities.

——(1993) *Establishing the Community Action programme 'SOCRATES'*, COM(93) 708, Luxembourg: Office for Official Publications of the European Communities.

——(1994) *Cooperation in Education in the European Union*, Education, Training Youth Studies no. 5, Luxembourg: Office for Official Publications of the European Communities.

Commission of the European Communities and the Organisation for Economic Cooperation and Development (1994) *Mobility in Higher Education: Pilot Project on Regional Cooperation in Reforming Higher Education*, Paris: European Commission/OECD.

Commission on University Career Opportunity (CUCO) (1994) *A Report on Universities' Policies and Practices on Equal Opportunities in Employment*, London: Committee of Vice-Chancellors and Principals.

Committee of Scottish University Principals (1992) *Teaching and Learning in an Expanding Higher Education System*, Edinburgh: Committee of Scottish University Principals.

Committee of Vice Chancellors and Principals (1992a) *Effective Learning and Teaching in Higher Education: a Series of Twelve Modules*, CVCP Universities' Staff Development and Training Unit, Sheffield: University of Sheffield.

——(1992b) *The Management of Higher Degrees Undertaken by Overseas Students (Code of Recommended Practice)*, London: CVCP.

——(1995a) *Economic Impact of International Students in UK Higher Education*, London: CVCP.

——(1995b) *Recruitment and Support of International Students in UK Higher Education: Code of Practice*, N/95/177, London: CVCP.

Connell, R. (1995) *Masculinities*, Cambridge: Polity Press.

Connell, T. and Hodson, N. (1995) 'English language support for overseas students', unpublished paper, City University, London.

Connor, U. and Kaplan, R. (eds) (1987) *Writing across Languages*, New York: Addison Wesley.

Coppock, V., Haydon, D. and Richter, I. (1995) *The Illusions of 'Post-Feminism': New Women, Old Myths*, London: Taylor and Francis.

Cortazzi, M. and Jin, L. (1995) *Teaching and Learning Across Cultures: China and the West*, paper presented to the Third Oxford International Conference on Education, Globalisation and Learning, New College, Oxford, 21–5 September.

——(1996) 'Cultures of learning: language classrooms in China', in H. Coleman (ed.) *Society in the Language Classroom*, Cambridge: Cambridge University Press.

Cowie, A. and Heaton, J. (eds) (1977) *English for Academic Purposes*, British Association of Applied Linguistics' Special English Language Materials for Overseas Students, Reading: University of Reading.

Craig, D. (1971) 'Education and Creole English in the West Indies', in D. Hymes (ed.) *Pidginisation and Creolisation of Languages*, Cambridge: Cambridge University Press.

Crano, S. and Crano, W. (1993) 'A measure of adjustment strain in international students', *Journal of Cross-Cultural Psychology*, 24, 267–83.

Craswell, G. (1994) 'Cross-cultural difficulties of international research and coursework students: notes for supervisors', unpublished paper, Study Skills Centre, Australian National University, Canberra.

Cross, A.G. (1985) 'Russian students in eighteenth-century Oxford (1766–75)', *Journal of European Studies*, 5, 91–110.

Currie, J. and Leggatt, T. (1965) *New Commonwealth Students in Britain*, London: Allen and Unwin.

Daniel, J. (1993) 'Mobility of minds and union of peoples', in T. Higgins and T. Cox (eds) *Student Mobility in Europe*, Cheltenham: Polytechnics Central Admissions System.

David, K. (1971) 'Culture shock and the development of self-awareness', *Journal of Contemporary Psychotherapy*, 4, 44–8.

De Groot, J. (1995) 'The drive for diversity', *Guardian Education*, November 28.

Delamont, S. (1980) *Sex Roles and the School*, London: Methuen.

Denicolo, P., Entwistle, N. and Hounsell, D. (1992) 'What is active learning? Module 1', *Effective Learning and Teaching in Higher Education*, Sheffield: Committee of Vice-Chancellors and Principals Staff Development and Training Unit.

Department for Education (1992) *UK Government Response to the EC Memorandum on Higher Education in the European Community*, London: Department for Education.

——(1994) *Students from Abroad in Great Britain, 1982–92*, Statistical Bulletin 15/ 94, Darlington: Government Statistical Service.

Department of Trade and Industry (1995) *Exporting Education: Education and Training Sector Group Newsletter, Issue 4*, London: Department of Trade and Industry.

Dirlik, A. (1994) 'The postcolonial aura: third world criticism in the age of global capitalism', *Critical Enquiry*, 20, 328–56.

Dore, R. (1976) *The Diploma Disease: Education, Qualification and Development*, London: Allen & Unwin.

Dunlop, F. (1966) *Europe's Guest Students and Trainees: a Survey on the Welfare of Foreign Students and Trainees in Europe*, Strasbourg: Council for Cultural Cooperation of the Council of Europe.

Dyhouse, C. (1984) 'Storming the citadel or storm in a tea cup: the entry of women into higher education, 1860–1920', in S. Acker and D. Piper (eds) *Is Higher Education Fair to Women?* Guildford: Society for Research into Higher Education and NFER-Nelson.

Ecclesfield, N. (1985) 'Responsibility in recruitment: the institution and its policy', in Further Education Staff College, *Coombe Lodge Report: Developing a Policy for Recruiting Overseas Students: Part I*, Coombe Lodge, Bristol: Further Education Staff College.

Edwards, R. (1993) *Mature Women Students: Separating or Connecting Family and Education*, London: Taylor and Francis.

Elbing, E. (ed.) (1970) *Behavioural Decisions in Organisation*, New York: Scott, Foresman and Co.

Elsey, B. (1990) 'Teaching and learning', in M. Kinnell (ed.) *The Learning Experiences of Overseas Students*, Buckingham: Society for Research into Higher Education and Open University Press.

Entwistle, N. (1992) *The Impact of Teaching on Learning Outcomes in Higher Education: a Literature Review*, Sheffield: Committee of Vice-Chancellors and Principals.

Entwistle, N. and Entwistle, A. (1991) 'Forms of understanding for degree examinations: the student experience and its implications', *Higher Education*, 22, 205–27.

Entwistle, N. and Hounsell, D. (1975) *How Students Learn*, Lancaster: University of Lancaster Institute for Research and Development in Post-Compulsory Education.

Evans, C. (1988) *Language People: the Experience of Teaching and Learning Modern Languages in British Universities*, Milton Keynes: Open University Press.

——(1993) *English People: the Experience of Teaching and Learning English in British Universities*, Milton Keynes: Open University Press.

Fan, R. (1990) 'Opportunities and challenges of the expansion plan for higher education', in *Higher Education in the 1990s: Development and Challenges*, Hong Kong: Publicity Committee of Lingnan College.

Farrant, J. (1981) 'Trends in admissions', in O. Fulton (ed.) *Access to Higher Education*, Guildford: Society for Research into Higher Education.

Featherstone, M. (ed.) (1990) *Global Culture: Nationalism, Globalization, and Modernity*, London: Sage Publications.

Federation of Hong Kong Students (1982) *Perspectives on Hong Kong Education*, Hong Kong: Wide Angle Publications.

——(1983) *Review of the Student Movement in Hong Kong*, Hong Kong: Wide Angle Publications.

Fenwick, K. and Moss, C. (1985) 'The role of the tutor: how far does welfare encroach on teaching?', in S. Shotnes (ed.) *The Teaching and Tutoring of Overseas Students*, London: UKCOSA.

Fernandez, M. (1988) 'Issues in counseling Southeast Asian students', *Journal of Multicultural Counseling and Development*, 16, 157–66.

Fisher, S. and Hood, B. (1987) 'The stress of the transition to university: a longitudinal study of psychological disturbance, absent-mindness and vulnerability to homesickness', *British Journal of Psychology*, 78, 425–41.

Fisher, S., Murray, K. and Frazer, N. (1985) 'Homesickness, health and efficacy in first year students', *Journal of Environmental Psychology*, 5, 181–95.

Flynn, J. (1991) *Asian Americans: Achievement Beyond IQ*, Hillsdale, NJ: Erlbaum.

Fulton, O. (ed.) (1991) *Access to Higher Education*, Guildford: Society for Research into Higher Education.

Furnham, A. (1979) 'Assertiveness in three cultures: multi-dimensionality and cultural differences', *Journal of Clinical Psychology*, 35, 522–7.

Furnham, A. and Alibhai, N. (1985) 'The friendship network of foreign students', *International Journal of Psychology*, 20, 709–22.

Furnham, A. and Bochner, S. (1986) *Culture Shock*, London: Methuen.

Furnham, A. and Tresize, L. (1983) 'The mental health of foreign students', *Social Science and Medicine*, 17, 365–70.

Further Education Staff College (1985) *Coombe Lodge Report: Developing a Policy for Recruiting Overseas Students: Part I*, Coombe Lodge, Bristol: Further Education Staff College.

Furukawa, T. and Shibayama, T. (1993) 'Predicting maladjustment of exchange students in different cultures: a prospective study', *Social Psychology and Psychiatric Epidemiology*, 28, 142–6.

——(1994) 'Factors influencing adjustment of high school students in an international exchange program', *Journal of Nervous and Mental Diseases*, 182, 709–14.

Galtung, J. (1981) 'Structure, culture and intellectual style: an essay comparing Saxonic, Teutonic, Gallic and Hipponic approaches', *Social Science Information*, 20, 6, 817–56.

Garden, R. (1987) 'The second IEA Mathematics Study', *Comparative Education Review*, 31, 47–68.

Gardiner, D. (1989) *The Anatomy of Supervision: Developing Learning and Practice Competence for Social Work Students*, Milton Keynes: Open University Press.

Gardner, H. (1989) *To Open Minds: Chinese Clues to the Dilemma of Contemporary Education*, New York: Basic Books.

Goldsmith, J. and Shawcross, V. (1985) *It Ain't Half Sexist, Mum: Women as Overseas Students in the UK*, London: World University Service and United Kingdom Council for Overseas Student Affairs.

Graddol, D., Thompson, L. and Byram, M. (eds) (1993) *Language and Culture*, Clevedon: Multilingual Matters.

Graham, J. (1987) 'English language proficiency and the perception of academic success', *TESOL Quarterly*, 21, 505–21.

Green, B. (1995) 'Proficiency in English of overseas students', in University of Newcastle, *Language Centre Information*, Newcastle upon Tyne: University of Newcastle.

Green, D. and Parker, R. (1989) 'Vocational and academic attributes of students with different learning styles', *Journal of College Student Development*, 30, 115–21.

Gudykunst, W. (1994) *Bridging Differences: Effective Intergroup Communication*, Thousand Oaks, CA: Sage Publications.

Guthrie, G. (1975) 'A behavioral analysis of culture learning', in R. Brislin, S. Bochner and W. Lonner (eds) *Cross-Cultural Perspectives on Learning*, New York: Wiley.

Habibah Elias and Wan Rafei Abdul Rahman (1994) 'Achievement motivation training for university students: effects on affective and cognitive achievement motivation', *Pertanika Journal of Social Science and Humanities*, 2, 115–21.

——(1995) 'Achievement motivation of university students', *Pertanika Journal of Social Science and Humanities*, 3, 1–10.

Hall, E. (1959) *The Silent Language*, Garden City, NY: Doubleday.

Hall, J. and Beil-Warner, P. (1978) 'Assertiveness of male Anglo and Mexican-American college students', *Journal of Social Psychology*, 105, 175–78.

Hammond, J. (1987) 'An overview of the genre-based approach to the teaching of writing in Australia', *Australian Review of Applied Linguistics*, 10, 163–81.

Hannerz, U. (1990) 'Cosmopolitans and locals in world culture', in M. Featherstone (ed.) *Global Culture: Nationalism, Globalization, and Modernity*, London: Sage Publications.

Harris, R. (1983) 'Social work education and the transfer of learning', *Issues in Social Work Education*, 3, 103–17.

——(1987) 'Problem solving as a vehicle for the development of core intellectual skills in social work students', *Issues in Social Work Education*, 7, 102–14.

——(1995) 'Overseas students in the United Kingdom university system', *Higher Education*, 29, 77–92.

Harris, R. (ed.) (1985) *Educating Social Workers*, Leicester: Association of Teachers in Social Work Education.

Harris, R. and Lavan, A. (1992) 'Professional mobility in the new Europe: the case of social work', *Journal of European Social Policy*, 2, 1–15.

Harvey L. (1995) 'The new collegialism: improvement with accountability', *Tertiary Education and Management*, 1, 153–60.

Hau, K. and Salili, F. (1991) 'Structure and semantic differential placement of specific causes: academic causal attributions by Chinese students in Hong Kong', *International Journal of Psychology*, 26, 175–93.

Hayes, E. and Flannery, D. (1995) *Adult women's learning in higher education: a critical review of scholarship*, paper presented to the 1995 Annual Meeting of the American Educational Research Association, San Francisco, CA.

Hays, R. (1972) 'Behavioral issues in multinational operations', in R. Hays (ed.)

(1972) *International Business: an Introduction to the World of the Multinational Firm*, Englewood Cliffs, NJ: Prentice Hall.

Held, D. and McGrew, A. (1993) 'Globalization and the liberal state', *Government and Opposition*, 28, 261–85.

Henkel, M. (1991a) *Government, Evaluation and Change*, London, Jessica Kingsley.

——(1991b) 'The new "evaluative state" ', *Public Administration*, 69, 121–36.

Hess, R. and Azuma, M. (1991) 'Cultural support for schooling: contrasts between Japan and the United States', *Educational Researcher*, 20, 2–8.

Higgins, T. and Cox, T. (eds) (1993) *Student Mobility in Europe*, Cheltenham: Polytechnics Central Admissions System.

Higher Education Funding Council for England (1996) *Assessors' Handbook; April– September 1996*, Bristol: Higher Education Funding Council for England, Quality Assessment Division.

Higher Education Quality Council (1995) *Managing for Quality Stories and Strategies; A Case Study Resource for Academic Leaders and Managers*, Swindon: Higher Education Quality Council.

Higher Education Statistics Agency (1995) 'Students in UK higher education', *Higher Education Digest*, 23, Autumn.

Hinds, J. (1987) 'Reader versus writer responsibility: a new typology', in U. Connor and R. Kaplan (eds) *Writing across Languages*, New York: Addison Wesley.

Ho, C. (1993) 'The state of the economy', in P-K. Choi and L-S. Ho (eds) *The Other Hong Kong Report*, Hong Kong: The Chinese University of Hong Kong.

Ho, D. Y-f. (1976) 'On the concept of face', *American Journal of Sociology*, 81, 867–84.

Hofstede, G. (1980) 'Motivation, leadership and organization: do American theories apply abroad?' *Organizational Dynamics*, 9, 42–63.

——(1984) *Culture's Consequences: International Differences in Work-Related Values*, Beverly Hills, CA: Sage.

——(1994) *Cultures and Organizations*, London: HarperCollins.

Holford, J., Gardner, D. and Ng, J. (1995) *The Hong Kong Adult Education Handbook 1995–6*, Hong Kong: Longman.

Holloway, S. (1988) 'Concepts of ability and effort in Japan and the United States', *Review of Educational Research*, 58, 327–45.

Hong Kong Education Commission (1986) *Education Commission Report no. 2*, Hong Kong: Government Printer.

——(1988) *Education Commission Report no. 3*, Hong Kong: Government Printer.

Hong Kong Government (1974) *Secondary Education in Hong Kong Over the Next Decade: White Paper*, Hong Kong: Government Printer.

——(1977) *Senior-Secondary and Tertiary Education: Green Paper*, Hong Kong: Government Printer.

——(1978) *Development of Senior-Secondary and Tertiary Education: White Paper*, Hong Kong: Government Printer.

——(1979) *Report of the Advisory Committee on Diversification*, Hong Kong: Government Printer.

——(1982) *A Perspective on Education in Hong Kong: Report by a Visiting Panel*, Hong Kong: Government Printer.

——(1986) *Address by the Governor at the Opening of the 1986–7 Session of the Legislative Council*, Hong Kong: Government Printer.

——(1989) *Address by the Governor at the Opening of the 1989–90 Session of the Legislative Council*, Hong Kong: Government Printer.

Hong Kong Government Education and Manpower Branch (1994) *Manpower 2001 Revised*, Hong Kong: Government Printer.

Hong Kong Government Secretariat (1981) *The Hong Kong Education System*, Hong Kong: Government Printer.

Hughes, R. (1976) *Borrowed Place, Borrowed Time: Hong Kong and its Many Faces*, London: Andre Deutsch.

——(1990) *Homes Far From Home: Housing for Overseas Students*, London: Overseas Students Trust.

Hutchinson, J. (1970) 'Notes on the African contextualisation of French teaching', in C. Brann (ed.) *French Curriculum Development in Anglophone Africa: a Symposium and Guide*, Occasional Paper no. 9, Ibadan: University of Ibadan Institute of Education.

Hyland, K. (1994) 'The learning styles of Japanese students', *Japanese Association of Language Teachers Journal*, 16, 55–74.

Hymes, D. (ed.) (1971) *Pidginisation and Creolisation of Languages*, Cambridge: Cambridge University Press.

Illich, I. (1973) *Deschooling Society*, Harmondsworth: Penguin Books.

International Association for the Evaluation of Educational Achievement (1988) *Science Achievement in Seventeen Countries: a Preliminary Report*, Oxford: Pergamon.

International English Language Testing System (1985) *The IELTS Handbook*, Cambridge and Canberra: University of Cambridge Local Examination Syndicate, the British Council and IDP Education, Australia.

Iredale R. (1992) *The Power of Change*, London: Overseas Development Administration.

Jao, Y. (1993) 'Monetary and financial affairs', in P-K. Choi and L-S Ho (eds) *The Other Hong Kong Report*, Hong Kong: The Chinese University of Hong Kong.

Jenkins, H. (ed.) (1983) *Educating Students from Other Nations*, San Francisco: Jossey-Bass.

Jin, L. (1992) 'Academic cultural expectations and second language use: Chinese postgraduate students in the UK: a cultural synergy model', unpublished PhD thesis, University of Leicester.

Jin, L. and Cortazzi, M. (1993) 'Cultural orientation and academic language use', in D. Graddol, L. Thompson and M. Byram (eds) *Language and Culture*, Clevedon: Multilingual Matters.

——(1995) 'A cultural synergy model for academic language use', in P. Bruthiaux, T. Boswood and B. Du-Babcock (eds) (1995) *Explorations in English for Professional Communication*, Hong Kong: City University.

——(forthcoming) 'The culture the learner brings: a bridge or a barrier?', in M. Byram and M. Fleming (eds) *Foreign Language Learning in Intercultural Perspective*, Cambridge: Cambridge University Press.

Johnson, G. (1994) 'Hong Kong from colony to territory: economic and social implications of globalization', in B. Leung and T. Wong (eds.), *25 Years of Social and Economic Development in Hong Kong*, Centre of Asian Studies Occasional Papers and Monographs no. 111, Hong Kong: University of Hong Kong.

Johnson, R. and Cheung, Y. (1991) *Reading literacy in Hong Kong in Chinese and English: a Preliminary Report on the IEA Study*, paper presented at the Annual Conference, Institute of Language in Education, Hong Kong.

Jordan, R. (1977) 'Identification of problems and needs: a student profile', in A. Cowie and J. Heaton (eds) *English for Academic Purposes*, British Association of Applied Linguistics' Special English Language Materials for Overseas Students, Reading: University of Reading.

Kagan, H. and Cohen, J. (1990) 'Cultural adjustment of international students', *Psychological Science*, 1, 133–37.

Kaplan, A. (1964) *The Conduct of Inquiry: Methodology for Social Research*, San Francisco: Chandler.

Karabel, J. and Halsey, A.H. (eds) (1977) *Power and Ideology in Education*, New York: Oxford University Press.

Keech, M. (1994) *Supporting for development: the QUT experience*, paper presented at the Australia Development Studies Network Symposium, Canberra, 23–4 September.

Kember, D. and Gow, L. (1991) 'A challenge to the anecdotal stereotype of the Asian student', *Studies in Higher Education*, 16, 117–28.

Kendall, M. (1968) *Overseas Students in Britain: an Annotated Bibliography*, London: Research Unit for Students' Problems and the United Kingdom Council for Overseas Student Affairs.

King, A. (1981) 'The administrative absorption of politics in Hong Kong', in A. King and R. Lee (eds) *Social Life and Development in Hong Kong*, Hong Kong: Chinese University of Hong Kong Press.

King, A. and Lee, R. (eds) (1981) *Social Life and Development in Hong Kong*, Hong Kong: Chinese University of Hong Kong Press.

Kinnell, M. (ed.) (1990) *The Learning Experiences of Overseas Students*, Buckingham: Society for Research into Higher Education and Open University Press.

Klineberg, O. and Brislin, R. (eds) (1983) *Handbook of Intercultural Training*, volumes I, II and III, New York: Pergamon.

Kolb, D. (1984) *Experiential Learning: Experience as the Source of Learning and Development*, Englewood Cliffs, NJ: Prentice-Hall.

Kolb, D. and Goldman, M. (1973) 'Toward a typology of learning styles and discipline demands on the academic performance, social adaptation and career choices of MIT seniors', MIT Sloan School Working Paper no. 688 (73), Cambridge, MA: Massachusetts Institute of Technology.

Krashen, D. (1982) *Principles and Practice in Second Language Acquisition*, Oxford: Pergamon.

Kratzing, M. (ed.) (1990) *Eighth Australasian Learning and Language Conference*, Queensland: Queensland University of Technology Counselling Services.

Landbeck, R. and Mugler, F. (1994) *Approaches to Study and Conceptions of Learning of Students at the University of the South Pacific*, Fiji: University of the South Pacific Centre for the Enhancement of Learning and Teaching.

Lau, S-K. and Kuan, H-C. (1988) *The Ethos of the Hong Kong Chinese*, Hong Kong: Chinese University of Hong Kong Press.

Le Page, R. (1964) *The National Language Question: Linguistic Problems of Newly Independent States*, Oxford: Oxford University Press.

Lee, N. (1996) *International Trade in Education: Investment in Human Capital or Cultural Imperialism? A Case Study of the Asia Pacific Region*, Nottingham: Occasional Paper of the Institute of Asian Pacific Studies, University of Nottingham.

Leech, F (1993) *Failed matrimony: why ELT projects fail*, paper presented to the Third Oxford International Conference on Education, Globalisation and Learning, New College, Oxford, 21–5 September.

Leki, L. (1995) 'Good writing: I know it when I see it', in D. Belcher and G. Braine (eds) *Academic Writing in a Second Language: Essays on Research and Pedagogy*, New Jersey: Ablex.

Leung, B. and Wong, T. (1994) *25 Years of Social and Economic Development in Hong Kong*, Centre of Asian Studies Occasional Papers and Monographs no. 111, Hong Kong: University of Hong Kong.

Leung, V., Lay, B., Ketchell, A., Clark, C. and Harris, R. (1995) 'Hong Kong social work students at the University of Hull', *Social Work Education*, 14, 44–60.

Lewins, H. (1990) 'Living needs', in M. Kinnell (ed.) *The Learning Experiences of Overseas Students*, Buckingham: Society for Research into Higher Education and Open University Press.

Lewis, I. (1984) *The Student Experience of Higher Education*, London: Croom Helm.

Lewis, V. and Habeshaw, S. (1990) *Interesting Ways to Promote Equal Opportunities in Education*, Bristol: Technical and Educational Services.

Li, K-w. and Lo, K. (1993) 'Trade and industry', in P-k. Choi and L-s. Ho (eds) *The Other Hong Kong Report*, Hong Kong: The Chinese University of Hong Kong.

Littlewood, W. (1981) *Communicative Language Teaching: an Introduction*, Cambridge: Cambridge University Press.

Littlewood, W. (1992) *Teaching Oral Communication*, Oxford: Blackwell.

Liu, S. (1995) *Contemporary Trend of Marketing Chinese Universities in Hong Kong: an Incoming Rival to British Counterparts*, Business Research Centre Papers on China, Series no. CP95005, Hong Kong: School of Business, Hong Kong Baptist University.

Livingstone, A. (1960) *The Overseas Student in Britain: with Special Reference to Training Courses in Social Welfare*, Manchester: Manchester University Press.

Louie, K. (1984) 'Salvaging Confucian education (1949–83)', *Comparative Education*, 20, 27–38.

Lundstedt, A. (1963) 'An introduction to some evolving problems in cross-cultural research', *Journal of Social Issues*, 19, 3–19.

Mac an Ghaill, M. (1994) *The Making of Men: Masculinities, Sexualities and Schooling*, Buckingham: Open University Press.

Maharaj, Z. (1995) 'Social theory of gender: Connell's gender and power', *Feminist Review*, 49, 50–65.

Maiworm F., Steube W. and Teichler U. (1993) *Learning in Europe: the ERASMUS Experience*, London: Jessica Kingsley.

Makepeace, E. (1989) *Overseas Students: Challenges of International Adjustment*, Standing Conference on Educational Development Paper 56, Birmingham: SCED Publications.

Marsella, A., Thorp, R. and Cibrowski, T. (eds.) (1979) *Perspectives on Cross-Cultural Psychology*, New York: Academic Press.

Martin, J., Powell, J. and Wieneke, C. (1981) 'The experiences of a group of older unqualified women at university', *Women's Studies International Quarterly*, 4, 117–31.

Marton, F. and Saljo, R. (1976a) 'On qualitative differences in learning I – outcome and process', *British Journal of Educational Psychology*, 46, 4–11.

——(1976b) 'On qualitative differences in learning II – outcome as a function of the learner's perception of the task', *British Journal of Educational Psychology*, 46, 115–27.

——(1984) 'Approaches to learning', in F. Marton, D. Hounsell and N. Entwistle (eds) *The Experience of Learning*, Edinburgh: Scottish Academic Press.

Maxey, K. and Preston, R. (1994) *Transferring Skill? The Overseas Student Returns Home*, Warwick: International Centre for Education in Development, Department of Continuing Education, University of Warwick.

May, M. and Bartlett, A. (1995) ' "They've got a problem with English": perceptions of the difficulties of international post-graduate students', in P. Thomas (ed.) *Teaching for Development: an International Review of Australian Formal and Non-Formal Education for Asia and the Pacific*, Canberra: National Centre for Development Studies, Australian National University.

May, M., Bartlett, A. and Holzknecht, S. (1994) *Discipline-Specific Academic Skills at Post-graduate Level: the Cement of Academia*, paper presented to the Higher Education Research and Development Society of Australasia Incorporated Conference, Higher Education in Transition, Canberra, 6–10 July.

May, R. (1970) 'The nature of anxiety and its relation to fear', in A. Elbing (ed.) *Behavioural Decisions in Organisation*, New York: Scott, Foresman and Co.

Maznah Baba (1993) 'Malay secondary school students' social support preferences', *Pertanika Journal of Social Science and Humanities*, 1, 1–9.

McKenna, E. (1987) 'Preparing foreign students to enter discourse communities in the US', *English for Specific Purposes*, 6, 187–202.

Medrich, E. and Griffith, J. (1992) *International Mathematics and Science Assessments: what have we learned?* Washington, DC: National Center for Education Statistics, US Department of Education.

Menges, R. and Svinicki, M. (1991) *College Teaching: from Theory to Practice*, San Francisco: Jossey-Bass.

Merton, R. (1938) 'Social structure and anomie', *American Sociological Review*, 3, 672–82.

Mirza, H. (1992) *Young, Female and Black*, London: Routledge.

Mo, T. (1978) *The Monkey King*, London: Andre Deutsch.

Monroe, S. (1982) 'Life events and disorder: event-symptoms associations and the course of disorders', *Journal of Abnormal Psychology*, 91, 14–24.

Moodley, R. (ed.) (1995) *Education for Transformation: Black Access to Higher Education*, Leeds: Thomas Danby Publications.

Morris, B. (1967) *International Community? A Report on the Welfare of Overseas Students*, London: National Union of Students of England, Wales and Northern Ireland and the Scottish Union of Students.

Morris, P. and Sweeting, A. (1991) 'Education and politics: the case of Hong Kong from an historical perspective', *Oxford Review of Education*, 17, 249–67.

Murphy, D. (1987) 'Offshore education: a Hong Kong perspective', *Australian Universities Review*, 30, 43–9.

Nash, D. (1967) 'The fate of Americans in Spanish setting: a study of adaptation', *Human Organization*, 26, whole no. 3.

Neave, G. (1988) 'On the cultivation of quality, efficiency and enterprise: an overview of recent trends in higher education in Western Europe 1986–8', *European Journal of Education*, 23, 211–22.

Nixon, U. (1993) 'Coping in Australia: problems faced by overseas students', *Prospect*, 8, 42–50.

Oberg, J. (1960) 'Cultural shock: adjustment to new cultural environments', *Practical Anthropology*, 7, 177–82.

Open University (1982) *Curriculum Evaluation and Assessment in Educational Institutions*, Course E364, Blocks 1, 2 and 6, Milton Keynes: Open University Press.

Organisation for Economic Cooperation and Development (1990) *Labour Market Policies for the 1990s*, Paris: OECD.

——(1993) *Higher Education and Employment: the Case of Humanities and Social Sciences*, Paris: OECD.

Othman Mohamed (1994) 'Malaysian students' learning style profile: implication for teacher-counselors' preparation', *Proceedings of the 41st International Council on Education for Teaching World Assembly*, Istanbul, August 19–22.

Park, R. (1974) *Perspectives in Social Inquiry: Collected Papers of Robert Ezra Park*, volumes 1–3, New York: Arno.

Pask, G. (1976) 'Styles and strategies of learning', *British Journal of Educational Psychology*, 46, 128–48.

Peace, J., Skinner, S., Murray, A. and Collins, J. (1994) *Guidelines on Increasing Women's Participation in Technical Cooperation Training*, London and Manchester: British Council and Overseas Development Administration.

Pearlin, L. (1985) 'Social structure and process of social support', in S. Cohen and L. Syme (eds) *Social Support and Health*, New York: Academic Press.

Pearson, R. (1986) *The Personal Support System Survey*, New York: Syracuse University.

——(1990) *Counseling and Social Support*, Beverly Hills, CA: Sage Publications.

Pederson, P. (1976) 'The Field of intercultural counseling', in P. Pederson, W. Lonner and J. Dragons (eds) (1976) *Counseling Across Cultures*, Honolulu: University of Hawaii Press.

Pederson, P., Lonner, W. and Dragons, J. (eds) (1976) *Counseling Across Cultures*, Honolulu: University of Hawaii Press.

Pelikan, J. (1992) *The Idea of the University*, New Haven, Conn.: Yale University Press.

Perry, W. (1988) 'Different worlds in the same classroom', in P. Ramsden (ed.) (1988) *Improving Learning: New Perspectives*, London: Kogan Page.

Phillips, D., Burke, E., Campbell, A. and Ingram, D. (1985) *The Formative Evaluation of Preparatory English Training of Sponsored Indonesian Students*, Canberra: Australian International Development Agency.

Piper, D. (1984) 'The question of fairness', in S. Acker and D. Piper (eds) *Is Higher Education Fair to Women?* Guildford: Society for Research into Higher Education and NFER-Nelson.

Political and Economic Planning (1955) *Colonial Students in Britain: a Report by PEP*, London: Political and Economic Planning.

——(1965) *New Commonwealth Students in Britain: with Special Reference to Students from East Africa*, London: Political and Economic Planning.

Preston, R. and Kandando, D. (1993) *The Situation of AET-Sponsored Namibians after their Return Home*, Namibian Institute for Social and Economic Research, University of Namibia, Windhoek: African Educational Trust.

Primrose, C. (1991) *Study Guide for Overseas Students*, Enterprise in Higher Education, Glasgow: University of Glasgow.

Randall, G. (1987) 'Gender differences in pupil–teacher interaction in workshops and laboratories', in G. Weiner and M. Arnot (eds) *Gender Under Scrutiny: New Inquiries in Education*, London: Unwin Hyman.

Random, M. (1987) *Japan, Strategy of the Unseen*, Wellingborough: Crucible.

Ramsden, P. (ed.) (1988) *Improving Learning: New Perspectives*, London: Kogan Page.

——(1992) *Learning to Teach in Higher Education*, London, Routledge.

Reed, B., Hutton, J. and Bazalgette, J. (1978) *Freedom to Study: Requirements of Overseas Students in the UK*, report prepared by the Grubb Institute for the Overseas Students Trust, London: Overseas Students Trust.

Report of the Committee on Higher Education (1963) Cmnd 2154, London, HMSO (Robbins Report).

Richards, J. (ed.) (1985) *The Context of Language Teaching*, Cambridge: Cambridge University Press.

Richards, J. and Sukwiwat, M. (1985) 'Cross-cultural aspects of conversational competence', in J. Richards (ed.) *The Context of Language Teaching*, Cambridge: Cambridge University Press.

Richardson, A. (1974) *British Immigrants and Australia: a Psycho-Social Inquiry,* Canberra: Australian National University Press.

Rivers, W. (1983) *Communicating Naturally in a Second Language,* Cambridge: Cambridge University Press.

Robbins, L. (1963) *Higher Education: Report of the Committee Appointed by the Prime Minister under the Chairmanship of Lord Robbins, 1961–3,* Cmnd 2154, London: HMSO.

Roberts, H. (1984) 'A feminist perspective on affirmative action', in S. Acker and D. Piper (eds) *Is Higher Education Fair to Women?* Guildford: Society for Research into Higher Education and NFER-Nelson.

Robertson, R. (1992) *Globalization: Social Theory and Global Culture,* London: Sage Publications.

Roccasalvo, J. (1981) 'The Thai practice of psychiatry and the doctrine of Annata', *Review of Existential Psychology and Psychiatry,* 27, 153–68.

Rogers, A. (1992) *Adults Learning for Development,* London: Cassell.

Rogers, Carl (1969) *Freedom to Learn,* Columbus, Ohio: Merrill.

——(1978) *Rogers on Personal Power,* London: Constable.

Rogers, Cathryn (1994) *Welfare Provision For International Students: a Guide to Evaluating their Needs,* London: United Kingdom Council for Overseas Student Affairs.

Rogoff, B. and Lave, B. (1984) *Everyday Cognition: its Development in Social Context,* Cambridge, MA: Harvard University Press.

Ross, R. and Trachte, K. (1990) *Global Capitalism: the New Leviathan,* Albany, NY: State University of New York Press.

Rusnani Abdul Kadir (1993) 'Counselor attractiveness as a function of similarity in locus of control', unpublished PhD thesis, Kansas State University.

Ryan, N. (1971) *The Cultural Heritage of Malaya,* Kuala Lumpur: Longman Malaysia.

Salili, F. (1994) 'Age, sex, and cultural differences in the meaning and dimensions of achievement', *Personality and Social Psychology,* Bulletin 20, 635–48.

Saljo, R. (1979) 'Learning about learning', *Higher Education,* 8, 443–51.

——(1982) *Learning and Understanding: a Study of Differences in Constructing Meaning from a Text,* Gothenburg: Acta Universitatis Gothenburgenis.

Samuelowicz, K. (1987) 'Learning problems of overseas students: two sides of a story', *Higher Education Research and Development,* 6, 121–34.

Sandhu, D. (1994) 'An examination of the psychological needs of the international students: implications for counselling and psychotherapy', *International Journal for the Advancement of Counselling,* 17, 229–39.

Saville-Troike, M. (1989) *The Ethnography of Communication,* 2nd edition, Oxford: Blackwell.

Schild, E. (1962) 'The foreign student as a stranger learning the norms of the host culture', *Journal of Social Issues,* 18, 41–54.

Schneider, M. and Fujishima, N. (1995) 'When practice doesn't make perfect: the case of a graduate ESL student', in D. Belcher and G. Braine (eds) *Academic Writing in a Second Language: Essays on Research and Pedagogy,* New Jersey: Ablex.

Scollon, R. and Scollon, S. (1995) *Intercultural Communication,* Oxford: Blackwell.

Searle, C. (1972) *The Forsaken Lover: White Words and Black People,* London: Routledge.

Searle, W. and Ward, C. (1990) 'The prediction of psychological and sociocultural adjustment during cross-cultural transition', *International Journal of Intercultural Relations,* 14, 449–64.

Sellitz, C. and Cook, S. (1962) 'Factors influencing attitudes of foreign students towards the host country', *Journal of Social Issues*, 18, 7–23.

Selye, H. (1977) *Stress in Health and Disease*, Boston, MA: Butterworth.

Sen, A. (1970) *Problems of Overseas Students and Nurses*, Slough: National Foundation for Educational Research in England and Wales.

Sewell, W. and Davidson, O. (1961) 'Scandinavian students' image of the United States', *Annals of the American Academy of Political and Social Science*, 295, 126–35.

Shaw, P. (1991) 'Science research students' composing processes', *English for Specific Purposes*, 10, 189–206.

——(1995) 'The rhetoric of solidarity in dissertation', unpublished paper presented to the TESOL Convention, Long Beach, CA.

——(1996) 'One-to-one work on dissertation: effectiveness of correction and efficiency of pedagogy', *Review of ELT*, forthcoming.

Shawcross, V., Grosser, K. and Goldsmith, J. (1987) *Women in Mind: the Educational Needs of Women Refugees in the UK*, London: World University Service.

Sherlock, M. (1995) 'Recruiting international students', *AUT Bulletin*, January.

Shotnes, S. (ed.) (1985) *The Teaching and Tutoring of Overseas Students*, London: UKCOSA.

Shumaker, S. and Brownell, A. (1984) 'Toward a theory of social support: closing conceptual gaps', *Journal of Social Issues*, 40, 11–33.

S. Husin Ali (1970) 'A note on Malay society and culture', in S. Takdir Alisjabana, Nayagam, X. and Wang Gung Wu (eds) *The Cultural Problems of Malaysia in the Context of Southeast Asia*, Kuala Lumpur: Department of Malay Studies, University of Malaya.

Skeggs, B. (1991) 'Challenging masculinity and using sexuality', *British Journal of Sociology of Education*, 12, 127–40.

Sklair, L. (1991) *Sociology of the Global System*, Hemel Hempstead: Harvester Wheatsheaf.

——(1994) *Social development: global perspectives*, paper presented to the Conference on Social Development in the Asia-Pacific Region, 19 November, Hong Kong: City University of Hong Kong.

Smalley, W. (1963) 'Culture shock, language shock and the shock of self-discovery', *Practical Anthropology*, 10, 49–56.

Smith, F. (1992) *To Think in Language, Learning and Education*, London: Routledge.

Smith, L. (ed.) (1987) *Discourse Across Cultures: Strategies in World Englishes*, New York: Prentice Hall.

Spender, D. (1982) *Invisible Women: the Schooling Scandal*, London: Writers and Readers.

——(1984) 'Sexism in teacher education', in S. Acker and D. Piper (eds) *Is Higher Education Fair to Women?* Guildford: Society for Research into Higher Education and NFER-Nelson.

Spender, D. and Spender, E. (1980) *Learning to Lose: Sexism and Education*, London: Women's Press.

Spolsky, B. (1977) 'The establishment of language education policy in multilingual societies', in B. Spolsky and R. Cooper (eds) *Frontiers of Bilingual Education*, Rowley, MA: Newbury House.

Spolsky, B. and Cooper, R. (eds) (1977) *Frontiers of Bilingual Education*, Rowley, MA: Newbury House.

S. Takdir Alisjabana, Nayagam, X. and Wang Gung Wu (eds) (1970) *The Cultural Problems of Malaysia in the Context of Southeast Asia*, Kuala Lumpur: Department of Malay Studies, University of Malaya.

Staff and Educational Development Association (1996) 'Accreditation of university teachers becomes a national issue', *The Competent Teacher*, 3, 1, Birmingham: Staff and Educational Development Association.

Stanworth, M. (1981) *Gender and Schooling: a Study of Sexual Divisions in the Classroom*, London: Unwin Hyman.

——(1987) 'Girls on the margins: a study of gender divisions in the classroom', in G. Weiner and M. Arnot (eds) *Gender Under Scrutiny: New Inquiries in Education*, London: Unwin Hyman.

Stapleton, P. (1995) 'The role of Confucianism in Japanese education', *The Language Teacher*, 19, 13–16.

Stevenson, H., Lee, S., Chen, C., Stigler, J., Hsu, C. and Kitamura, S. (1990) *Context of Achievement : a Study of American, Chinese, and Japanese Children*, Monographs of the Society for Research in Child Development, serial no. 221, volume 55, Chicago: University of Chicago Press.

Stone, L. (ed.) (1994) *The Education Feminism Reader*, London: Routledge.

Stoner, J., Aram, J. and Rubin, I. (1972) 'Factors associated with effective performance in overseas work assignments', *Personnel Psychology*, 25, 303–18.

Sue, S. and Okazaki, S. (1990) 'Asian-American educational achievements: a phenomenon in search of an explanation', *American Psychologist*, 44, 349–59.

Sue, S. and Zane, N. (1987) 'The role of culture and cultural techniques in psychotherapy: a critique and reformulation', *American Psychologist*, 42, 37–45.

Sutherland, G. (1995) 'Gender deficit and tradition', *Times Higher Education Supplement*, October 13.

Svensson, L. (1977) ' "Symposium: learning processes and strategies III", on qualitative differences in learning III, study skill and learning', *British Journal of Educational Psychology*, 47, 233–43.

Swales, J. (1990) *Genre Analysis: English in Academic and Research Settings*, Cambridge: Cambridge University Press.

Swedish National Board of Universities and Colleges (1992) *Business Administration and Economics Study Programmes in Swedish Higher Education: an international perspective*, Stockholm: National Board of Universities and Colleges.

Sweeting, A. (1990) *Education in Hong Kong, Pre-1841 to 1941 – Fact and Opinion: Materials for a History of Education in Hong Kong*, Hong Kong: University of Hong Kong Press.

——(1993) *A Phoenix Transformed: the Reconstruction of Education in Post-War Hong Kong*, Hong Kong: Oxford University Press.

Tajfel, H. and Dawson, J. (eds) (1965) *Disappointed Guests: Essays by African, Asian, and West Indian Students*, London and Oxford: Institute of Race Relations and Oxford University Press.

Taylor, L. (1993) Keynote speech delivered to the Conference on Equality Training and Training Evaluation in Further and Higher Education. University of Bradford, 13–14 December.

Taylorson, D. (1984) 'The professional socialization: integration and identity of women PhD candidates', in S. Acker and D. Piper (eds) *Is Higher Education Fair to Women?* Guildford: Society for Research into Higher Education and NFER-Nelson.

Teichler, U. (1991) *Experiences of ERASMUS Students: Select Findings of the 1988–9 Survey*, ERASMUS Monograph 13, Kassel: Wissenschaftliches Zentrum für Berufs und Hochschulforschung der Gesamthochschule.

——(1994) 'Student mobility in Europe', in G. Bradley and B. Little (eds) *Quality and Europe: Papers Presented at a Conference*, London: Quality Support Centre and the Open University.

Teichler, U. and Maiworm, F. (1994) *Transition to Work: the Experiences of Former ERASMUS Students*, London: Jessica Kingsley.

Thomas, K. (1990) *Gender and Subject in Higher Education*, Buckingham: Society for Research into Higher Education.

Thomas, P. (ed.) (1995) *Teaching for Development: an International Review of Australian Formal and Non-Formal Education for Asia and the Pacific*, Canberra: National Centre for Development Studies, Australian National University.

Times Higher Educational Supplement (1994) 'Short change', editorial, *Times Higher Educational Supplement*, 30 September, 11.

Tornbiorn, I. (1982) *Living Abroad: Personal Adjustment and Personnel Policy in an Overseas Setting*, Chichester: Wiley.

Trow, M. (1994) *Managerialism and the Academic Profession: Quality and Control*, QSC Higher Education Report no. 2, London: Quality Support Centre.

Truax, D. and Carkhuff, R. (1967) *Toward Effective Counseling and Psychotherapy: Training and Practice*, Chicago and New York: Aldine Atherton.

United Kingdom Council for Overseas Student Affairs (1986a) *Towards a Policy on International Education*, London: UKCOSA.

——(1986b) *Responsible Recruitment*, London: UKCOSA.

——(1989) *The UKCOSA Manual: Working with Overseas Students*, London: UKCOSA.

——(1992) *Orientation Within the Institution: a DIY Guide to Welcoming International Students*, London: UKCOSA and the Council for International Education.

——(1995a) *International Students: Their Families in the UK and Marriage*, Guidance notes for students 1995–6, London: UKCOSA.

——(1995b) *Annual Review 1994–5*, London: UKCOSA.

United Nations Educational, Scientific and Cultural Organisation (1953) *The Use of Vernacular Languages in Education*, Monographs on fundamental education VIII, Paris: UNESCO.

——(1995) *Policy Paper for Change and Development in Higher Education*, Paris: UNESCO.

Universities Grants Committee (1994) *University Statistics Vol. 1: Students and Staff 1993–4*, Cheltenham: Universities' Statistical Record.

University and Polytechnic Grants Committee of Hong Kong (1993) *Higher Education 1991–2001: An Interim Report*, Hong Kong: UPGC.

University of Newcastle (1995) *Statement of Good Practice in Teaching*, unpublished, Newcastle upon Tyne: University of Newcastle.

Unterhalter, E. and Hayton, A. (1993) *Homeward Bound: a Pack for Tutors Organising Courses for Students Returning to their Home Countries after Studying in the UK*, London: United Kingdom Council for Overseas Student Affairs.

van Vught, F. (1993) 'Towards a general model of quality assessment in higher education', in J. Brennan and F. van Vught (eds.), *Questions of Quality: in Europe and Beyond*, Quality Support Centre Higher Education Report no. 1, London: Quality Support Centre and the Open University.

van Vught, F. and Westerheijden, D. (1993) *Quality Management and Quality Assurance in European Higher Education: Methods and Mechanisms*, Luxembourg: Office for Official Publications of the European Communities.

Vroeijenstijn, T. (1994) *Improvement and Accountability: Navigating between Scylla and Charybdis*, London: Jessica Kingsley.

Walden, J. (1993) 'The Implementation of the Sino-British Joint Declaration', in P-k. Choi and L-s. Ho (eds) *The Other Hong Kong Report*, Hong Kong: The Chinese University of Hong Kong.

Wallace, P. (1981) 'Overseas students: the foreign policy implications', in P.

Williams (ed.) *The Overseas Student Question: Studies for a Policy*, London: Heinemann for the Overseas Students Trust.

Wan Rafaie Abdul Rahman (1980) 'Peranan motivasi pencapaian dalam pembentukan usahawan: satu kajian di kalangan murid-murid sekolah di Malaysia dan United Kingdom' (Role of achievement motivation in entrepreneurship formation: a case study among school children in Malaysia and the United Kingdom), unpublished paper presented to the Seminar on Psychology and Society, Universiti Kebangsaan Malaysia, Bangi, 10 February.

Wang, Y. (1982) 'The Essence of the Chinese University', in Federation of Hong Kong Students, *Perspectives on Hong Kong Education*, Hong Kong: Wide Angle Publications.

Watkins, D., Regmi, M. and Astilla, E. (1991) 'The Asian-learner-as-rote-learner: stereotype, myth or reality?' *Educational Psychology*, 11, 21–34.

Watts, A. (1972) *Diversity and Choice in Higher Education*, London: Routledge & Kegan Paul.

Wehrly, B. (1988) 'Cultural diversity from an international perspective, part 2', *Journal of Multicultural Counseling and Development*, 16, 3–15.

Weiner, G. (1993) 'Ethical practice in an unjust world: educational evaluation and social justice', in J. Blackmore and J. Kenway (eds) *Gender Matters in Educational Administration and Policy*, London: Falmer Press.

Weiner, G. and Arnot, M. (eds) (1987) *Gender Under Scrutiny: New Inquiries in Education*, London: Unwin Hyman.

Wheeler, S. and Birtle, J. (1993) *A Handbook for Personal Tutors*, Buckingham: Society for Research into Higher Education and Open University Press.

White, R., Martin, M., Stimson, M. and Hodge, R. (1991) *Management in English Language Teaching*, Cambridge: Cambridge University Press.

Wilkin, M. (1995) *Learning to Teach in Higher Education*, Centre for Educational Development, Appraisal and Research, Coventry: University of Warwick.

Williams, G., Woodhall, M. and O'Brien, U. (1986) *Overseas Students and their Place of Study: Report of a Survey*, London: Overseas Students Trust.

Williams, J., Cocking, J. and Davies, L. (1989) *Words or Deeds? A Review of Equal Opportunity Policies in Higher Education*, London: Commission for Racial Equality.

Williams, P. (1981) 'Introduction', in P. Williams (ed.) *The Overseas Student Question: Studies for a Policy*, London: Heinemann for the Overseas Students Trust.

——(1982) *A Policy for Overseas Students*, London: Overseas Students Trust.

——(1985) *They Came to Train: a study of responses to their training experiences of study fellows coming to Britain under the British Technical Cooperation Programme*, London: HMSO.

Williams, P. (ed.) (1981) *The Overseas Student Question: Studies for a Policy*, London: Heinemann for the Overseas Students Trust.

Willis, P. (1977) *Learning to Labour: How Working Class Kids get Working Class Jobs*, London: Saxon House.

Wilson, L. (1994) 'Mobility for Central and Eastern Europe: the ERASMUS model and the TEMPUS experience', in Commission of the European Communities and the Organisation for Economic Cooperation and Development, *Mobility in Higher Education: Pilot Project on Regional Cooperation in Reforming Higher Education*, Paris: European Commission/OECD.

Woldgang, A. (ed.) (1979) *Non-Verbal Behaviour*, London: Academic Press.

Wolpe, A. (1988) *Within School Walls: the Role of Discipline, Sexuality and the Curriculum*, London: Routledge.

Wong, P.M. (1983) 'What kind of Hong Kong citizens has the curriculum of economics and public affairs produced?' *Ming Pao Monthly*, 18, 56–9.

Woodhall, M. (1981) 'Overseas students', in O. Fulton (ed.) *Access to Higher Education*, Guildford: Society for Research into Higher Education.

Woods, R. and Woods, S. (1995) 'Dialogues on development: what roles for postgraduate education?', in P. Thomas (ed.) *Teaching for Development: an International Review of Australian Formal and Non-Formal Education for Asia and the Pacific*, Canberra: National Centre for Development Studies, Australian National University.

Wu, K. (1992) *Higher Education in Hong Kong: Investment in Science and Technology During the Time of Political and Economic Change*, World Bank Document no. PHREE/92/70.

Yau, R., Leung, K. and Chau, T. (1993) *Education in Hong Kong: Past and Present*, Hong Kong: Urban Council.

Young, L. (1994) *Crosstalk and Culture in Sino-American Communication*, Cambridge: Cambridge University Press.

Yum, J. (1988) 'The impact of Confucianism on interpersonal relationships and communication patterns in East Asia', *Communication Monographs*, 55, 374–88.

Yusoff Ismail (1982) *A Study of the Relationships between Achievement Motivation and Learning Styles of a Group of Malaysian Students attending Northern Illinois University*, unpublished doctoral dissertation, Northern Illinois University.

Yusoff Ismail (1986) 'Motivasi pencapaian dan gaya pembelajaran di kalangan Siswazah Diploma Pendidikan' (Achievement motivation and learning styles among Diploma of Education graduates) *Jurnal Psikologi Malaysia*, 2, 95–118.

Zwingmann, C. and Gunn, A. (1963) *Uprooting and Health: Psycho-Social Problems of Students from Abroad*, Geneva: World Health Organisation.

Index

Printed in the United Kingdom
by Lightning Source UK Ltd.
124720UK00009B/8/A